D1058602

Education Myths

Education Myths

What Special Interest Groups Want You to Believe about Our Schools— And Why It Isn't So

By Jay P. Greene
with
Greg Forster
and
Marcus A. Winters

Foreword by James Q. Wilson

ROWMAN & LITTLEFIELD PUBLISHERS, INC.
Lanham • Boulder • New York • Toronto • Oxford

ROWMAN & LITTLEFIELD PUBLISHERS, INC.

Published in the United States of America
by Rowman & Littlefield Publishers, Inc.
A wholly owned subsidiary of The Rowman & Littlefield Publishing Group, Inc.
4501 Forbes Boulevard, Suite 200, Lanham, Maryland 20706
www.rowmanlittlefield.com

PO Box 317
Oxford
OX2 9RU, UK

British Library Cataloguing in Publication Information Available

Library of Congress Cataloging-in-Publication Data

Education myths : what special interest groups want you to believe about our schools, and why it isn't so / Jay P. Greene.
p. cm.
Includes bibliographical references and index.
ISBN 0-7425-4977-1 (cloth : alk. paper)
1. Education—United States. I. Greene, Jay P., 1966-
LA210.E445 2005
379.73—dc22 2005006729

Printed in the United States of America

∞™ The paper used in this publication meets the minimum requirements of American National Standard for Information Sciences—Permanence of Paper for Printed Library Materials, ANSI/NISO Z39.48–1992.

To our mentors who taught us how to distinguish myth from fact: Paul Peterson, Morris Fiorina, Steven Smith, Norma Thompson, and Richard Vedder;

To our colleagues who helped us express the facts more clearly: Larry Bernstein, Matthew Ladner, Patrick Wolf, and Henry Olsen;

To our employer, the Manhattan Institute for Policy Research, its president, Larry Mone, and its many supporters for giving us just one charge: follow the facts;

And to our families who supported and encouraged us in writing this book: Aleza, Avi, Deborah, and Jonah Greene; Charles and Myrna Greene; Irene and Joel Spalter; Beth Forster; Sue Forster; and Raymond and Catherine Winters;

To these and many others we owe an enormous debt of gratitude.

Contents

Foreword *James Q. Wilson* ix

Introduction 1

PART I: RESOURCES

1 The Money Myth—*"Schools perform poorly because they need more money."* 7

2 The Special Ed Myth—*"Special education programs burden public schools, hindering their academic performance."* 21

3 The Myth of Helplessness—*"Social problems like poverty cause students to fail; schools are helpless to prevent it."* 39

4 The Class Size Myth—*"Schools should reduce class sizes; small classes would produce big improvements."* 49

5 The Certification Myth—*"Certified or more experienced teachers are substantially more effective."* 59

6 The Teacher Pay Myth—*"Teachers are badly underpaid."* 71

PART II: OUTCOMES

7 The Myth of Decline—*"Schools are performing much worse than they used to."* 87

8 The Graduation Myth—*"Nearly all students graduate from high school."* 95

9 The College Access Myth—"*Nonacademic barriers prevent a lot of minority students from attending college.*" 105

PART III: ACCOUNTABILITY

10 The High Stakes Myth—"*The results of high-stakes tests are not credible because they're distorted by cheating and teaching to the test.*" 117

11 The Push-Out Myth—"*Exit exams cause more students to drop out of high school.*" 127

12 The Accountability Burden Myth—"*Accountability systems impose large financial burdens on schools.*" 135

PART IV: CHOICE

13 The Inconclusive Research Myth—"*The evidence on the effectiveness of vouchers is mixed and inconclusive.*" 147

14 The Exeter Myth—"*Private schools have higher test scores because they have more money and recruit high-performing students while expelling low-performing students.*" 157

15 The Draining Myth—"*School choice harms public schools.*" 167

16 The Disabled Need Not Apply Myth—"*Private schools won't serve disabled students.*" 179

17 The Democratic Values Myth—"*Private schools are less effective at promoting tolerance and civic participation.*" 191

18 The Segregation Myth—"*Private schools are more racially segregated than public schools.*" 201

Conclusion 217

Notes 225

Index 251

About the Author 267

Foreword

James Q. Wilson

Education occupies a privileged position in American life, but that privilege, though it confers many benefits, also imposes some real costs. So committed are Americans to the value of education that they will support almost anything that seems to help that endeavor. Any suggestion that the legislature spend more money on schools or offer higher salaries to teachers is likely to have decent support; any measure on a state ballot designed to sell bonds to fund more schools has a good chance of passing. When unions representing school teachers run radio ads calling for more money, they get a respectful reception.

Contrast the status of education with that of other public policy issues. The public is skeptical of proposals to fix Social Security. It is deeply split on questions of gun control and drug abuse. It usually opposes American military adventures abroad, at least until the president orders one. Bills suggesting that we expand free trade are likely to be dead on arrival.

The privileged status of education means that legislators and their constituents are disposed to believe almost any argument that appears designed to help public schools. Higher teacher salaries? Smaller classrooms? Tougher teacher certification standards? Special education for handicapped students? Not every proposal along these lines will pass, but they all begin their legislative odyssey with a head start.

Most people are not aware that for decades serious scholars have been trying to find out what changes, if any, will make any difference in how well our students learn. In 1966 James S. Coleman, a sociologist, published a major report about what shaped school achievement. Formally known as the Equality of Educational Opportunity Report, it soon became known as the Coleman Report. It was one of the largest social science research projects ever carried out in this country. More than half a million school children were tested and information was gathered about four thousand schools that they attended and some sixty thousand teachers who taught them. Perhaps because its findings were so unexpected, it was published on the weekend of the Fourth of July when not many people pay much attention to what is in the newspapers.

The first goal of the report was to find out to what degree black and white school children attended separate schools. That question was easily answered: almost all did. Not many people found that to be controversial. But the second finding of the report altered scholarly understanding of schooling forever: do inputs into a school (money, buildings, laboratories, teacher salaries) affect the outputs from that school (student achievement)? The answer was that almost none do.

Ponder this for a moment. How much money we spend on schools does not affect how well the schools perform. Of course, if there were huge differences in spending so that in some American schools only $10 was spent on each pupil and in other schools $10,000 was spent on each one, there would be important differences in outputs. You cannot get much schooling for $10 a head. But for the financial differences that actually exist among American schools, spending more money has no discernible effect. Since the Coleman Report there have been dozens of additional studies of this relationship, and almost all have come to the same conclusion.

The finding has scarcely influenced public debate. Today, as in 1966, improving schools is thought to mean spending more on them. Now, there were some problems with the Coleman Report; if you wish to learn more about them, read *On Equality of Educational Opportunity*, a massive, multiauthored study of the report edited by Frederick Mosteller and Daniel Patrick Moynihan (Random House, 1972). But those problems do not alter Coleman's fundamental finding—namely, that you cannot predict school outputs just by knowing school inputs.

Since 1966 many new ideas for improving school achievement have been developed: tougher tests, smaller classes, stricter teacher certification, charter schools, and voucher programs designed to let parents pick public or private schools with somebody (a foundation, the government) paying part of the tuition. Happily, scholarly attention to this subject has not flagged; there are many studies of the effects on school outputs of all of these inputs.

But one thing has not changed: the educational establishment and much of public opinion persists in thinking that better inputs will produce better outputs. This book, by Jay P. Greene, is a splendidly written summary of what scholars have learned set against what many people suppose. It lists eighteen myths about public schools and summarizes the evidence showing that each of these myths is entirely wrong or seriously open to question.

For example, we learn once again that increased school spending does not improve student achievement, that stricter teacher certification does not improve teaching, that there is as yet no reason to think that having tougher student tests leads to cheating or causes students to drop out of school, or that smaller class size always leads to better student performance. And there is a review of the evidence that suggests that voucher programs usually improve student performance, at least for some students, especially the least advantaged ones.

The argument of this book is not that nothing works, but that some things work better than others. Most parents already know that there are differences in the quality of public schools. Many pick places to live based on the reputation of the schools in that town. My own grandchildren attend very good public schools found in certain small suburbs.

Many people, and not just rich ones, send their children to private schools in the belief, supported by a lot of evidence, that private schools (most of which are rather poor, church-related enterprises) do a better job of teaching students that many big-city school systems. James Coleman, after issuing his report on educational opportunity, published another book suggesting that, even after controlling for pupil backgrounds, private schools did a better job than public ones. And these private schools are generally not like lushly endowed and quite expensive Andover or Exeter; they are typically Catholic schools with small tuitions that are named after a saint.

There are important differences between good and bad public schools. In a book published in 1990, John E. Chubb and Terry M. Moe found that the good ones tend to be smaller ones with a less intrusive bureaucracy, teacher unions with not much influence over who is hired and who is dismissed, and parents who are better educated. To oversimplify just a bit, good schools are more likely to be found in small towns and suburbs than in big cities. That is probably why my grandchildren are getting a good education.

There is a great deal one can learn about schools that has solid scholarly backing. This book from Jay Greene and the Manhattan Institute is an excellent place to start.

Introduction

Why myths dominate education policy, and how evidence can dispel them

Myths aren't lies. They're beliefs that people adopt because they have an air of plausibility, people want to believe they're true, and they are consistent with at least some pieces of evidence. But, of course, myths aren't true—or at least they're not the whole truth. This book identifies, catalogues, and rebuts eighteen common myths that dominate education policy. Dispelling these myths would open the door to substantial improvement of our nation's schools.

Just because someone believes in or promotes a myth doesn't mean that person is a fool or a liar. Myths usually have a lot going for them. They're plausible—they're generally consistent with how people think the world works. They're things people want to believe—it's often more comfortable to believe a myth than to challenge it. And they're consistent with some evidence—a myth wouldn't get very far unless there were some facts people could point to that seemed to justify it.

Unfortunately, much of what people believe today about education is as mythological as anything from Homer or Aesop, even if it isn't nearly as poetic. Education policy is dominated by myths. Some of the more prominent education myths are that schools perform poorly because they need more money, that high-stakes testing only leads to teaching to the test and manipulation of the results, that the research on school choice is mixed and inconclusive, and that school choice leads to increased segregation. These myths, like many others, are plausible, attractive, and not entirely without some empirical support. Suburban school districts that spend more money also tend to be the districts with higher student achievement, teachers do appear to change classroom content and practices in response to high-stakes testing, school choice researchers have contentious disagreements on some questions, and the idea of universal public education is clearly in keeping with the principle of equal opportunity for everyone. Nonetheless, these and many other common beliefs about education are myths.

The people promoting these myths may not be fools or liars, but the myths themselves do real harm to children. They cause us to misunderstand the nature of the problems in our schools, to continue engaging in practices that shortchange students, and to resist the adoption of effective reforms that would improve education. For example, if not for education myths we wouldn't think that schools fail because they lack adequate resources, we wouldn't continue paying ineffective teachers the same as effective ones, and we would support proven reforms like accountability and school choice. Before we can bring about real improvement in schools, we have to start by dispelling the education myths that facilitate mediocrity and block progress.

People believe these education myths for a variety of reasons. Because it involves children, education is a highly emotional issue, which tends to cloud people's thinking. And it doesn't help that people tend to assume they already know about education policy just because they went to school themselves or they have a child going through school. Public perceptions of education policy tend to be distorted by people's subjective experiences in the classroom, from which they may draw the wrong lessons if they don't step back and look at the facts objectively.

But by far the most important reason myths dominate education policy is that they are promoted by organized interests. These interest groups fundamentally shape education policy, just as similar groups fundamentally shape every other kind of policy. In a democracy, policymaking is primarily the result of alliances between, and deliberations among, various organized interest groups. To gain an advantage in debates over policy, interest groups promote myths that support their positions. Of course, if systematic evidence supports their positions, interest groups will use that as well. Their goal is simply to advance their agendas; they are relatively indifferent to whether their claims are based on myths or facts. Thus, evidence does inform policy deliberations and can affect the relative strength of each interest group, but it is usually not the sole or even predominant influence over policy outcomes. This is the way democratic governance works, and education policymaking is not immune to its normal practices and problems.

Though it can be ugly, this democratic process usually works pretty well. But it is malfunctioning on education because most people fail to appreciate the role interest groups play in shaping education policy. Education policymaking is no different from other policymaking in a democratic system, but people prefer to think that it is different because it involves our children. We care much more about our children than about roads or buildings, so how could education policy be governed by the same process of competition among organized interests that governs the construction of highways or the zoning of land? Rather than face this uncomfortable reality, most people are inclined to view the actors in education policy debates as wise, disinterested experts even when they are obviously interested parties. This allows them to believe that education policymaking is really a discussion among professional experts rather than a political struggle among organized interest groups.

Education practitioners, such as teachers, school administrators, and professors at education schools, are not necessarily reliable judges of an education policy's merits. Just as doctors are not neutral parties in health policy discussions, education practitioners are not neutral parties in education policy discussions, since education policy affects their interests. Also, people with direct experience often lack the proper perspective to assess questions of policy, just as a soldier on the front line may be a poor judge of the merits of a military strategy. While reporters regularly consult education practitioners for their opinions about education policy, we should be careful not to treat their claims as though they were comprehensive assessments made by neutral experts.

And if the practitioners themselves aren't necessarily objective, their professional associations certainly won't be. These organizations exist to promote the collective interests of their members. We should expect the policy positions of organizations like teachers' unions, school board associations, and education bureaucracies to reflect their members' interests, just as the policy positions of the American Medical Association reflect the interests of doctors. No one should treat these organizations as anything other than what they really are—interest groups that seek to advance their agendas regardless of the evidence.

In this book, we have attempted to adjudicate which education policy claims are supported by the evidence and which are myths. We are not just naysayers knocking down everything in sight as a myth. We identify a number of policies that are supported by the evidence; indeed, one of the major harms inflicted by education myths is that they block the adoption of promising reform policies. And we recognize that not everyone will agree with all our assessments of the evidence. We encourage our readers to listen to the assessments of others. Some people will even say that we are the mythmakers, and that the beliefs we are calling myths are actually supported by a full consideration of the evidence. As long as the debate is based strictly on the evidence, we welcome it. We trust that informed readers will be able to compare the various claims about the evidence and draw the appropriate conclusions.

PART I

Resources

CHAPTER I

The Money Myth

"Schools perform poorly because they need more money."

If people know anything about public schools, it's that they are strapped for cash and would perform significantly better if only they had more money. They know this because they hear it so often. Car bumpers across America declare that "It will be a great day when our schools get all the money they need and the Air Force has to hold a bake sale to buy a bomber." Author Jonathan Kozol has produced a series of best-selling books portraying urban schools as desperately underfunded. The National Education Association declares that there is "a lack of resources in schools and classrooms across the country."[1] The Education Commission of the States warns that "school finances across the country are teetering on horrendous."[2] The *New York Times* editors can say, without much fear of being contradicted, that "providing quality education for all America's children will take . . . a great deal of money."[3] In 2003 a New York state appeals court found that the state had not spent enough money on New York City schools to provide them with an adequate education, and ordered the state to open up its treasury and spend $14 billion more.

The assertion that schools need more money is so omnipresent that most Americans simply accept the truth of the claim unconsciously. They don't think about whether schools are inadequately funded any more than they think about whether the living room couch is still in the living room. The premise that schools need more money has become the furniture of our national thought about education.

That's why just about every education policy debate quickly turns into a debate about spending more money. Do parents want schools to set higher standards of academic achievement? The education columnist for the *New York Times* replies that to do so we must spend more money, solemnly intoning that "higher standards and adequate finances cannot be separated."[4] Do people want schools to be held accountable for their performance? Schools cry out that they cannot perform better without more money. "The dollars are just not there for the laserlike work necessary to take care of all children," says the superintendent of a suburban school district where schools were identified as failing, echoing his colleagues across the country.[5] Do some cities want to experiment with pilot school voucher programs? That, too, inevitably becomes an argument about school spending; as a *Boston Globe* column put it, "vouchers would not be an issue if we properly funded public schools."[6]

The pervasiveness of this assumption that schools are inadequately funded says more about the state of our public thought about education than anything else. It is simultaneously the most widely held idea about education in America and the one that is most directly at odds with the available evidence. Our nation's experience over the past thirty years has shown that a lack of resources is not one of the major problems affecting our schools' performance. The idea that underperforming schools would succeed if only we gave them more funding—the Money Myth—is simply unsupported.

Defining the Money Myth

To say that it is a myth that schools are inadequately funded is not at all to deny that there is a relationship between spending and school performance. If we reduced school spending to zero, that would certainly have an impact on student outcomes! But it is one thing to say that schools need adequate resources in order to perform well, a proposition that everyone agrees with; it is quite another thing to say that if we gave schools more money than they currently get, they would produce substantially better results than they currently produce. The former statement is self-evidently true—by definition, if school spending is not "adequate" then schools will not perform well. The latter statement, by contrast, is an empirical claim concerning facts that can be measured and evaluated.

Before we examine the evidence on school spending, it is important that we define what it means to say that schools are "inadequately funded." The truly relevant question for voters and policymakers is whether increases in spending levels would produce a substantial degree of improvement in student performance. Thus, schools are "inadequately funded" in the relevant sense only if there are reasonable grounds to believe that spending more money on education would produce better education outcomes.

One major reason people find it plausible that schools are inadequately funded is that they know many schools aren't performing well. But while adequate funding is a necessary condition for school success, it is far from sufficient by itself. There are factors besides spending that contribute to school performance. Institutional incentives are one example—if schools are not rewarded for performing well, they have little incentive to succeed regardless of how much money they have available. If schools are failing, inadequate funding is only one possible explanation; poor performance alone tells us nothing about whether spending levels are contributing to the problem.

Examining the Record on Spending and Performance

Few people are aware that our education spending per pupil has been growing steadily for fifty years. According to the U.S. Department of Education, at the end of World War II public elementary and secondary schools in the United States spent a total of $1,214 per student in inflation-adjusted 2001–2002 dollars. By the middle of the 1950s that figure had roughly doubled to $2,345. By 1971–1972 it had almost doubled again, reaching $4,479. And in the thirty years since then, it has doubled a third time, climbing to $8,745 in 2001–2002 (see figure 1.1).[7]

It would be difficult to measure the effects of these spending increases on student outcomes during the period before the early 1970s, when the federal government began conducting standardized tests on nationally representative samples of students. To do so we would have to rely on such measures as classroom grades or performance on college entrance exams during this period, which would be unwise. Grades are highly subjective and variable from place to place and even from teacher to teacher, while college exams are taken by a subset of students that is not representative of the student population as a whole.

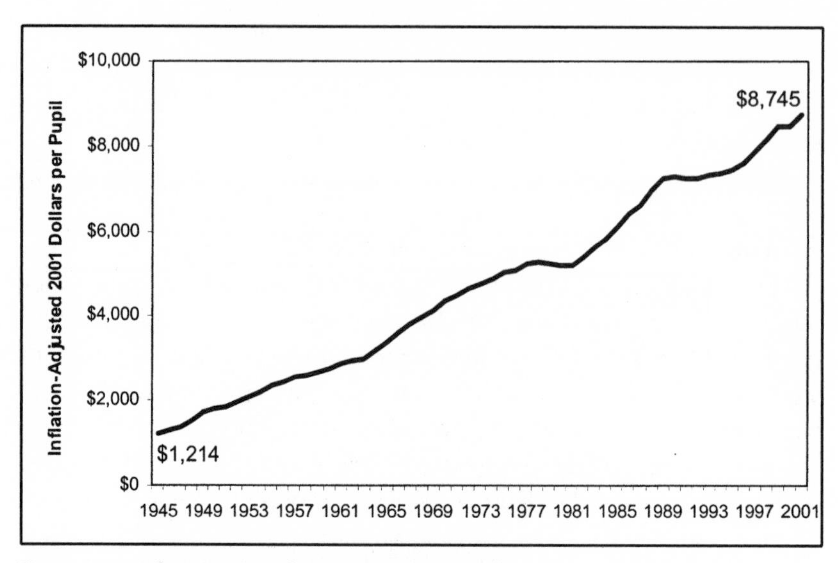

Figure 1.1. Education Spending Has Grown Rapidly
Note: Before 1970 data are only available for odd-numbered years. Data for 2000 and 2001 are estimates.
Source: *Digest of Education Statistics 2002*, U.S. Department of Education, Table 166.

In any event, the effects of early spending increases are not necessarily relevant today. Knowing whether it made a difference fifty years ago to raise per-pupil spending from about $1,000 to $2,000 in today's dollars does not give us any information on whether it would make a difference now to raise per-pupil spending from about $9,000 to $10,000. The law of diminishing marginal returns tells us that each new spending increase will buy us less improvement in outcomes than the last one did—just as the difference between a $50,000 home and a $250,000 home is much greater than the difference between a $1 million home and a $1.2 million home.

But the record since the early 1970s, when the National Assessment of Educational Progress (NAEP) began, is a different matter. Here we have a reliable, objective, and properly representative measurement of student outcomes to tell us what effect spending increases have had. During this period inflation-adjusted spending per pupil doubled from $4,479 to $8,745, so if more money were going to produce better results then we would expect to see very significant improvement during this period.

This has not happened. For twelfth-grade students, who represent the end product of the education system, NAEP scores are basically flat over the past thirty years. The average NAEP reading score was 285 in 1971 and 288 in 1999; the average NAEP math score was 304 in 1973 and 308

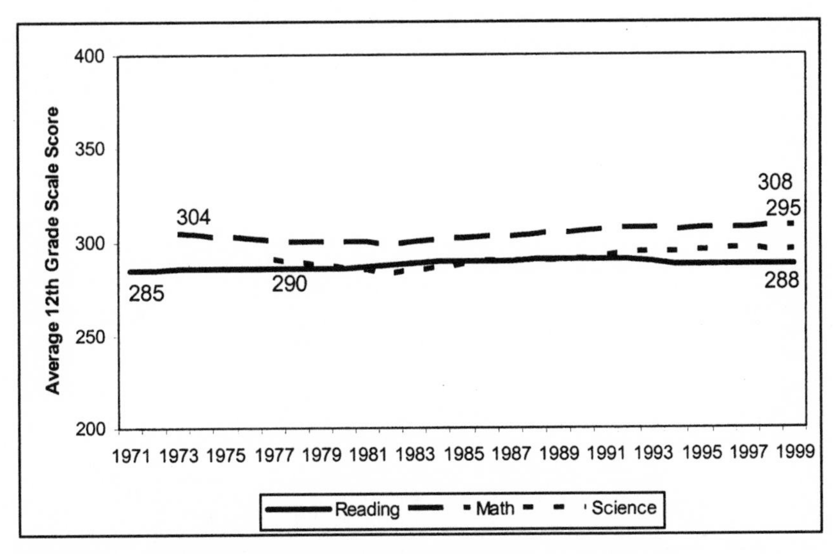

Figure 1.2. NAEP Scores Are Flat
Source: Campbell, Hombo, and Mazzeo, "NAEP 1999, Trends in Academic Progress: Three Decades of Student Performance," U.S. Department of Education.

in 1999; and the average NAEP science score was 290 in 1977 and 295 in 1999 (see figure 1.2).[8] The high school graduation rate was also flat during this period. In 1971–1972 high school graduates made up 75.6 percent of the seventeen-year-old population, while in 1999–2000 they made up 70.3 percent, while early estimates for 2000–2001 and 2001–2002 indicate that the rate may have gone back up by one or two points (see figure 1.3). If so, this would leave it very close to the level it had been at thirty years earlier.[9]

These small gains—three to five points on the NAEP out of a scale of 500—do not represent significant progress. They are certainly trivial compared to the magnitude of the increase in education spending over the same period. It is clear from the evidence of our national experience that simply adding more money to the public school system produces no significant improvements.

This evidence is strongly confirmed by the existing body of academic research. Although a relatively small number of social science studies have found a positive relationship between more spending and better results, the large majority of such studies have found no evidence of such a relationship. Eric Hanushek of Stanford University examined every available study on the relationship between spending and educational outcomes that conformed

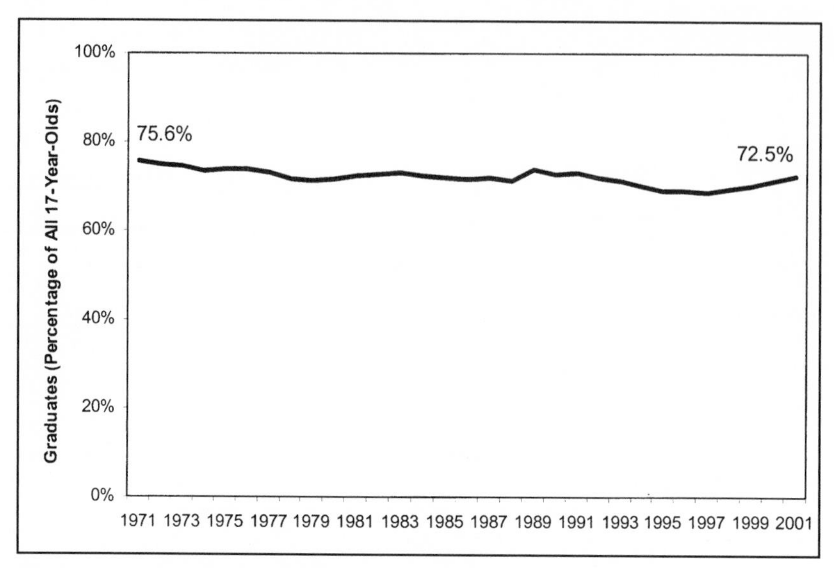

Figure 1.3. High School Graduation Rates Are Flat
Note: Data for 2000 and 2001 are estimates.
Source: *Digest of Education Statistics 2002*, U.S. Department of Education, Table 103.

to basic social science methods—a total of 163 studies—and found that only twenty-seven had identified a statistically significant relationship between increased per-pupil spending and student performance. He concludes that "unless one weights it in specific and peculiar ways, the evidence from the combined studies of resource usage" shows that "any evidence of effective resource usage is balanced by evidence of other, naturally occurring, situations in which resources are squandered."[10] Other researchers analyzing the same set of studies with somewhat different methods have argued that the studies justify concluding that more school spending does affect student performance, but the size of the effect they identify is so small that it is dwarfed in comparison to the large increases in school spending over the past thirty years.[11] To show such a tiny effect from such a large increase in spending does not justify the Money Myth.

It is possible, of course, that the additional funds put into the system over the past thirty years would have produced major improvements, if not for other problems that prevented the system from making good use of all the extra money it received. These problems might include structural inefficiencies or perverse institutional incentives. It is also possible that if only these other problems were removed, not only would the past increases in spending be freed to produce improvements, but providing the system with still further additional funds would also produce further improvements. If so, this only makes it all the more important to deal with those other problems and free the system to start making good use of the money it receives rather than focusing on the alleged need to supply the system with even more spending increases.

Rescuing the Money Myth from the Facts

Various arguments have been put forward by academics and policymakers seeking to rescue the Money Myth from the considerable evidence against it. One of the most common and most widely believed is the argument that much of the increase in funding over the past thirty years has gone to services for disabled students provided through special education programs. On this view, spending increases would have improved student performance if only they had gone to general education instead of being diverted to special education. We will set aside this argument for the moment; it will be fully addressed in chapter 2.

Another method by which some seek to justify the Money Myth is to claim that large portions of spending in the school system are not really relevant to education, and thus the true amount that is spent on education is much lower than it appears to be. For example, Richard Rothstein has long claimed that the amount of money going to "regular education" has been growing much more slowly than total education spending. In a report for the Economic Policy Institute he shows that "regular education spending" has grown slowly—if we exclude from the category of "regular education" all spending on administrative costs, dropout prevention, programs serving at-risk youth, bilingual education, lunch and breakfast subsidies, student activities, security and violence prevention, attendance control, health programs, counseling, and various other programs. Once we take away all these expenses, Rothstein claims, we can see that the amount we spend on "regular education" is really not so big.[12]

Unfortunately, this approach to school spending does not stand up under scrutiny. Additional money spent on these other programs should be improving student performance, just as additional money spent on "regular education" would, if it is not being spent wastefully. If we are spending more on services to at-risk youth and dropout retention then we should expect that to affect student outcomes, as more of the students targeted by these programs stay in school and perform better. If we are spending more on classes for students who have limited English proficiency then we should expect that to affect student outcomes, as those students learn English faster and also do better in other subjects. If we are spending more money on school security then we should expect that to affect student outcomes, as reduced violence in school frees students to learn in a secure environment. Whenever we spend more money on any school program, we have a right to expect a return on that investment for our students, just as we do if we spend more money on teachers and textbooks.

A similar mistake was made by former Secretary of Education William Bennett when he claimed that "too much money has been diverted from the classroom; a smaller share of the school dollar is now being spent on student classroom instruction than at any time in recent history." Bennett said that "administrative bloat" and "the bureaucratic 'blob'" are "draining our school resources."[13] It is true that teachers' salaries make up a smaller share of all education spending than they used to, but the portion of education spending that doesn't go to teachers' salaries includes much more than just administrative costs; it includes textbooks, equipment, teachers' employment benefits, and other items directly relevant to "classroom instruction." And even if administrative costs are rising as a share of education spending, that would be just fine if it were leading to an increase in test scores as schools became better administered. The real problem isn't whether money flows to this or that category of school spending; the real problem is that increased spending isn't producing significant improvements.

Still another method for salvaging the Money Myth is to claim that spending has gone up without raising outcomes because students are harder to teach than they used to be. In their book *The Manufactured Crisis*, David Berliner of Arizona State University and Bruce Biddle of the University of Missouri claim that students today have higher disability rates, are more likely to speak a native language other than English, have greater health-care needs, and are more likely to be poor than in the past, rendering them less easily teachable than they used to be.[14] But most of these claims don't withstand scrutiny. Berliner and Biddle present no evidence that the health-care needs of students have worsened; in fact, children's health has actually improved quite a bit. The child mortality rate, a good indicator of physical health generally, has improved 66 percent in the past thirty years.[15] The evidence they put forward to show that student disabilities and poverty have worsened is based on misleading measurements of those factors. The question of disabilities we will set aside so we can look at in greater detail in chapter 2. As for poverty, Berliner and Biddle only make it appear to have increased by arbitrarily choosing to begin their analysis in 1977 and end it in 1988. While poverty did get a little worse between those two particular years, it is important to remember that poverty is constantly getting better and worse as the business cycle takes the economy up and down. If we take a longer view, we see that there is a broader upward trend behind the short-term ups and downs of poverty: between 1970 and 2001, family incomes for those in the lowest quintile of income peaked and then turned downward again four times, but despite this they saw an overall increase of roughly 10 percent.[16] Of the factors cited by Berliner and Biddle, only the percentage of students not speaking English as their native language is substantially worse than it used to be.

Most important, Berliner and Biddle do not attempt to systematically measure the overall level of students' advantages and disadvantages. Instead, they isolate a few factors on which they claim conditions have worsened and present only those factors to the reader. As a result, their depiction of changes in the characteristics of the student population over time is highly selective. An accurate evaluation of students' overall teachability would have to include an examination of other factors, such as preschool attendance, on which conditions may have improved. The relevant question is not whether the level of poverty (or any other particular problem) has gone up but whether students are or are not less teachable on the whole than they used to be.

Jay Greene and Greg Forster of the Manhattan Institute have developed a systematic method for measuring the overall level of disadvantages in the student population. They combined sixteen social factors that affect student achievement, such as poverty, family structure, health, and students who don't speak English well, into a single measurement they call the Teachability Index. They found that students are actually more easily teachable today than they were thirty years ago—levels of the characteristics they measured were on the whole about 9 percent higher in 2001 than in 1970.[17]

In order to salvage the Money Myth by appealing to a decline in student teachability, the myth's advocates would have to show that students got roughly twice as hard to teach over the period when education spending doubled and outcomes were flat. While the Teachability Index may not be a highly precise measurement, it is a reasonably good one. In light of the evidence it provides about the well–being of students during this period, it does not appear plausible that students could have gotten twice as hard to teach. It is not even very plausible that they could have gotten much harder to teach at all.

Finally, some argue that education spending has risen while student performance has been flat because of changes in the labor market. Specifically, talented and well-educated women used to have few professional opportunities outside of teaching, whereas now they have much greater potential for success in other occupations. Since women make up most of the teaching workforce, this has made it harder to hire high-quality teachers; to get the same quality teacher you now need to pay more, because the women who teach now have better opportunities elsewhere.[18]

This is probably true to some extent, but it is largely beside the point. The large increase in education spending over the past thirty years cannot be attributed to teachers' compensation. Average teachers' salaries have risen only slightly faster than inflation—from $41,573 in 1970–1971 to $44,604 in 2001–2002 in inflation-adjusted dollars.[19] Instead, the increase in spending has gone to other areas. For example, the public school system employs a much larger number of teachers relative to the student population. In 1970 it employed one teacher for every 22.3 students, but in 2001 it employed a teacher for every 15.9 students.[20] Changes in the labor market for teachers cannot explain why very large spending increases on things other teachers' compensation have not produced significant improvements in school performance.

Foundations of the Money Myth

At this point one might reasonably ask: if it is true that the Money Myth is unfounded, why is it so widely believed? Hanushek suggests two reasons. The first is simply that for various reasons people don't want to believe that large amounts of additional money have been spent without producing significant results. They tend to pay attention to the small amount of evidence that confirms their expectations rather than the large amount of evidence that runs against their expectations. "The suggestion that differences in resources are unrelated to student performance . . . defies common sense, conventional wisdom, the hopes of parents and policymakers, and the apparent self-interest of many participants in the schooling system. Given this background, it is not surprising that any evidence that appears to suggest that 'resources count' gets unduly wide attention."[21] He also suggests the Money Myth came to be accepted because the rise in per-pupil spending since 1970 was less noticeable due to the shrinking number of students in U.S. schools during that time; although spending per pupil was rising dramatically, total spending rose much more slowly due to the lower number of students actually in the system.[22]

There are other reasons as well. The Money Myth survives in part because people are frequently confused about what is or is not a sign of inadequate funding. The "bake sale" bumper sticker is a perfect example—just because schools hold bake sales doesn't mean they're inadequately funded. Any bureaucratic institution, whether it is desperately strapped for cash or lavishly funded, will seek to increase its budget if it can do so in a cost-effective manner. Ultimately, the "bake sale" bumper sticker is more an aesthetic statement than a real assessment of funding priorities—especially since the United States actually spends much more on education than it does on the military.[23]

Another factor fueling the Money Myth is the common tendency to accept anecdotes about needy schools without much critical thought. In his best-selling *Savage Inequalities*, Kozol profiles a New York City school that meets in a converted roller-skating rink. The school has no windows. "Textbooks are scarce and children have to share their social studies books. . . . The carpets are patched and sometimes taped together."[24] Elsewhere, a PTA official advocating higher school spending writes of her school: "My big frustration is the lack of money for computer teachers and science teachers. Belvedere had two computer labs, but now we're down to one. No money. We don't have a science lab anymore. No money."[25] A teacher asking for more school spending writes, "I work in a school that has not been refurbished or modernized since it was built in the early 1950s."[26]

The trouble with this sort of anecdotal reasoning is not only, or even primarily, that the poor condition of a few schools is not necessarily representative of the condition of schools generally. Much more important than this is that such anecdotes are a distraction from what should be the crucial issue: if we gave these schools more money, would they improve?

Or are other problems preventing these schools from making good use of the money they get? If schools are plagued by structural or institutional problems, then funding increases may not necessarily produce the fresh carpets, new textbooks, and better classroom equipment they are intended to produce.

These anecdotes are particularly effective in swaying public opinion when they are coupled with claims that there is a gap in spending between urban schools and suburban schools. Kozol in particular relies on the assumption that any funding inequality between urban and suburban schools constitutes prima facie proof that urban schools are inadequately funded. Hence the name of his book, *Savage Inequalities*—inequalities in funding are "savage" because they cause urban schools to fail.

Scholars disagree over whether there really is a funding gap between urban and suburban schools. For example, Abigail and Stephan Thernstrom of the Manhattan Institute argue that "Kozol's allegations about the unfair distribution of school resources were not accurate generalizations in 1991, and in subsequent years educational spending has soared, with a disproportionate share of the additional resources going to high-minority, high-poverty schools."[27]

But regardless of whether there is a gap between urban spending and suburban spending, the existence of such a gap would not prove that giving urban schools more money would result in improvement. It may be that other problems would prevent urban schools from making good use of the additional funds. Kozol doesn't address this possibility. Similarly, Rothstein asks: "If money does not matter" to school performance, "why do wealthy suburbs tax themselves so highly for expensive schools?"[28] One possible explanation is that suburban schools can make better use of the funds they receive because they are not plagued by the same structural and institutional problems that urban schools face. Thus, a suburban school might reach the point of diminishing marginal returns—where further spending does not produce significant improvements—at a higher level of spending than an urban school would.

Of course, some may believe that it is just inherently wrong for some schools to have more money than others do. This, however, is an entirely separate issue. The age-old political question of whether those who have more money ought to be permitted to keep it has no bearing on the question of whether our urban schools are performing poorly because they lack money rather than for other reasons such as structural inefficiencies or perverse institutional incentives.

No doubt there is plenty of room for debate on how best to reform our school system. However, that debate can't happen in a constructive way until Americans realize that schools are not inadequately funded—they would not perform substantially better if they had more money. The empirical evidence simply doesn't allow for this to be the case. The sooner people realize how the Money Myth is distorting their view of the school system, the sooner we can have a productive debate on how to make that system better.

CHAPTER 2

The Special Ed Myth

"Special education programs burden public schools, hindering their academic performance."

How did the Money Myth we examined in chapter 1 get to be so widespread? One of the most important ways is through popular misunderstanding of special education programs. When angry parents demand to know why the public school system produces such lackluster results, education experts often seek to redirect their anger, claiming that the real problem is a budget crisis caused by soaring special education costs. Don't blame the schools, they say in effect; rising numbers of handicapped kids are to blame. This is the Special Ed Myth, a close cousin of the Money Myth.

But disabled students are not a valid excuse for the school system's failure to perform better. There has been a remarkable level of nominal growth in special education programs, but the evidence indicates it is being caused by artificial category shifting rather than by any real change in the frequency or severity of student disabilities. That is, more students today are labeled "special education" students, but this is because of changes in the way we label students rather than because more students suffer from real disabilities than did before. There may be a number of factors contributing to this change in labeling practices, but the most important cause seems to be perverse incentives arising from the special education funding system.

What's more, there have been very large increases in funding for special education in the last quarter-century, but they have not produced improvements in special education outcomes. The common image of disabled students as hopeless cases who can't learn is simply wrong—most disabled students have mild disabilities that shouldn't prevent them from making educational progress if they get the extra help they need. Such progress, if it were occurring, would be visible in graduation rates and national test scores, since special education students are included in those measurements. Its absence clearly indicates that the school system is not performing adequately.

Foundations of the Special Ed Myth

It isn't hard to see why people believe in the Special Ed Myth, given that the number of kids in our schools classified as disabled has been increasing steadily for twenty-five years. In the 1976–1977 school year, when federal programs for disabled students had just been enacted, only 8.3 percent of all public-school students were enrolled in special education programs. By the 2000–2001 school year, that number had risen to 13.3 percent, an increase of over 50 percent.[1] This growth, far from showing signs of slowing down, actually accelerated during the 1990s.[2]

It's also true that this has caused a significant increase in the amount of money spent on activities classified as special education programs. Federal law requires states to fund services for disabled students, so as the number of students classified as disabled has grown, spending on activities classified as special education programs has grown as well. Estimates of what portion of the overall growth in educational spending has gone to special education programs range from less than 20 percent to almost 40 percent, but no one doubts that spending on programs labeled "special education" has grown substantially.[3]

If we don't look any further than these superficial observations, it certainly appears plausible that the growth of special education has eaten up a large amount of educational spending, draining those dollars from school budgets. And once we accept the Special Ed Myth, the Money Myth becomes more plausible. If a large portion of the increased education spending since 1970 has been siphoned out of school budgets by special education, that would help explain why we're spending almost twice as much money on schools and seeing the same educational outcomes.

Former *New York Times* education columnist Richard Rothstein relies crucially on the Special Ed Myth to justify the Money Myth. For Rothstein, we shouldn't include the rising amount of money spent on special education when we look at whether student outcomes are benefiting from increased spending. "Education of the handicapped is worthwhile," he writes, "but it is dishonest to suggest that special education funds should produce academic gains for regular students and, when they do not, claim proof that money spent on public schools is wasted."[4] David Berliner of Arizona State University and Bruce Biddle of the University of Missouri make a similar argument in their influential book *The Manufactured Crisis.* "Have enrollments in special education recently climbed?" they ask. "The answer is an unequivocal *yes*!" And since special education students cost more to educate, special education growth "is a major reason why local school budgets have increased." They echo Rothstein in arguing that this increase in school budgets should not be expected to produce improvements in student outcomes. "It makes no sense at all to argue that extra funds needed for *special* education programs should produce gains in achievement scores for *regular* students—but this is exactly what the arguments of some critics have implied."[5]

A Closer Look at the Facts

The problem with the Special Ed Myth is that its account of the growth of special education programs is misleading. When we inspect the data more closely, we see that the growth of special education enrollment has not been caused by an actual increase in the number of disabled students, but rather by changes in diagnostic practices. The evidence does not support the conclusion that either the number of disabled students or the severity of their disabilities has grown. Rather, the standard for what counts as a disability has been lowered. A student who might have been called "slow" a quarter century ago because he had difficulty learning would now be far more likely to be called "disabled."

This makes a crucial difference in our understanding of how special education money is spent. If student disabilities had truly increased by over 50 percent, it might have made sense that we are spending more money and seeing no overall improvement in student outcomes; the benefits from the increase in funds would have been offset by the increased challenges of serving a student population with greater disabilities. But if the student body has not significantly changed in terms of the number or severity of student disabilities, spending more money on education ought to produce better results regardless of how many students are formally classified as disabled. Simply putting a "disabled" label on certain students and a "special education" label on the programs that serve them doesn't excuse schools from educating those students effectively.

Has There Been Real Growth in Disabilities?

The underlying premise of the Special Ed Myth is that the growth of enrollment in special education programs is caused by real growth in the occurrence of disabilities in children. By this account, there are simply more disabled students than there used to be, and those students have more costly disabilities. For example, school superintendents Sheldon Berman and Perry Davis, Ann Koufman-Frederick of the Massachusetts Association of School Superintendents, and neurologist David Urion of Boston's Children's Hospital defend the special education system by arguing that there has been real growth in student disabilities caused by broad social forces outside schools' control. They point to three factors in particular: improvements in medical technology, deinstitutionalization of children with serious difficulties, and increases in childhood poverty.[6]

This account simply isn't consistent with the facts. The authors argue that there are now more children with mental retardation and other neurological disorders because improved medicine saves more low-birth-weight babies. It is true that the number of babies expected to develop retardation later in life due to birth conditions has grown, but the total number of students classified as mentally retarded has undergone a dramatic drop—from about 961,000 in 1976–1977 to about 599,000 in 2000–2001.[7] That's not just a drop in the percentage of all students with mental retardation, but an absolute reduction; as a percentage of all students, this reduction is even greater. Any growth in neurological disorders caused by increased numbers of surviving low-birth-weight babies has been more than offset by improvements in the prevention of such disorders in other areas, such as improved prenatal medicine, safer child car seats, and reductions in exposure to lead paint. While medical improvements will certainly cause some number of children to survive with disabilities where in a previous era they would have died, it also generally causes other children to avoid developing disabilities where in a previous era they would have become disabled.

Deinstitutionalization of students with severe problems also can't be driving the growth of special education enrollment, because that growth has not occurred among students with severe disabilities. While not all categories of severe disability have dropped dramatically, as the mental retardation category has, severe disabilities have not increased. In fact, virtually all of the growth of special education enrollment in the past quarter-century can be attributed to learning disabilities, a mild category. The percentage of all public-school students classified as learning disabled has more than tripled, from 1.8 percent in 1976–1977 to 6.0 percent in 2000–2001. Over the same period, the percentage of students with all other types of disability has been roughly constant; it was 6.5 percent in 1976–1977 and 7.3 percent in 2000–2001 (see figure 2.1). The dramatic growth of special education in the past quarter-century has been driven by learning disabilities, not by the kind of severe problems that might cause a child to be institutionalized.

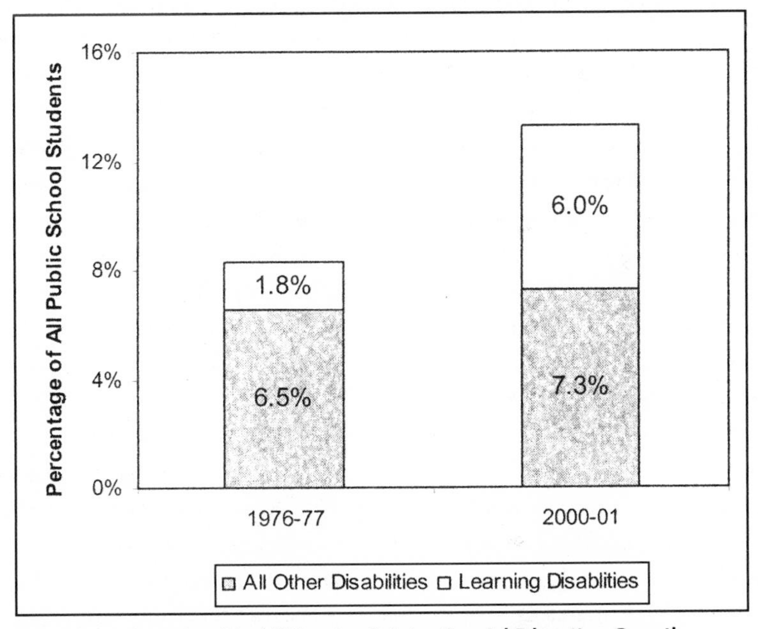

Figure 2.1. Learning Disabilities Are Driving Special Education Growth
Source: Digest of Education Statistics 2002, U.S. Department of Education, Tables 52; and calculations based on data from "24th Annual Report to Congress on the Implementation of the Individuals with Disabilities Education Act," U.S. Department of Education, and Digest of Education Statistics 2002, U.S. Department of Education, Table 37.

At first brush, childhood poverty seems like a more promising explanation for the growth of special education. If early childhood poverty is rising, the disadvantages associated with poverty may cause more children to have, or to be diagnosed as having, disabilities. In particular, growing childhood poverty might increase the number of children diagnosed as learning disabled. Research on child development has reached a consensus on the vital importance of a child's early years in his educational development.[8] Since poor children are likely to receive less stimulation and less help learning, they would face more frequent learning problems due to inadequate early development. Federal law does state that children should not be classified as learning disabled due to learning problems that arise from life circumstances such as poverty. However, in practice it is difficult to separate students who have learning problems because of poverty from students who have learning problems because of bona fide disabilities. So, a rise in the childhood poverty level would make a plausible explanation for the growth in the number of diagnoses of learning disabilities.

There's only one problem with this hypothesis—childhood poverty hasn't actually increased. The percentage of children under six living in poverty was 18.1 percent in 1977 and 18.5 percent in 2002. This difference is far too tiny to explain an over 50 percent increase in special education enrollment over the same period.[9] There were fluctuations in the childhood poverty rate during this period, as it rose during recessions and then declined again during economic recoveries. But the growth of special education enrollment has not tracked these movements in the childhood poverty rate, even if we allow for a time lag between increases in childhood poverty and in special education enrollment. Childhood poverty has regularly oscillated back and forth while special education enrollment has grown on a smooth and steady upward curve.

What's more, childhood poverty reached its last peak in 1992 and has been on a downward trend ever since. If childhood poverty had been causing the growth of special education, we would expect to have seen special education enrollment rates falling by the end of the 1990s. But special education enrollment actually rose at an ever-faster rate throughout that decade.[10]

Even these figures understate the case, because the average poor person today is less poor than the average poor person of 1977. The standard for what counts as "poor" goes up over time as society gets richer. In 1977 the average family in the lowest quintile of income earned $12,908 in inflation-adjusted 2001 dollars, compared to $14,021 for the average family the lowest quintile in 2001.[11] The Census' poverty threshold rose substantially in inflation-adjusted terms during the same period, reflecting this upward movement in the income of the poor.[12] Since the number of children below the poverty line has been relatively stable and the material conditions of those who do live below the poverty line have improved, we should expect to see fewer disabled students because of poverty, not more.

Faced with this dramatic rise in learning disabilities with no clear medical cause, some have even speculated that there might be something in the water. "The data we have seen about lead and mercury contamination in our food and water suggest that the effects they have on the fetus and children may have contributed to the increasing number of children in special education with attention and learning disorders," writes Senator Hillary Clinton.[13] But lead and mercury exposure appear to have been decreasing, not increasing, during the period when diagnoses of learning disabilities have tripled.[14] Perhaps more importantly, if increased lead and mercury exposure—or any other environmental factors—were causing increases in learning disabilities they would also be causing increases in mental retardation. As we have seen, mental retardation diagnoses have declined precipitously. An explosion in learning disability diagnoses coinciding with a collapse in mental retardation diagnoses would be difficult to account for by any medical factor.

There does not appear to be any medical explanation consistent with the facts for why the actual occurrence of disabilities in children would be rising. But this does not mean we should conclude that there must be some other, unknown factor inflicting disabilities on millions of children. There is a far more plausible explanation for rising special education enrollments. The real occurrence of childhood disabilities may not actually have grown; instead, it might be the case that more students are being classified as disabled when there has been no change in the number of students who actually are disabled.

Do Improved Diagnosis or Parental Pressure Cause Category Shifting?

One factor that might cause this to occur would be improved diagnosis of disabilities. For example, the number of students diagnosed as autistic is rising, and this may be attributable to improved diagnosis of autism rather than to an actual increase in the occurrence of autism itself.[15] Also, growth in the number of students placed in special education under the catchall category "other health disorders" may be attributable to more widespread recognition of attention-deficit disorder and related disorders (while most students with such disorders are not placed in special education, some students with severe cases are).

But despite these particular instances where improved diagnosis is probably playing a role, it is unlikely that improved diagnosis is very important as an overall cause of growth in special education. The autism and "other health disorders" categories are not nearly large enough that their growth could explain the dramatic expansion of special education over the last quarter-century. Only about one-tenth of the growth in special education enrollment between 1976–1977 and 2000–2001 occurred in those two categories.[16] As for other categories of disability, we have no reason to believe that schools have significantly improved their diagnosis of most types of disabilities—particularly during the 1990s, the period of the most rapid growth.

This leaves us with a less benign explanation. If the rate at which students are diagnosed as disabled is growing but improved diagnosis is not the main reason, it follows that schools are increasingly diagnosing students as disabled and placing them in special education for reasons unrelated to those students' genuine need for special education services.

Why would schools place more students in special education regardless of whether they truly need it? One possibility is parental pressure; some parents may seek to have their children diagnosed as disabled in order to get them extra attention in class and special accommodations on tests, including college entrance exams. Plausible as this explanation may seem to some, there is not much solid scientific evidence to tell us how often such parental pressure really occurs. While there are some advantages to being placed in special education, there are also considerable disadvantages, including the stigma of the special education label and the reduced level of academic achievement that would normally follow from holding a student to lower expectations in the classroom.

Does High-Stakes Testing Cause Category Shifting?

Another possibility—one that has been the subject of empirical study—is that education policy can create perverse incentives that alter schools' behavior. Schools and their special education staff exercise an overwhelmingly decisive influence over the diagnosis of students. While students can be placed into special education based on a diagnosis from a doctor outside the school system, in practice most students are placed in special education based on a diagnosis from within the school. Any incentive for schools to distort this process may have a profound impact on the actual pattern of diagnosis.

As more states have adopted test-based accountability programs, some researchers have identified these programs as a possible cause of more frequent disability diagnoses. The goal of such high-stakes testing programs is to provide schools with healthy incentives; if students do poorly on the test, schools can be held accountable. But these programs can also create perverse incentives—specifically, an incentive to game the system by labeling low-performing students as disabled in order to exempt them from mandatory testing. When low-performing students are exempt from testing, their schools' average test scores are artificially inflated. Some states have attempted to mitigate this problem by requiring that special education students who are considered testable (that is, not so severely disabled that they are unable to take the test) be included in mandatory testing, but schools could still game the system by labeling testable students untestable.

Examining a high-stakes statewide test in Texas, Donald Deere and Wayne Strayer of Texas A&M University found that students who failed the test in one year were more likely to be classified as exempt from the test (either as special education students or limited English proficient students) the next year; that schools were more likely to classify minority students as exempt if this would reduce the number of minority students tested to a low enough level that the school's minority test scores would not be reported separately; and that when the state started counting the scores of special education students who did take the test toward schools' accountability ratings, the percentage of special education students who were classified as exempt from the test went up, reversing a downward trend.[17] David Figlio of the University of Florida and Lawrence Getzler of the Virginia Department of Planning and Budget, examining a high-stakes test in Florida, found that special education enrollment went up after the introduction of the test, that students in tested grades were more likely than students in untested grades to be placed in special education, that lower-scoring students were more likely to be placed in special education, and that severe disability categories did not rise after the introduction of the test.[18] Finally,

Brian Jacob of Harvard University found that in Chicago schools the percentage of students exempted from testing through special education rose faster after the introduction of high-stakes testing, and most quickly among lower-scoring students.[19]

However, these findings are limited—and in most cases seriously undermined—by problems arising from their research methods. Most obviously, each of these studies is confined to one state or city. This point is much more important than it may seem to be at first glance, because it means that none of these studies can control for the national trend in special education enrollment, or in any other way compare states with and without high-stakes testing (although a few of the findings do compare students who are and are not subject to high-stakes testing within the same state).

Special education enrollment grew nationwide throughout the 1990s. What's more, the nationwide rate of growth accelerated as the decade progressed. Thus, it tells us very little to say that special education enrollment in a given state or city grew faster in years after it adopted high-stakes testing than it did in the years before. This only proves that the state or city in question behaved in a manner consistent with the national trend.

We could just as easily use the same method to link almost any event to growth in special education. For example, special education enrollment in Texas grew faster in the years after the Dallas Cowboys won the 1996 Super Bowl than it had in previous years. Following the method used by both Figlio and Getzler's study and Jacob's study, we could conclude that the Cowboys' victory caused public schools to classify as disabled thousands upon thousands of innocent Texas children who otherwise wouldn't have received that label. But it is more likely that Texas's acceleration of special education growth after 1996 was simply a reflection of the nationwide trend toward faster and faster special education growth during the 1990s.

Likewise, a correlation between low student test scores and special education enrollment—which is found by all three of the studies listed above—doesn't tell us as much as one might think. If a low-performing student is more likely than other students to be placed in special education, it may well be because schools are pushing low-performing students into special education to remove them from the testing pool. But it also stands to reason that students with genuine disabilities will have lower test scores than other students, so it may be that low-performing students are more likely to be diagnosed with disabilities because those are the students who actually *have* disabilities.

Deere and Strayer try to account for this problem by comparing more than one set of paired years—that is, they look not only at whether students are more likely to be diagnosed as disabled one year after performing poorly on the state test, but also at whether they are more likely to be diagnosed after two or three years of performing poorly. However, this does nothing to overcome the problem; it only proves that when schools put low-performing students into special education, they do not always do so after only one year of low performance. In fact, this reflects the procedure schools are supposed to follow—a single low test score should not immediately put a student into special education. Deere and Strayer's finding is simply a multiyear correlation between low test scores and special education enrollment, which is still just as easily attributable to real disabilities in low-performing students as it is to schools' desire to remove those students from the testing pool.

In contrast to these local studies that do not control for the national trend or otherwise compare states that do or do not have high-stakes testing, two national studies have compared states with different policies and found no evidence of a connection between high-stakes testing and growth in special education enrollment. One, conducted by Eric Hanushek and Margaret Raymond of Stanford University, looked only at states with high-stakes testing but controlled for the national trend in special education enrollment. This control serves to implicitly compare states with high-stakes testing to states without high-stakes testing.[20] The other, conducted by Jay P. Greene and Greg Forster of the Manhattan Institute, directly compared states with and without high-stakes tests.[21] Both studies found that states with high-stakes tests did not see any faster growth in special education than states without high-stakes tests.

Do Funding Incentives Cause Category Shifting?

Another source of perverse incentives favoring growth in special education enrollment is school funding systems. In most states, special education is funded in such a manner that school districts receive more money if their special education programs are larger. Funding is either directly based on the number of students in special education, or it is based on something else (such as the number of special education teachers) that is in turn based on the number of special education students. This provides school districts with a financial reward for placing students in special education. Some education officials even call this funding system "the bounty system," because it provides schools with extra money for each additional child diagnosed.

This system creates a perverse financial incentive for schools to put as many students as possible into special education. Unpleasant as it is to suggest that something as important as placing students into special education might be driven by financial considerations, the hard reality is that incentives alter people's behavior. If placing students into special education is financially advantageous, we can reasonably expect that school systems will seek to influence the rate at which students are diagnosed. This need not involve flagrant or obvious abuse of the system; schools can respond to these incentives in ways that are subtle and hard to detect. For example, if a low-performing student is examined and diagnosed as not having a disability, the school might seek to have that student reexamined, and continue conducting reexaminations until the diagnosis comes out differently.

Some might object that funding for special education could not create this kind of perverse incentive because placing a student in special education creates costs at least equal to the new funding it generates. This view misunderstands what truly is and is not a "cost" of placing a child in special education. A true cost is an expenditure that would not have occurred if the student had not been placed in special education. Many of the apparent costs of special education are not truly costs because they represent money that the school would have spent anyway; the only difference is that the spending is labeled "special education" spending rather than ordinary spending.

For example, consider a school whose administrators decide to devote more resources to helping students who are falling behind in reading. If the school simply provides these students with extra reading help, the school must bear the cost of this program itself. But if the same school redefines those students as "learning disabled," and can therefore label its new reading program as a "special education" service, the state government will help pay. This is financially advantageous for the school because it brings in new state funding to cover "costs" for services that the school was going to have to pay for anyway.

Furthermore, there are many fixed costs associated with special education that do not increase with every new child. If a school hires a full-time special education reading teacher or speech therapist, it will pay the same cost whether that teacher handles three students a day or ten. But if funding is provided on a per-student basis, the school will collect a lot more money from the state for teaching ten special education students than it would for teaching three.

Sixteen states have sought to combat the problem of perverse financial incentives by adopting an alternative to the traditional "bounty" system that might be called the "lump-sum" system. In these states, funding for special education is not based on the size of special education programs. Typically, each school district gets funds for special education based on the total number of students enrolled in the district rather than the number of special education students. If a district places a larger percentage of its students into special education, it does not get a larger amount of state funding. Extra funds are usually available for students whose disabilities require extraordinarily expensive services, but these represent only a tiny portion of all special education students.

Greene and Forster studied the effects of funding incentives on special education enrollment by comparing the growth of special education in states with bounty funding systems and those with lump-sum funding systems. They found that the special education enrollment rate grew significantly faster in the 1990s in states with bounty funding systems. While states that adopted lump-sum funding saw their average special education enrollments grow from 11.1 to 12.4 percent of all students, states with bounty funding saw average special education enrollment grow from 10.5 to 12.8 percent (see figure 2.2). The difference was so large that 62 percent of the growth of special education enrollment in bounty-system states over the course of the decade was attributable to funding incentives. This accounts for about 390,000 extra students in special education programs, resulting in additional special education spending of over $2.3 billion per year. High-stakes testing programs were not associated with faster growth in special education.[22]

These findings confirm that the number of disabled children is not really getting bigger. Instead, special education programs have grown for the simple reason that this growth, far from bleeding money from school budgets, is profitable for schools because it brings in state funding for programs

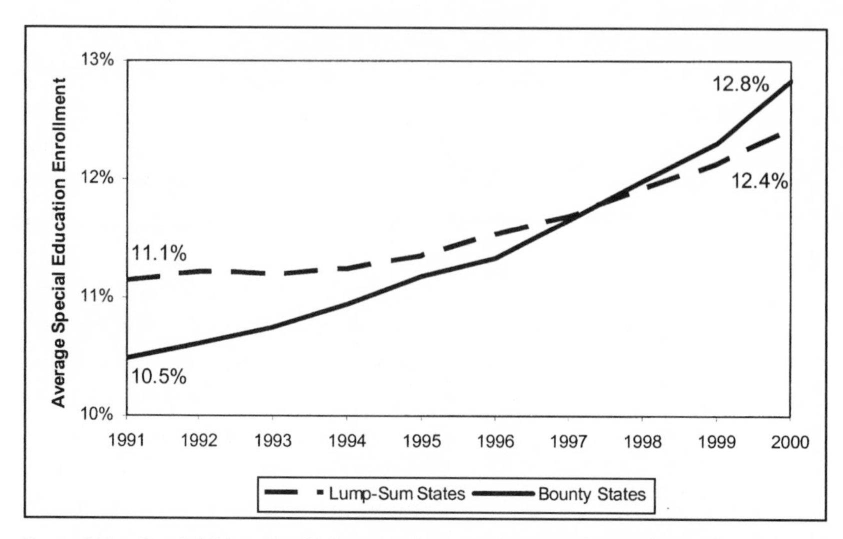

Figure 2.2. Special Education Is Growing Faster in States with Bounty Funding Systems
Note: "Lump-Sum States" includes states that switched from bounty funding to lump-sum funding at some time before 2000.
Source: Greene and Forster, "Effects of Funding Incentives on Special Education Enrollment," Manhattan Institute.

schools would otherwise have to pay for themselves. Thus, not only is the Special Ed Myth false, it is the reverse of the truth: special education is not draining school budgets, it's inflating them.

More Spending Should Produce Better Results

Surprisingly, the point that growth in special education can be attributed to category shifting was once all but conceded by the chief proponent of the Special Ed Myth. In a 1995 report on school spending for the Economic Policy Institute, Rothstein wrote:

> Growth in special education spending may mask a shift in regular education funds resulting from a willingness by some districts to classify as 'special' children whom [sic], in 1967, were considered within the normal span of learning styles teachers confront. New classifications may result from greater sensitivity to causes of learning difficulties, a desire to relieve regular teachers of disciplinary problems or the burden of special attention some children

> require, or an attempt to take advantage of state reimbursement formulae that allot more dollars per pupil for special education students. . . . Lines between special and regular education placements are indistinct.[23]

Unfortunately, Rothstein does not adjust his larger claims about school spending to account for the category shifting he describes here. The main thesis of the report is a repetition of the argument he has made elsewhere: large spending increases haven't improved school performance mainly because they have been diverted from "regular education" to various other budget items, among which special education plays a prominent role. The report's executive summary describe, with figures and details, the large increases in special education spending since 1967. This clearly conveys the impression that schools are burdened with more disabled students than they used to have, and thus that increased spending on disabled students should not be expected to produce improved student performance. He draws the crucial distinction between increased enrollment in special education programs and real growth in the occurrence of student disabilities only once, on page 51 of the report.

Contrary to Rothstein's assertions, spending more money on the same students should produce better results regardless of the categories into which we put students. Rearranging the labels we put on kids doesn't provide an excuse for spending ever-greater amounts on them without seeing any improvement, but that is the implicit premise of Rothstein's argument for the Special Ed Myth—that only money spent on "regular education" should be expected to produce results.

Special Education Students Can Learn

Some claim that it is unreasonable to expect to see educational improvements in special education students if more money is spent on them. One teacher told the Associated Press: "These children are going to plateau at a certain level—that is the nature of a disability. . . . These kids are not going to grow out of it, not going to grow up and be OK."[24] The popular perception of "disabled children" doesn't help—for most people that phrase conjures up images of children with very severe disabilities, hopeless cases who can't be expected to improve. Many people's attitudes seem to be that spending money on these students' education may be noble, but in terms of the results we can expect to achieve it is not ultimately all that different from shoveling bags full of hundred dollar bills into a furnace.

Of course, if this view of things were true it would call into question the wisdom of spending any money at all on special education. Fortunately, however, it simply is not the case for a large majority of special education students that they cannot be expected to learn. Most students in special education have relatively mild disabilities. As we saw in figure 2.1, the "learning disabled" category alone accounts for half of all special education students. Many others have disabilities, like speech and language impediments, that can be largely overcome with the right intervention in all but the most severe cases. "Many of the children who have been dumped into special education classes . . . are teachable children," noted a *New York Times* lead editorial. "Among those with disabilities, perhaps as many as 70 percent are teachable children who suffer from learning or language-related disorders."[25] Even many students with more serious disabilities should be making educational progress if they're getting the help they need—there's no good reason that a blind child or a deaf child shouldn't be learning if his school is doing its job. While it is true, as the teacher said to the Associated Press, that disabled students will not "grow out of" their disabilities, it isn't true that they can't learn at all, and it is certainly false that all of them are already achieving at the highest possible level. The number of students who cannot make measurable educational progress is very small.

Special Education Students' Progress Can Be Measured

Of course, because of the major category shifting that has occurred, it's important that we include special education students when we evaluate how our schools are doing. Rothstein, Berliner, and Biddle are right when they assert that extra spending on special education will not necessarily produce improvements in the performance of students who are not in special education. They seem to be implying that the data we use to measure school performance do not include special education students. If that were true, they would be correct in their assertions that we have a distorted view of how schools are doing.

But this premise is false. We can evaluate the performance of our schools with data that do include special education students. While there is no way to perfectly measure the academic performance of special education students, that does not mean those students are entirely absent from our measurements. The available data include special education students more than well enough to ensure that we can see whether the very large increase in school spending over the past thirty years is producing results. Problems with the data on special education students, while real, are not nearly so serious that they would obliterate any sign of improvements from the doubling of per-pupil spending—if significant improvements were in fact occurring.

To begin with, high school graduation rates include special education students. Many special education students can graduate from high school with a regular diploma rather than a special education diploma if they get the extra help they need. With the large increase in school spending, including major new funding for special education, we ought to see more students successfully graduating. And yet, according to the best available calculation of graduation rates that goes back far enough for a meaningful comparison, the high school graduation rate has been flat or worse. It was 75.6 percent in 1971–1972 and 70.3 percent in 1999–2000. Early estimates for 2000–2001 and 2001–2002 show that the rate may have recovered by one or two percentage points in those years; if that turns out to be so, the graduation rate will have recovered to the point where it will have been close to flat even as per-pupil spending has doubled.[26]

Test scores from the National Assessment of Educational Progress (NAEP) also include special education students. Obviously not every special education student is included, because not every student is capable of taking the test. However, more than enough disabled students take the NAEP for improvements in their performance to be visible if they were occurring.

In fact, even as enrollment in special education has grown substantially throughout the 1990s, the percentage of students excluded from taking the NAEP because of disabilities has not risen. (Data on NAEP exclusions for special education were not systematically gathered before the 1990s.) On NAEP exams where no accommodations for student disabilities were allowed, the rate at which students were excluded from the test because of disabilities generally stayed around 6 or 7 percent. After NAEP began allowing certain accommodations for some types of disability in 1998, the rate went down. On tests where accommodations have been permitted, exclusions from the math test have stayed consistently at 4 percent, while exclusions from the reading test (where fewer accommodations are possible) have fluctuated between 4 and 7 percent.[27]

This indicates that the growth in special education enrollment has mainly occurred among students who do take the NAEP despite their special education diagnoses. Shifting these students into the special education category has not removed them from the pool of students whose outcomes are measured by the NAEP. Thus, advocates of the Special Ed Myth are incorrect when they imply that the growth of special education spending should not be expected to produce gains on the NAEP. The new special education students on whom that additional money is spent are taking the NAEP, so if the money were producing results we would expect to see that reflected in NAEP scores.

Blaming disabled children for the education system's failure to perform simply doesn't stand up to scrutiny. The typical student in special education is just a kid who needs some extra help to learn. Spending significantly more money on helping these students ought to produce visible results, and if it doesn't, we ought to conclude that the problem is with the school system and not with the students.

CHAPTER 3

The Myth of Helplessness

"Social problems like poverty cause students to fail; schools are helpless to prevent it."

Everyone is familiar with the process by which obstacles and difficulties lying in the path to a certain goal are inevitably transformed into excuses for giving up on that goal entirely. A politician on the campaign trail will solemnly promise to adhere to a particular policy, but will later cite some new or complicating factor as an excuse to disregard this promise if doing so is politically expedient. A child will eagerly take up the study of a musical instrument—usually one that costs his parents a lot of money—only to declare it uninteresting and drop it the instant he discovers that practicing is tedious and slow to yield results. And every workplace has at least one employee who keeps finding excuses not to do difficult tasks.

Unfortunately, education is not exempt from what we might call the "law of convenient helplessness," the iron law of human behavior by which any difficulty becomes an excuse for inaction. Schools frequently cite a variety of social problems like poverty, broken homes, and bad parenting as excuses for their own poor performance. There is no doubt that many of our schools face big challenges caused by these problems. Even though material poverty has lessened—poor people today have higher incomes and a better standard of living than poor people a generation ago—other social problems that create obstacles to student learning have proven to be more persistent. For some, the existence of these challenges means that any effort to improve education is doomed to failure. A surprising number of commentators believe in the Myth of Helplessness—that failing schools cannot be improved so long as social problems persist. Some of them seem to think that the very idea of a "failing school" is misleading, since it is really society that has failed. But the evidence clearly establishes that schools can make a difference in students' level of educational achievement in spite of social problems.

Social Problems as an Excuse for Inaction

Richard Rothstein, former education columnist for the *New York Times*, is one of the foremost champions of the Myth of Helplessness. In one column, he laments that "parents today, by a ratio of three to one, tell pollsters that all children should be held to identical standards." He assures us that he doesn't want to go back to the days when schools believed that poor black children couldn't learn at all. But he complains that this myth has been replaced by "a new, equally dangerous one: that . . . all children, regardless of background, can achieve to the same high standards if only schools demand it. . . . We cannot seriously believe this."[1] It is unreasonable, he writes, to expect poor and minority students to read and do math up to a defined minimum standard when they have not benefited from the superior parenting skills and resources of middle-class families.

Rothstein's successor as *New York Times* education columnist, Michael Winerip, has followed his lead in promoting the Myth of Helplessness. Commenting on the federal No Child Left Behind Act, he argues that whether schools meet federal standards will be determined by the condition of their local neighborhoods. He quotes a state education official complaining that his state "will have good schools punished just because they're from poor areas."[2] In another article, he goes even further, asserting that schools are helpless to change poor educational outcomes in the absence of huge new infusions of money to hire better teachers and make classes much smaller. Any other explanation for school failure is simply a distraction—worse, it's blaming the victim: "Blaming public schools, their principals and teachers for losing the education war feels a lot like blaming the ground troops for losing the Vietnam War."[3]

Rothstein and Winerip are the most prominent advocates of the Myth of Helplessness, but unfortunately, that myth goes far beyond their columns.

Indeed, in some ways Rothstein and Winerip are voices of moderation compared to many other mainstream education commentators. They sometimes concede that schools are not totally helpless in the face of difficult social problems; others are not so conciliatory.

Commentator Geoff Rips reminds us that "the public school is responsible for all children who appear at its door: from families kicked off the welfare rolls, from homes with teenage moms or dads, from homes with parents who work two or three jobs, and from homes of the comfortable, the educated, the read-to." He laments that "there are all kinds of standards for measuring schools and [the] schoolchildren coming out" of them, even though "there are no standards governing the lives of children going in—let's say for health care or housing or family income."[4] By this reasoning, unless all students begin from the same starting point it's wrong to expect them to reach any defined minimum endpoint.

Washington Post columnist Richard Cohen thinks that student failure is inherent in poverty itself and is unrelated to the performance of the school system. "It's just plain folly to demand that a school, where a kid spends part of the day, be held accountable for what happens the rest of the day. Poverty—its culture, its effects—is what molds too many kids. The doleful statistics that really matter are produced even before a kid gets to school. . . . None of these factors is the fault of the schools."[5] Even making allowances for the hyperbole that is normal in newspaper columns, Cohen's position is extraordinary. He attributes the gap in educational performance between rich and poor entirely to poverty, disregarding any role that schools themselves might play in exacerbating that gap. Is it really impossible that one reason poor students don't perform as well is that schools disproportionately fail to serve them effectively? Cohen seems to think so. Schools can't do everything, but there are many things that they can do, if they don't do what they can then student failure is, at least in part, "the fault of the schools."

The Myth of Helplessness is also often promoted by political conservatives. Writing in the *Wall Street Journal*, James Heckman of the University of Chicago and Amy Wax of the University of Pennsylvania argue that "reform must look to private behavior more than public policy" to address the unequal performance of black students, because family dysfunction allegedly causes black children to arrive at school hopelessly behind their white peers. They argue that approaches like school reform won't do much to alleviate inequality until black parenting is improved. However, their only evidence regarding the role of schools is that "black underachievement . . . is present even in the best schools and is only weakly correlated with indicators of school quality, such as per-student expenditures, class size or racial composition." The problem here is that Heckman and Wax are relying upon "indicators of school quality" that do not actually indicate school quality.[6] Higher spending and smaller classes do not reliably improve student outcomes (see chapter 1 and chapter 4, respectively), and having more white students does not make a school more effective at educating its students.[7] Observing that more money, smaller classes, and more white students do not improve student outcomes hardly warrants the conclusion that there is nothing schools can possibly do to raise student outcomes. Disadvantages of various kinds may cause black students to be further behind when they first enter the schoolhouse door, but it does not therefore follow that no matter what the school does those students will be just as far behind when they leave twelve years later.

No one would deny that learning is more difficult for some students than it is for others because of factors that are beyond schools' control. Poverty, broken homes, lack of English proficiency, poor parenting, and any number of other factors pose serious educational challenges for some students. If the advocates of the Myth of Helplessness were merely cautioning us to be mindful of these difficulties, or exhorting us that while we seek to improve schools we must also try to alleviate other social problems, no one could disagree with them.

But they go far beyond just reminding us of the challenges resulting from social problems; they use these problems as an excuse to oppose school reforms. Rothstein's position is that no school reform can ever be effective as long as social problems persist: "It would be comforting to think that schools alone could raise achievement for low-income students, but such a shortcut is illusory." If low-income minority students perform poorly, it's because of poverty: "If the past is any guide, rising unemployment will cause children's school performance to decline, but commentators will attribute the drop entirely to poor teachers, low standards or overcrowded schools." And if those same low-income minority students do well, it's because of a strengthening economy: "School leaders take pride in the test-score improvements of recent years for low-income children. But school reforms may not have been entirely responsible for such gains in the strong economy of the 1990s."[8] Winerip also uses his column to oppose school reforms, as do other, more strident advocates of the Myth of Helplessness.

For those who embrace this myth, the difficulties caused by social problems have become an excuse for inaction. Even Rothstein and Winerip, who do occasionally say that there is room for improvement in schools even if social problems are not alleviated, never allow these admissions to translate into concrete support for any proposal that would change the educational status quo. The Myth of Helplessness predominates—social problems are always seen as more powerful than anything schools might do to overcome them.

Consider the radicalism inherent in Rothstein's seemingly moderate position. He says that the old practice of sweeping poor black children into dead-end programs and the new practice of holding all children to the same academic standards are "equally dangerous." That is a remarkable statement—requiring that schools provide disadvantaged students with exactly the same level of education as other students is as bad for them as allowing schools to segregate them into classes where they receive no academic education at all.

Evidence of Promising Reforms

Of course, if the Myth of Helplessness were well founded in empirical evidence then it wouldn't matter how radical it was. But for the evidence to support the Myth of Helplessness and its attendant across-the-board opposition to changes in the educational status quo, it would have to show that no change in the status quo is effective at raising student performance in spite of the challenges posed by social problems. This is not the case. In fact, some school systems do a strikingly better job than others at overcoming the challenges posed by student disadvantages, and there are a variety of educational strategies and reforms that have been shown to work better than the status quo, even for the most disadvantaged students. Poverty, broken homes, and other social problems no doubt pose significant challenges, but the evidence simply doesn't leave room for the conclusion that these challenges are insurmountable.

Some School Systems Do Better Than Others

If the influence of disadvantages on student achievement were as overwhelming as the Myth of Helplessness implies, we would expect to see little variation in levels of achievement at schools serving similar student populations. That is, if two populations of students are similar with regard to their disadvantages, we would expect them to have similar educational outcomes—highly advantaged students would have consistently high achievement, while highly disadvantaged students would have consistently low achievement. On the other hand, if schools can make a sizeable difference in students' academic outcomes in spite of their disadvantages, we might see substantial variation among the achievement of similarly disadvantaged student populations.

Jay Greene and Greg Forster of the Manhattan Institute performed a simple analysis to test the evidence on this question. First, they developed a systematic method for measuring levels of advantages and disadvantages in the student population. They combined measurements of sixteen social factors that researchers agree affect student outcomes, such as poverty, family structure, health, and students who don't speak English well. They call their combined measurement the Teachability Index, since it measures the overall "teachability" of the student population. Then they tested its validity by examining its statistical relationship with student outcomes; they found that the Teachability Index is a reliable predictor of student outcomes, indicating that it does in fact measure students' teachability.

Armed with this tool, they compared each state's student characteristics to its level of academic achievement. Specifically, they used each state's Teachability Index score to predict the level of achievement its students would be expected to reach given their level of disadvantages, and then compared each state's actual achievement to its predicted achievement. They found a large degree of variation in how well the school systems in the various states overcome student disadvantages. For example, Texas's schools perform much better than their student demographics would predict. Levels of student disadvantages were 19.8 percent worse than the national average in Texas; Greene and Forster found that Texas's student achievement is 110 percent of what one would expect it to be given its highly disadvantaged students. This ranks Texas fourth among the states in academic outcomes adjusted for student characteristics—a good deal higher than the thirty-second place its raw test scores produce. Not every state with similarly disadvantaged student populations did as well as Texas; Louisiana's students have disadvantages 16.5 percent worse than the national average, but performed at only 93 percent of even the low level of achievement one would expect given its disadvantaged students. This ranks Louisiana forty-first in the nation in student achievement adjusted for student characteristics.[9]

Greene and Forster's findings suggest that student achievement depends on more than just the levels of advantages and disadvantages that students face. This would naturally prompt us to ask what factors other than student advantages might produce higher educational outcomes. If we examine the evidence, we find that a number of school strategies have been shown to raise student achievement, even among particularly disadvantaged student populations.

Accountability Programs

One type of reform that has been shown to work is school accountability, also known as "high-stakes testing." This type of program measures each school's performance through standardized testing and then provides rewards for schools that perform well and sanctions for schools that perform poorly. The goal is to give schools an incentive to educate all students well. Accountability has become something of a lightening rod for sharp criticism, especially from proponents of the Myth of Helplessness; Winerip in particular has been unrelenting in his attacks on high-stakes tests.

But the evidence shows that accountability works. Margaret Raymond and Eric Hanushek of Stanford University have demonstrated that states with high-stakes tests made significantly better test score improvements on the National Assessment of Educational Progress (NAEP), a highly reliable basic-skills test administered nationally by the U.S. Department of Education. Examining math scores, they found that high-stakes tests made a statistically significant difference in boosting both fourth-grade and eighth-grade scores over time. They also tracked a cohort of students from fourth grade in 1996 to eighth grade in 2000 and found that this cohort had made significantly better improvements in states with high-stakes testing.[10] These findings contradict the findings of a widely publicized study by Audrey Amrein and David Berliner of Arizona State University; Raymond and Hanushek expose a startling number of gross errors and fundamental breaches of scientific procedure in the Amrein and Berliner study.[11]

Another study, by Martin Carnoy and Susanna Loeb of Stanford University, came to similar conclusions. Carnoy and Loeb rated the strength of each state's accountability system according to the seriousness of its sanctions for failing schools, counting states with no sanctions as having the weakest accountability. They found that stronger accountability systems were associated with higher NAEP scores in both fourth and eighth grades, and that the improvements were even greater for black and Hispanic students than for white students. They also found no significant relationship between the strength of accountability systems and the extent to which students were "held back" in their grades rather than promoted.[12]

The evidence also shows that high-stakes testing works not only in comfortable suburban schools, but also in failing schools with large numbers of poor and minority students. A study of high-stakes testing in Florida by Greene and Marcus Winters of the Manhattan Institute found that when chronically failing schools were threatened with sanctions if their test scores didn't improve, they made very impressive gains compared to the performance of all other schools, while similar low-performing schools not threatened with the same sanctions did not make similar gains.[13] This is a point of particular importance, since one of the most frequent criticisms of high-stakes testing—especially from Rothstein and Winerip—is that poor students can't pass the same high-stakes tests that middle-class students can. But the opposite is actually occurring: accountability systems force school systems to focus their efforts on the failing schools and poor minority students who need help most.

School Choice

Another kind of school reform that can help overcome the educational challenges caused by social problems is school choice. Five school voucher programs, all of them restricted to low-income students, have been studied by what is called the "random assignment" method. Random assignment is the gold standard for social science research; it provides highly reliable results because it compares groups of students that are virtually identical in every respect except whether or not they received a treatment, in this case whether or not they used a voucher. All five programs were found to have a statistically significant beneficial effect on the test scores of participating students (see chapter 13 for a detailed discussion of this research).[14]

School choice is a particularly important reform for the low-income and minority students who are facing larger challenges because of social problems. Comfortable middle-class families already exercise school choice when they choose where to live; they have the financial means to decide what neighborhood to live in based partly on the quality of the local schools. This gives neighborhoods an incentive to provide good schools, because if they don't then families will move away and property values will go down. But low-income families cannot exercise this form of school choice, so their schools can simply take them for granted. Offering school vouchers to these families gives urban schools in poor neighborhoods the same positive competitive incentives that suburban schools already face (see chapter 15 for a detailed discussion of the effect of school vouchers on public school systems).

Other Promising Reforms

High-quality early instruction is yet another education policy shown to produce positive results in spite of social problems. Research particularly supports early intervention for young children who have difficulty learning to read. A consensus has emerged among researchers that giving extra help to students who are behind in reading in first and second grades significantly reduces the number of those students who are later diagnosed as learning disabled. This is particularly relevant for the poor minority students who are the most likely to have trouble learning to read. A group of eight specialists led by G. Reid Lyon of the National Institutes of Health has called for dramatic reforms in the special education system given the large body of evidence that early reading intervention prevents the onset of educational dysfunctions that are often attributed to learning disabilities.[15]

Research has also shown that another form of early intervention, high-quality preschool programs, can produce significantly better outcomes for poor minority students facing social problems. A longitudinal study of the Perry Preschool Project tracked a set of poor black preschoolers who were randomly assigned to two groups: one that attended preschools using the "active learning" program of the High/Scope Educational Research Foundation and another that attended no preschool. Students who received the preschool program performed better in school, were more likely to graduate from high school (65 percent of participants graduated, versus 45 percent in the control group), were more likely to be employed at age forty (76 percent versus 62 percent), had higher incomes, were more likely to own homes and cars, were less likely to go to jail or deal drugs, had longer-lasting marriages, and were less likely to bear children out of wedlock.[16]

The educational method known as "direct instruction" has also been shown to improve student performance. Direct instruction seeks to convey a highly specific set of knowledge and skills to students through carefully planned lessons. There is empirical evidence that direct instruction improves test scores, raises academic achievement, and results in better student attitudes and behavior.[17]

All of these strategies have been shown to effectively improve student performance. What's more, they have all been shown to work even for the poor minority students who face the largest educational challenges. In some cases, these strategies have been shown to work especially well for these disadvantaged students. And these strategies—accountability, choice, early intervention, and direct instruction—are only four examples of effective school reforms. Other strategies could also be effective in improving student outcomes.

This evidence stands in marked contrast to the Myth of Helplessness. To believe that school reform can't succeed because of the challenges posed by social problems, we would have to believe that no strategy—not these examples and not any other kind of reform—will work. The evidence shows otherwise, and in light of this, we can see the serious consequences of the Myth of Helplessness. It uses the educational disadvantages faced by many students to justify blocking reforms that have been shown to alleviate those very disadvantages.

Social problems present our schools with serious challenges. Nonetheless, schools are not helpless. The evidence shows that there are many effective strategies for improving student performance, even—and sometimes especially—for the poor minority students who bear the brunt of these challenges. The Myth of Helplessness should not be allowed to stand in the way of reforms that promise to help those students who need it most.

CHAPTER 4

The Class Size Myth

"Schools should reduce class sizes; small classes would produce big improvements."

In September 2003 the president of the Arkansas teachers' union contacted the *Arkansas Democrat-Gazette* to request a correction. One of the paper's editorials, he said, had seriously mischaracterized the union's position on class sizes. Teachers are naturally very concerned with how education policy affects the number of children in each classroom. The union wanted to set the record straight: the teachers of Arkansas were firmly in favor of larger classes.

Larger classes? Yes, the paper's editors explained, the teachers' union supported an increase in class sizes because it would benefit both teachers and students. Larger classes mean hiring fewer teachers, and less money spent on hiring teachers means more money available for raising teachers' salaries. Better pay would attract higher-quality teachers who might otherwise take jobs in other fields, and would also attract better teachers into Arkansas from other states. A top-quality teacher in front of a somewhat larger class, the union reasoned, would provide a better education than a lousy teacher in front of a small one.[1]

This isn't the kind of argument Americans are accustomed to hearing when it comes to class sizes. Just about everybody agrees on the Class Size Myth: that smaller classes would produce much better results and that class size reduction is a badly needed reform. In fact, the research that shows benefits from class size reduction finds effects that are smaller than most people realize, and there is some reason to doubt whether class size reduction really produces even these benefits. There are also problems with implementing class size reduction on a broad scale because of the limited teaching labor pool—what works in a small, controlled experiment may not work when applied wholesale to millions of students because there may not be enough good teachers to go around.

What's more, any serious reduction in class sizes would require us to invest a very large amount of money, so we could only produce smaller classes by taking resources away from other educational priorities (such as teachers' salaries, as the Arkansas union noted). Smaller classes would almost certainly leave insufficient funds left over for other, much more promising reform strategies. Success in reducing class sizes would be a Pyrrhic victory—more would ultimately be lost than gained.

Growing Interest in Class Size Reduction

The typical view of class size policy is expressed in a *Chicago Tribune* feature story on the issue: "The advantages of small classes seem intuitive; who wouldn't want children to learn in a small class? Parents crave them, teachers love them, and policymakers push for them." The article's headline shared that same enthusiasm: "Schools Think Small, Win Big."[2] The editorial board of the *New York Times* has also endorsed smaller classes.[3] Best-selling author Jonathan Kozol makes class size one of the main counts in his indictment of urban school quality. "We are badly overcrowded," he quotes one urban principal as saying. "Ideal class size for these kids would be fifteen to twenty. Will these children ever get what white kids in the suburbs take for granted?"[4]

As popular discontent with the state of education has grown, class sizes have emerged as a key political issue. In 2002 Florida voters approved by referendum a state constitutional amendment mandating major reductions in class sizes. "Smaller classes are not the only answer, but they are an indispensable part of the solution to the crisis facing Florida's public schools," declared a report written by supporters of the amendment.[5] The Florida governor's race that year lost sight of just about all other issues and turned into a debate over class sizes. In 2003 class sizes became a central issue in New York. First, a push to reduce class sizes became a key issue in state budget battles that spring. Later in the year a long, drawn-out political fight emerged in New York City over a proposed ballot initiative to create a commission on class size policy. What is perhaps most telling of the power of the Class Size Myth is this: leaders on both sides of the Florida governor's race and the New York referendum debate all agreed that smaller classes were a desirable reform.

Teachers' unions have been particularly aggressive in the claims they make for the virtues of small classes, the position of the Arkansas union notwithstanding. "NEA supports a class size of fifteen students in regular programs and even smaller in programs for students with exceptional needs," declares the National Education Association.[6] The American Federation of Teachers declares that "compelling evidence demonstrates that reducing class size, particularly for younger children, will have a positive effect on student achievement overall and an especially significant impact on the education of poor children."[7] Given that shrinking class sizes means hiring more teachers, and thus putting more money into the pockets of teachers' unions, it is hardly surprising that these unions are the loudest supporters of class size reduction.

The STAR Project

The Class Size Myth is not totally baseless. Research does give us reason to believe that there might be some benefits to smaller classes. But if the research supporting smaller classes is correct, the benefits of class size reduction are only moderate. And whether this research is in fact correct is still very much open to debate. There is certainly no way to justify the strong claims made by political activists that the benefits of small classes are solidly proven.

Discussions of the research on small classes center around the STAR project, an experiment conducted in the 1980s by the state of Tennessee. Students were randomly assigned to one of three types of classes as they progressed from kindergarten through third grade. The first type of class was regular sized (around twenty-four students) with one teacher; the second was regular sized with both a teacher and a teacher's aide; the third was small (around fifteen students) with one teacher.

The random assignment of students to different types of classes made the STAR project a unique opportunity to conduct high-quality research on the effects of small classes. As Eric Hanushek of Stanford University has shown, research on class sizes that looks at schools under normal, nonexperimental conditions has failed to produce solid evidence that class sizes have a positive effect on student performance.[8] However, these studies are somewhat less reliable than random assignment studies. When students are randomly assigned to different types of classes, the result should be that the students in each type of class are virtually identical in every respect other than the size of their classes. If the random assignment is properly implemented, this makes very highly reliable research possible.

The study found that students in the small classes showed a one-time benefit in test scores as compared to students in regular-sized classes (there was no significant difference between the regular-sized classes that did or did not have a teacher's aide). The increase was equal to fewer than 0.2 standard deviations.[9] For a student who started at the 50th percentile—in the exact middle of the performance spectrum—this increase would be the equivalent of an improvement of less than 8 percentile points, which would bring the student up to a level between the 57th and 58th percentile.

Follow-up research finds similar effects. For example, students who were in small classes under the STAR project went on to be somewhat more likely to take a college entrance exam, indicating plans to attend college. Among regular-class students, 40 percent took the SAT or ACT exam, versus 43.7 percent among small-class students.[10]

This benefit may not amount to an educational revolution, but it is not trivial. If we could be reasonably sure that this increase in performance truly did result from reduced class sizes, and if we could be reasonably sure that large-scale class size reduction would reproduce these small-scale results, and if we could accomplish such large-scale reduction without making disproportionately severe sacrifices of our other educational priorities, then class size reduction would be as solidly supported as proponents of the Class Size Myth claim it is. Unfortunately, the evidence does not allow us to reach any of these conclusions.

Reasonable Doubts about STAR's Findings

The first problem with the Class Size Myth is whether we can be confident that the better performance observed in students who attended small classes in the STAR program really followed from class size reduction and not from a flaw in the program's method. Unfortunately, there were a number of shortcomings in the way the STAR program was implemented.[11] These flaws raise reasonable doubts about the accuracy of the study's findings. The most important flaw is that students were not tested when they entered the program. Such point-of-entry tests would establish a baseline for each student's performance as it stood before the experiment began. Without this baseline measurement, we cannot confirm that the STAR project's random assignment method was successfully carried out.

For the experiment's results to be accurate, all three experimental groups must have been performing at about the same average level before the experiment began. If the random assignment method was properly carried out, that should have been the case. And even if some variation in student performance crept in despite random assignment, researchers could have used the baseline test scores to correct for this distortion. But without baseline testing, we cannot confirm that the students in the three experimental groups were in fact performing at the same level before the experiment began, nor can we make the necessary statistical corrections if they were not starting at the same level. If the students assigned to smaller classes were higher-performing students to begin with, their higher test scores would be attributable to this preexisting advantage and not to smaller classes.

This matters because of an anomaly in the research findings: the improvement in test scores was a one-time benefit. That is, as students remained in different-sized classes year after year, the gap between the two types of classes did not grow. Students who had been in smaller classes for four years were no further ahead of their peers in regular-sized classes than they had been after only one year of smaller classes. This is an unusual and unexpected finding, because if smaller classes really do improve student performance we would generally expect to see these benefits accrue over time.

It is possible that smaller classes really do convey a one-time benefit to student performance. However, the lack of baseline scores in the study introduces another possibility. It may be that parents of higher-scoring students managed to get their children assigned to the smaller classes in violation of the random assignment method schools were supposed to follow.

Most parents strongly desire smaller classes for their children. The STAR project set up different-sized classes in every school, such that students in regular-sized classes were going to school every day next to their peers in smaller classes. It is reasonable to expect that parents would have tried to get their children assigned to the smaller classes. And the parents most likely to succeed in exercising such influence over schools would be the more affluent and better-educated parents, whose children would have somewhat higher test scores due to the social advantages they enjoy.

If this did happen, it would represent a fundamental compromise in the integrity of the study. It would not totally repudiate the possibility of benefits from smaller classes—it may be that the higher test scores in STAR's smaller classes were partly attributable to higher-performing students in the study sample and partly attributable to beneficial effects from the smaller classes. Nonetheless, given that the benefits apparently resulting from the STAR project were moderate to begin with, this problem raises serious doubts about whether the true effects of smaller classes are large enough to be worth pursuing as a policy.

The Track Record of Large-Scale Class Size Reduction

The second problem with the Class Size Myth is that even if we assume small classes produced all of the gains found by the STAR project, other evidence suggests that reducing class sizes does not produce similar gains when implemented on a wider scale. The nation as a whole has seen a very significant drop in the student-teacher ratio with no improvement in performance. According to the U.S. Department of Education, from 1970 to 2001 the number of students per teacher nationwide dropped from 22.3 to 15.9, a 29 percent reduction.[12] But test scores and graduation rates are flat over the same period.[13]

It is possible that this national picture does not tell the whole story. Counterintuitive as it may seem, this large drop in the national student-teacher ratio may not have translated into a substantial reduction in class sizes. A national teacher survey finds that between 1961 and 1996 average elementary school classes shrank from twenty-nine to twenty-four students while average high school classes grew from twenty-eight to thirty-one students.[14] Even if we consider only the reduction in elementary school classes, it is only a 17 percent reduction, much less than the drop in the teacher-student ratio. One reason shrinking teacher-student ratios may not have reduced class sizes very much is that schools are hiring more teachers but those teachers have fewer hours of classroom instruction per day. That would reduce the teacher-student ratio without reducing class sizes.

We can get a clearer picture of the effects of large-scale class size reduction by looking at its track record in California. In 1996, persuaded by the STAR project that smaller classes would raise its students' very low test scores, the state appropriated $1 billion to reduce elementary school class sizes. Advocates of the Class Size Myth hold up this program as a model—*New York Times* education columnist Michael Winerip published an article praising small classes under the headline "Miracles of Small Class Size Unfold Each Day in California."[15]

But six years later, a Rand Corporation study showed that California students who attended larger elementary school classes had improved at about the same rate as students in smaller classes. California's overall educational performance had gone up, but this need not have been due to smaller classes—the state had also undertaken a number of other major education reforms at the same time it was reducing class sizes. The study concluded that no link could be shown between smaller class sizes and improvement in test scores.[16] This gives us stronger evidence that widespread implementation of class size reduction doesn't improve student performance.

Why doesn't class size reduction produce higher student achievement when it is applied on a large scale? One possibility is that class size reduction simply doesn't have a substantial effect on student performance. However, there is another possible reason. Even if class size reduction does produce improved performance under the optimal conditions of a small, controlled experiment like the STAR project, labor pool problems may prevent this success from being reproduced on a large scale.

When implemented throughout a large school system such as the entire state of California, reducing class sizes requires hiring a very large number of new teachers. To take the class size benchmarks of the STAR project as an example, reducing classes from an average of twenty-four students to an average of fifteen students entails a 37.5 percent reduction in class sizes, implying a corresponding increase in the teaching workforce. Accomplishing this for the STAR project didn't require massive new hiring since there were only about six thousand students involved in the project. Accomplishing the same result across a whole state, to say nothing of the entire nation, implies a very big increase in teacher hiring. To implement its class size reduction program, California expanded its teaching workforce from 62,226 teachers to 91,112 in just three years.[17]

Research has shown that teacher quality has a large impact on student performance.[18] Hiring more people means digging deeper into the labor pool, and that means accepting a lower level of quality in the people we hire. If you want to hire six chefs for a classy new restaurant, you can demand only the very highest-quality labor—you could hire Emeril, Wolfgang Puck, and the four Iron Chefs. But if you want to hire sixty thousand chefs for a new worldwide chain of restaurants, you're simply going to have to accept a lower quality of worker. Large-scale class size reduction cannot be accomplished without running afoul of this problem.

The Cost of Class Size Reduction

Finally, the third problem with the Class Size Myth involves not what we get from smaller classes but what we have to give up in order to implement them. Obviously any plan for education reform will carry a price tag, but the cost of a serious reduction in class sizes would be exceptionally high—well above the range that most people might expect.

Any talk about the costs of an education policy causes some people great distress; they think schools should be immune from having to worry about costs. However, we have no choice but to talk about costs when we talk about education. Cost is just a shorthand way of talking about the sacrifices that have to be made in order to implement a policy. There is only a certain amount of money available for schools. That amount can be raised if taxpayers can be convinced to direct more money away from other priorities and into education, but the amount available will always be limited. Policymakers must therefore make hard choices about how the limited pool of money will be spent. Every dollar spent on class size reduction is a dollar that will not be available for teachers' salaries, new books, better equipment, or the implementation of other school reform policies—and this will be true no matter how many total dollars the school system has.

Caroline Hoxby of Harvard University has quantified just how large the cost of class size reduction would be. Using 2000–2001 spending and enrollment figures, she calculated that the cost of a 10 percent reduction in class sizes would be about $615 per pupil. Hoxby calculates that per-pupil spending in that year was $8,157, so $615 per pupil represents 7.5 percent of school spending.[19] That may not sound like much, but bear in mind that this is only the cost of a 10 percent reduction in class sizes. If classes began at twenty-four students, a 10 percent reduction only gets us to 21.6 students per class. Given that the STAR program had to reduce classes all the way to fifteen students to get even moderate results, it is unlikely that a 10 percent reduction in class sizes would produce substantial improvements in student performance. The cost of a 37.5 percent reduction in class sizes, such as the reduction modeled in the STAR project, would be about 3.75 times as large, or $2,306 per pupil. That would represent 28.3 percent of education spending—a remarkable price tag.

In the end, even if all the claims made to promote the Class Size Myth were right, improving student performance by reducing class sizes is a little bit like driving from Los Angeles to San Francisco by way of Pittsburgh. Given that there are other reform strategies that are more promising and less costly, the modest benefits of class size reduction simply can't justify the very large sacrifices that would have to be made.

CHAPTER 5

The Certification Myth

"Certified or more experienced teachers are substantially more effective."

Receiving professional certification in some field of endeavor is generally regarded as a reliable sign of expertise. That's because professional credentials in most occupations are given to those who have proven that they have what it takes to perform their duties well. Few people would be seen by a doctor who wasn't board certified or consult a lawyer who hadn't passed the bar, because people trust that these forms of certification reliably establish that those who possess them will do a better job than those who don't. And because this is true in most professions, we tend to assume it is true in all professions, treating any process of professional certification as though it were closely connected to real-world performance.

This tendency to assume that all professional credentials are created equal leaves us vulnerable to the Certification Myth—the belief that teachers with professional credentials are more effective in the classroom. Unfortunately, not all forms of professional certification actually are reliable indicators that those who possess them will perform substantially better in their chosen fields. Teacher certification is one of the most clear-cut cases we have of a mismatch between the process required to obtain a professional credential and actual job performance. While the evidence does clearly establish that teacher quality makes a big difference in students' academic achievement, it also indicates that there is not much relationship between teacher quality and teacher credentialing. The presence or absence of a teaching certificate on a teacher's resume does not make a noticeable difference in the classroom. Even an advanced degree in education from a graduate school does not establish that a teacher will perform better when it comes to student achievement.

Another aspect of the Certification Myth is the belief that more experienced teachers are more effective. In this case, the story is a little more complicated—it appears that teachers do get a little more effective in their first few years of teaching as they learn how to cope in the classroom. However, after those first few years teachers do not tend to get more effective with further years of experience. There is even some evidence that teachers get less effective in the later stages of their careers, perhaps because of adverse incentives arising from the inability of most schools to fire veteran teachers even when their performance is very poor.

The Certification Myth is often taken for granted among both researchers and politicians. In a study of charter schools, Bruce Fuller of the University of California at Berkeley and his coauthors assert that California charter schools have lower "teacher quality" than regular public schools because their teachers are less likely to be certified and on average have fewer years of experience. The study simply takes for granted that measuring teacher certification and years of experience is the same as measuring teacher quality.[1] A California legislator, alarmed by the drop in teacher quality caused by massive teacher hiring as part of that state's class size reduction program, introduced a bill to pour extensive resources into academic training for teachers. He commented: "Frankly, I would rather have my child in a classroom of thirty students with an excellent teacher than a classroom of twenty students with a poor teacher."[2] Like Fuller and his coauthors, he assumed that more teacher credentialing would mean better teachers.

The Certification Myth has enormous consequences for our education system because teachers' salaries are based almost entirely on their credentials and years of experience. If certification and experience are not reliable indicators of the qualities that actually make for good teaching—intelligence, familiarity with classroom procedures, communication skills, self-confidence, diligence, and so on—then those qualities will go unrewarded. By failing to reward these desirable skills, policies based on the Certification Myth will drive good teachers away from teaching while attracting and retaining others who possess teaching credentials and years of experience but may not be good teachers. Caroline Hoxby and Andrew Leigh of Harvard University find that since 1960 this perverse teacher pay system has been the main cause of significant declines in the academic abilities of those who have entered the teaching profession.[3] In particular, the educational pay system rewards teachers richly for getting master's degrees in education—both by paying their graduate school tuition costs and by raising their pay considerably once they complete a degree—even though it is one of the strongest and most consistent findings in the research on teacher quality that these degrees are irrelevant to classroom performance.

The Evidence

The research on teaching confirms what most people's experiences would lead them to expect: teacher quality is a very important factor in students' academic achievement. For example, Steven Rivkin of Amherst College, Eric Hanushek of the University of Rochester, and John Kain of the University of Texas at Dallas, analyzing a large set of high-quality student data in Texas, conclude that "there can be little doubt that teacher quality is an important determinant of achievement."[4] Other research has led to similar conclusions.[5]

It's easy for researchers to determine that teachers make a difference, but it is a more difficult matter to determine exactly what makes one teacher better than another. To show that teacher quality matters, all researchers have to do is measure whether or not students who have different teachers consistently perform at different levels. If some teachers' students regularly outperform other teachers' students, we can conclude that teacher quality has an important impact on classroom outcomes. But figuring out just what it is that makes a good teacher good requires us to sort out a variety of possible factors and determine which ones are consistently related to higher student performance.

Researchers cannot examine the role played by every possible factor, for the simple reason that not every factor can be easily measured and evaluated. We all know from our own experiences that a teacher who is genuinely enthusiastic about teaching, and about the material being taught, is more engaging and interesting. It stands to reason that teacher enthusiasm probably causes higher student achievement. But teacher enthusiasm is difficult to quantify, so there is no scientific evidence addressing this question.

There are three major factors that the research has been able to measure and evaluate scientifically. These are professional credentials, teaching experience, and academic ability. Few will be surprised to learn that research supports the conclusion that teachers' academic ability—measured, for example, by scores on basic skills tests—makes a substantial positive contribution to their classroom effectiveness. In at least some cases, teachers who hold degrees in the fields they teach also tend to perform better.[6] However, the research on professional credentials and teaching experience does not lend itself to similarly optimistic conclusions.

Professional Credentials

There are two main types of professional teaching credentials: a teaching certificate and an advanced degree in education. Every state has some procedure for professional certification of teachers. Typically, a teacher becomes certified by taking college-level education courses designed to convey knowledge of pedagogical theory and familiarity with classroom procedures. The purpose of this certification is to distinguish teachers who have a certain set of specialized knowledge and skills from those who do not possess this body of specific educational knowledge. An advanced degree in education, such as a master's degree, is also intended to reflect the acquisition of specialized knowledge—in this case, the knowledge taught in graduate schools of education.

Whether these professional credentials are reliable indicators that a teacher will be more successful in the classroom is one of the most important questions on the educational research agenda. Unfortunately, the quality of the research on this urgent question is often very poor. A vast amount of the research on the relationship between teacher credentials and teacher quality is fundamentally compromised by methodological faults, including violations of such basic scientific procedures as ensuring an adequate sample size and controlling for student background characteristics.[7] If we want to know what the evidence really shows on teacher certification, we must be careful to reject studies that deviate from accepted social science practices.

Hanushek (now at Stanford University) examined every available study of whether a teacher's credentials are an accurate predictor of his job performance that followed basic scientific methods and found that only a tiny number of them had identified a statistically significant relationship between teacher education and student performance. Of 171 scientifically sound studies on teacher education, only nine found a significant positive relationship with student performance. He also found five studies that observed a statistically significant *negative* relationship between teacher education and student performance. Other researchers analyzing the same set of studies with somewhat different methods have argued that the studies justify concluding that teacher credentials affect student performance, but the size of the effect they identify is very small. Hanushek also performed another overview that was more strictly limited, including only research that used the very highest quality of data and the most reliable methods of analysis; of the thirty-three top-quality studies of teacher education he identified, none finds a significant relationship with student performance.[8] Another review of studies conforming to basic social science methods, conducted for the Abell Foundation, found that teachers holding master's degrees did not produce higher student performance (except for high school teachers with master's degrees in the subjects they taught, as opposed to degrees in education) and that among new teachers traditional certification makes no difference in student performance.[9]

This body of research finding no substantial benefit to professional education credentials is confirmed by recent research. A large study of California students by Julian Betts, Kim Rueben, and Anne Danenberg of the Public Policy Institute of California found that the impact of teacher certification on student achievement is very small, amounting to only one-tenth of the impact of students' socioeconomic background. The effects of teacher education more generally were even smaller, and were more statistically uncertain.[10] The Texas study mentioned above found that advanced degrees had no effect on student achievement: "Similar to most past research, we find absolutely no evidence that having a master's degree improves teacher skills."[11] Two separate analyses of data from the National Assessment of Educational Progress (NAEP) also found that master's degrees did not improve student performance.[12] Dan Goldhaber's research for the Urban Institute found that "only about 3 percent of the contribution teachers made to student learning was associated with teacher experience, degree attained, and other readily observable characteristics" combined.[13] Paul Decker, Daniel Mayer, and Steven Glazerman of Mathematica Policy Research recently conducted a large study of Teach For America, which lets recent college graduates become teachers without obtaining traditional credentials. They found that in one year, students taught by nontraditionally credentialed teachers made significantly greater gains in math (equivalent to an extra month of instruction) and kept pace in reading gains.[14]

If, as the evidence indicates, there is no substantial relationship between teacher credentials and performance in the classroom, current education policy is misguided in a way that can only be inflicting serious harm on teacher quality. Almost without exception, teachers must be certified or be working toward certification in order to teach. This onerous requirement will drive promising candidates away from teaching, while attracting candidates who are good at getting certificates rather than good at teaching. "Increasing the number of requirements prospective teachers must meet has been shown to reduce the supply of applicants and potential teachers, while guaranteeing little in the way of effectiveness," Hanushek writes. "Many college students, it appears, are dissuaded from considering teaching because of the course and training requirements that states place on entry into teaching."[15]

The current pay system, which rewards teachers for seeking out master's degrees in education, must also harm teacher quality by artificially redirecting time and money toward earning these degrees. This reduces the time and money available for other efforts that might actually make a difference in the classroom. The system accomplishes this perverse redistribution of resources both by paying teachers' tuition costs while they work on their master's degrees and by substantially increasing their salaries once their degrees are complete. That's why 42 percent of teachers had master's degrees and a further 5 percent had other advanced educational degrees in the 1999–2000 school year.[16] Working on advanced degrees and other credentials is a way of life for teachers; a full 50 percent of all teachers had earned college credits in the previous three years as of 1996. Of course, some of those credits were the undergraduate work of young teachers just out of college, but the overwhelming majority were not—the median experience for teachers at the time was fifteen years and only 2 percent of teachers were in their first year of teaching.[17] One of the NAEP studies cited above pointedly concludes that while "for universities and colleges, providing teachers with master's degrees produces significant income," such a degree "seems to have little effect on improving teachers' abilities to raise achievement," and therefore the enormous amount of money spent to encourage teachers to pursue these degrees "is arguably one of the least-efficient expenditures in education."[18]

Teaching Experience

Researchers have also investigated the relationship between years of teaching experience and students' academic achievement. Here the story is less straightforward. Most studies do not find a significant relationship between teacher experience generally and student achievement. Some research does find a weak but significant relationship, but researchers examining the impact of teaching experience at different stages in a teacher's career find important variations that prevent us from having confidence in the existence of even a weak general relationship between teacher experience and student performance.

Teaching experience is harder to evaluate than it might at first seem to be. Teachers with the same number of years of experience are, for the most part, teachers who entered the profession at the same time. Because of this, they may have similar characteristics that are not related to experience. Goldhaber notes that "teacher experience implicitly captures the effects of the prevalent graduation requirements and labor market conditions at the time when teachers were hired."[19] Any such similarities in incoming teacher cohorts can show up in studies as though they were the effects of teaching experience. There is also the problem that veteran teachers are more likely to be able to choose which schools they teach in, and will choose to teach in better schools; this might cause higher student test scores to be falsely associated with teacher experience.[20] In order to minimize the effects of these problems, it is all the more important that we take into account only the research that follows proper social science procedures.

In addition to reviewing the scientific research on teacher education, Hanushek also reviewed the research on teacher experience. He found 207 scientifically sound studies on teacher experience, of which twenty-nine found a statistically significant positive relationship with students' academic achievement. That is not as dismal a result as he found for teacher education, but it is still a relatively small number of positive findings. The overwhelming majority of the available research does not find a general relationship between teacher experience and student achievement. However, in his separate review of the highest-quality research, he found that fourteen out of thirty-six studies identify a significant relationship between teacher experience and student performance.[21] This provides stronger support for the existence of such a relationship. Elsewhere Hanushek has stated that "experienced teachers are, on average, more effective at raising student performance than those in their early years of teaching."[22]

Some recent studies have found less evidence for this conclusion. The California study examined the role of teacher experience and found that its impact on student achievement was infinitesimal—only one-thirtieth as large as the impact of students' socioeconomic background.[23] One of the studies of NAEP data, conducted by Harold Wenglinsky of the Educational Testing Service, found no relationship at all between teacher experience and student achievement.[24]

How do we explain these mixed findings? More sophisticated studies of teacher experience have explained them by separately examining the effect of teaching experience at different stages in a teacher's career. If the effect of teaching experience is nonlinear—that is, if some of a teacher's years of experience improve that teacher's performance but others do not—then studies looking at "teacher experience" generally might sometimes see a weak effect and sometimes see none at all.

The Abell Foundation's review of the available research reports that a number of studies have found that teaching experience only improves teachers' performance in the first two or three years of teaching, and may actually be associated with a decline in teachers' performance at the end of their careers.[25] This decline in later years may be due to the strong tenure protections built into almost all teacher contracts. Since veteran teachers' jobs are so well protected, they have little incentive to strive for a higher level of performance.

The finding that only the first few years of teaching improve performance is confirmed by two recent studies. The Texas study found no effect on student achievement for teacher experience generally, but it did find that teachers with at least two years of experience performed better than teachers with fewer than two years. Even here, the size of the effect they identified was very small; the authors write that "the magnitudes of the effects of these variables pale in comparison to the total effect of teacher quality."[26] The other NAEP data study, conducted for the RAND Foundation by David Grissmer, Ann Flanagan, Jennifer Kawata, and Stephanie Williamson, finds that while teacher experience generally had a weak effect on teachers' performance, additional years of teaching had no effect on performance for teachers who had more than two years of experience.[27]

Thus, the evidence seems to indicate that teachers get a little more effective in their first few years as they get up to speed in the classroom, but that after this initial period teachers do not tend to get more effective with more years of experience. This evidence raises serious doubts about the public school system's practice of basing teacher pay very heavily upon years of experience throughout their careers. This practice ensures that teachers are always getting raises for additional years of experience, but the incremental raise for each particular year of experience is very small. The result is that teachers receive relatively small raises in their second and third years, when the evidence suggests their performance has improved somewhat, while teachers in their twentieth and thirtieth years continue to collect annual raises based on experience (over and above raises for the cost of living) even though the evidence gives us little reason to think that those teachers are getting any better. Thus, while there may be a real relationship between teaching experience and performance, the current system still gives inadequate compensation to young teachers while overcompensating older ones. This will tend to drive away good teachers who are young while encouraging poor teachers who are old to stay in their jobs longer.

Foundations of the Certification Myth

Research does not provide much evidence for the Certification Myth, but people, especially members of the education establishment, fiercely resist giving it up. The Education Law Center, an advocacy group, filed a federal civil rights complaint in March 2004 on grounds that minority students were less likely to be taught by certified teachers.[28] Any suggestion that certification to teach might be made available through an alternative means—for example, through a test that evaluates both the acquisition of basic academic skills and knowledge of classroom procedures—is met with stern protests. "No paper-and-pencil test can assess the personality, interpersonal skills, and beliefs of a potential teacher," said an education school dean responding to one such proposal in Georgia. A member of a state educational advisory panel concurred: "Offering the test out will get us more teachers, but it will not get us more teachers with staying power."[29]

Naturally, the fiercest defenders of the Certification Myth are the certified and experienced teachers themselves. When Michigan adopted new standards for teacher qualifications reflecting an emphasis on teachers' academic ability rather than their credentials or years of experience, the *Detroit News* profiled some highly credentialed and experienced teachers who would not be considered "highly qualified" unless they passed a skills test. "It's a slap in my face that I have to go back and take a test," said one teacher with a master's degree and thirty years' experience. "It's insulting. I've paid my dues." Another teacher, a seventeen-year veteran with a master's degree, declared: "It's totally an insult." Adding further embarrassment, this forty-four-year-old teacher was serving as a professional mentor to a twenty-three-year-old colleague who was already "highly qualified" under the new standards. The credentialed-and-experienced teacher declared that she was offended because "if you were to do this to any other profession, they wouldn't stand for it."[30]

In this last comment, she was speaking for many of her peers. Teachers and other education professionals often lament that their credentials do not produce in others the same level of deference to their professional judgment that, say, doctors' credentials do. Referring to charter schools that hire noncertified teachers, a district superintendent argued that "it's like hiring someone who's not a doctor to run a hospital."[31] A thirty-six-year veteran teacher complained about accountability programs in the same terms: "If I were a neurosurgeon, they wouldn't dream of telling me what procedures I have to carry out."[32]

It is certainly true that certified teachers are not looked upon in the same way that licensed doctors are, and it is worth looking at the reasons why professional credentials are regarded so highly in professions such as medicine and law. Credentials in these fields are difficult to obtain, but that is not the main reason people value them so highly. It takes about twice as many years to get a Ph.D. as it does to get an M.D. or J.D., and professional training in some other fields takes even longer still. Yet most of these other credentials are not nearly as highly respected as an M.D. or J.D.; there is no medical or legal equivalent of the common belief that Ph.D. stands for "Piled High and Deep." Medical and legal credentials are valued so highly not because of the years required to obtain them but because the professions of medicine and law have proven that they can successfully control the quality of their practitioners through meaningful licensure. Such controls are useful and appropriate in these fields because we know that the M.D. and the J.D., along with the procedures for board licensure and admission to the bar, reliably indicate the possession of necessary professional skills and are consistent predictors of on-the-job performance. To return to the neurosurgeon example, the reason politicians don't legislate what procedures neurosurgeons must use is because the medical profession does an adequate job of promoting safe and effective neurosurgical procedures while punishing doctors who use dangerous or ineffective ones. If it didn't—if neurosurgeons regularly butchered their patients and got away with it—legislatures would surely impose regulatory controls on neurosurgical procedures.

It is only natural for people to assume that educational credentials would similarly reflect people's professional abilities. Teachers must pass through a variety of college-level courses to obtain certification, and of course they must take graduate-level courses to obtain a master's degree. By all rights, those who have invested so much time and money in their training should be better prepared to teach. David Berliner of Arizona State University and Bruce Biddle of the University of Missouri argue that we ought to allow teachers to do what they think is best in the classroom rather than trying to reform the education system, because teachers are similar to "doctors, lawyers, clergymen, psychologists, and other professionals" and we ought to defer to their professional judgment. After all, "most [teachers] have completed many years of higher education; most have a good deal of technical knowledge they can use and express; and most have sincere moral commitments to the welfare of the students and communities they serve. They have typically earned the right to be treated as knowledgeable professionals, and the quality of their efforts—and the academic achievements of our students—depend ultimately on whether they receive this treatment."[33] For Berliner and Biddle, teachers who have taken a lot of college classes on how to teach simply must be better at teaching—so much better, in fact, that we ought not even question their professional judgment on how to make education better.

Regrettably, it appears that the college classes that produce teaching credentials do not actually make people into better teachers. This certainly seems counterintuitive. Nonetheless, there are two reasons that could explain why it is the case.

First, it could be that these credentials do not necessarily indicate actual acquisition of the skills that candidates are supposed to acquire in order to receive them. In other words, it may be that colleges are turning out education graduates who haven't learned what they were supposed to learn. As Hanushek puts it, "the number of semester hours of courses in pedagogy required to teach at a certain level can be specified [in certification requirements], but neither the quality of the courses nor the behavioral outcomes of prospective teachers can be guaranteed."[34]

Second, it could also be the case that the skills taught in education courses are not effective in improving classroom performance even for those who do acquire them. The main focus in education courses is the study of pedagogical theory, and it is possible that the formal study of pedagogy might not contribute substantially to a teacher's ability to actually teach. It is certainly true in many other fields that the study of theory, although important for scholars, does not contribute much to professional performance. Economic theory is not the main focus in schools of business administration, legal philosophy is even less important in law schools, and biological theory (which includes, for example, debates over evolution) is either peripheral or totally absent in medical schools.

Of course, these two reasons for a disconnect between teacher credentialing and teacher quality are not mutually exclusive. Both could be true to some degree. The important point is that education courses do not produce more effective teachers, either because they do not teach effectively or because they do not teach the right material, or for both reasons.

High quality teachers are crucial to improving student performance, but the Certification Myth keeps most people in the dark about what really makes for a quality teacher. And since education policy reflects this myth, the incentives created by the way we hire and pay teachers are badly out of alignment with what we need to attract and retain truly excellent candidates to the field of teaching. We can never improve the quality of our teachers until we stop deliberately hiring and financially rewarding teachers according to qualifications that are irrelevant to their performance. Just how much we're paying for these ineffective qualifications will be the subject of chapter 6.

CHAPTER 6

The Teacher Pay Myth

"Teachers are badly underpaid."

At the height of the Internet boom, when real estate prices in Silicon Valley and the rest of the San Francisco area were rising significantly, local newspapers presented residents with story after story describing how teachers could no longer afford to live there. "Teachers . . . increasingly are fleeing Silicon Valley for more affordable locales," claimed one story. "Some keep their jobs but take on exhausting commutes," while others were simply leaving. The article profiles one teacher who moved to North Carolina partly "to be able to afford a nice apartment," and another who worked a second job after hours.[1] "We don't have any margin of error," declared a teacher quoted in another story. "Hopefully, we won't have anything go wrong with our lives."[2] The *Los Angeles Times* covered San Francisco's housing troubles with just a hint of *schadenfreude*: "Silicon Valley Paying the Price for Its Own Success," read the headline on one story, which reported that "teachers . . . are priced hopelessly out of the market and must commute hours every day."[3] A *Seattle Times* column worried that Seattle's prosperity might prove to be equally disastrous. "What will become of the area," it asked, "if tomorrow's teachers . . . [leave] in favor of towns where they're not forever destined to be the working poor?" A Seattle Chamber of Commerce member lamented that "we could get to be like San Francisco."[4] Some Silicon Valley school districts even considered building housing units themselves and then renting them to teachers at subsidized rates. "The valley's red-hot economy, which has made it the envy of the world, also has pushed housing prices and monthly rents out of the price range of young teachers," proclaimed an article about one such plan. "Many leave the valley after a few years, in search of more affordable locations where they can teach, buy a home and raise a family."[5]

The story resonated with local residents not only because they were themselves feeling the pinch of higher housing prices, but also because they all knew—or believed, at any rate—that teachers are badly underpaid. Given this, it made perfect sense to them that the rising housing market would squeeze teachers first and worst. How could struggling, underpaid teachers hope to keep up in a city of dot-com millionaires?

There was only one problem with the story: it wasn't true. Several years later, when the media hype surrounding the Internet boom was a fading memory, the *San Jose Mercury News* analyzed housing data from that period. "Teacher Housing Crisis a Myth," announced the headline. "For years, Silicon Valley has taken as gospel that teachers are among those hardest hit by the region's housing crisis," but at the peak of the Internet boom 96 percent of Silicon Valley's teachers lived there, and about two-thirds owned their own homes. "In this respect, teachers fare far better than the average Silicon Valley worker, including those with college degrees." Not only that, but "teachers also owned homes at a higher rate than many other professions, including software engineers, network administrators and accountants." The article reported that one of the main reasons teachers were so much better off than those in other professions was "pay scales" for teaching.[6]

This is only one especially dramatic instance of the Teacher Pay Myth—the belief that teachers are underpaid compared to workers in similar professions. While high-profile suburban legends like the San Francisco teacher housing crisis are rare, assertions that teachers are underpaid are not. *Washington Post* columnist Richard Cohen has declared the situation to be so dire that teachers ought to be excused from paying any income taxes.[7] When a court ruled that New York City was not adequately meeting its constitutional obligation to educate all students, *New York Times* columnist Bob Herbert turned out a column dripping with sarcasm: "Forget . . . that teachers (even with the most recent raise) are underpaid."[8] Certainly, the teachers' unions are not shy about claiming, like one spokesman for the National Education Association, that "it's easier to earn more money with less stress in other fields."[9] And the Teacher Pay Myth is often affirmed by the political right as well: no less a figure than First Lady Laura Bush, herself a former public school teacher, has said that for teachers, "salaries are too low. We all know that. We need to figure out a way to pay teachers more."[10]

But the facts tell a different story than the Teacher Pay Myth. The average teacher's salary does seem modest at first glance: about $44,600 in 2001–2002 for all teachers.[11] Starting teachers' salaries are a little harder to calculate; using U.S. Department of Labor data, Michael Podgursky of the University of Missouri at Columbia estimates that the median teacher under thirty makes about $29,000.[12] But when we take an accurate account of what teachers are paid for their labor and compare it to what workers of similar skill levels in similar professions are paid, we find that teachers are not shortchanged. This continues to hold true when we take employment benefits like medical coverage and retirement plans into account. The high value we place on education gives us emotional reasons to believe that teachers ought to be paid more regardless of how much they actually make, but that does not change the facts. It is simply not the case that teachers are less richly rewarded for their work than those in similar professions.

Measuring Teachers' Labor

One reason for the prominence of the Teacher Pay Myth is that people often fail to account for the relatively low number of hours that teachers work. Simply comparing the annual salaries of teachers with the annual salaries of other professionals will produce a misleading result if we fail to examine the amount of work each employee is doing. A person who makes $100 for working eight hours is not as well paid as a person who makes $100 for working four hours, even though they both receive the same amount of money. We must compare hourly compensation rather than annual compensation if we want to get an accurate picture.

It seems obvious, but it is easily forgotten: teachers work only about nine months per year. During the summer they can either work at other jobs or use the time off however else they wish. If they work at other jobs, they will make more money, but official statistics on teacher salaries will not convey this information. If they use the time for other purposes, that is a different kind of benefit but it is still a benefit. Time off from work is as much a form of compensation as a paycheck—as anyone who has ever had to count vacation days knows. If a teacher makes $45,000 for nine months of work while a nurse makes $45,000 for twelve months of work, clearly the teacher is much better paid. Nurses would certainly consider it to be a generous raise if they were offered three months' vacation each year at the same annual salary. However teachers use their summer months off, when we examine how well teachers are paid we should not include those months as work time.

Accurately accounting for the number of hours teachers work goes a long way toward dispelling the Teacher Pay Myth, because it eliminates simplistic comparisons of annual salaries. For example, David Berliner of Arizona State University and Bruce Biddle of the University of Missouri claim that "for years, teachers have been paid low salaries" because of "sexist prejudices." They argue that "the fact that most teachers are women becomes an excuse to pay lower average salaries for teaching than for other comparable occupations," and that this phenomenon has not been widely noticed because "most of those who write about the salaries of teachers are, after all, men." In support of this large claim, they point out that the annual salaries of accountants are higher than those of teachers.[13] But when we compare hourly earnings instead of annual salaries, we find that teachers are actually substantially better paid than accountants. The U.S. Department of Labor reports that on average elementary school teachers earn $30.75 per hour and secondary school teachers earn $31.01 per hour, while accountants and auditors earn $23.35 per hour.[14] This means teachers are paid about one-third more than accountants. Unfortunately, the data are not sufficient for us to determine whether this gap is caused by discrimination against people who wear pocket protectors.

Looking at teacher pay in a way that properly accounts for work time can unearth facts that adherents of the Teacher Pay Myth would find quite shocking. For example, a *Chicago Sun-Times* article on the salaries of union leaders reported that Deborah Lynch, the head of the Chicago teachers' union, made about $111,000 a year. That's reasonable for the head of a union in a major city. But consider how she justifies it: "Our [union] officers make what a teacher would make, but for an eight-hour day and a twelve-month year."[15]

Most people would probably be stunned at the suggestion that ordinary teachers make the equivalent of a six-figure salary. But teachers do earn that much if they stay in the system long enough and take advantage of programs that pay their graduate school tuition for them. In 1999–2000 the average teacher with a master's degree (which 42 percent of all teachers have) and thirty to thirty-four years of teaching experience made a base salary of $54,244.[16] The most recent data available, from 1996, indicate that teachers' school days are 7.3 hours long and they work 180 days per year (figures that have been virtually unchanged since 1961).[17] This adds up to 1,314 hours per year. If the same teachers worked eight-hour days for a full year, taking two weeks of vacation and another ten paid holidays per year, that would add up to 1,928 hours. Doing the math, we find that this produces an equivalent full-time average base salary of $79,591. Given that this is an average, we would expect teachers in expensive cities (like Lynch's Chicago) to make substantially more. So, it is quite plausible that some teachers are making the equivalent of Lynch's six-figure salary. In fact, Frederick Hess of the American Enterprise Institute, relying on federal survey data, estimates that in 2004 between 15,000 and 20,000 teachers actually did make over $100,000—not that they made the equivalent of that much if they had worked full time, but that they actually were paid that much for the time they did work.[18]

Obviously most teachers are not making this much. However, that's only because most teachers don't yet have thirty years' experience. Even the average teacher's salary doesn't appear sub-par when translated into its full-year equivalent. Following the same calculation used above, the national average teacher's salary of $44,600 translates to the full-time equivalent of $65,440—not enough to buy a house in Bill Gates's neighborhood, but certainly enough to keep the wolves from the door.

Some argue that when teacher pay is calculated on an hourly basis, the figures are distorted because teachers perform an unusually large amount of work away from the job site, primarily at home—grading papers on the weekend, for instance. Sylvia Allegretto, Sean Corcoran, and Lawrence Mishel of the Economic Policy Institute argue that Labor Department statistics do not accurately measure hours of offsite work by teachers. They claim that teachers work many hours offsite, and that when we account for this we can see that teachers are underpaid.[19]

To support this claim they cite a large amount of survey data and other self-reported data establishing that teachers undertake significant amounts of offsite work in addition to their contractually mandated hours of onsite work. But no one doubts that many teachers do offsite work. The problem is that people in other professions also do offsite work. The only important question is whether teachers do significantly more offsite work than others.

Out of all the discussion of offsite work they provide, only once do Allegretto, Corcoran, and Mishel actually address the question of whether teachers do more offsite work than others. They assert in passing that their analysis of survey data finds that "teachers report an average of 43.9 weekly hours" of total work, onsite and offsite, while "nonteaching professionals' hours reported corresponded more closely to the traditional forty-hour work week."[20] The vagueness of this assertion makes it impossible for us to evaluate the validity of their claim. Exactly how many hours per week did nonteaching professionals say they worked? It could have been forty-two or even forty-three hours, and the claim that this "corresponded more closely to the traditional forty-hour work week" would still be technically accurate. Since these researchers are writing in support of the idea that teachers are underpaid, it seems certain they would have reported the exact figure instead of making a vague assertion if the exact figure really established a significant difference between the work hours of teachers and nonteachers. Given the margin of error one must allow for with survey data, the difference between forty-two and forty-four hours would be too little to justify the conclusion that there truly is a substantial difference in offsite work done by teachers and nonteachers. In the absence of the specific data that researchers are supposed to provide when they make this kind of claim, we have no reason to accept this vague assertion as a research finding.

While it is difficult to study this question empirically, there are a number of good reasons to think it is not likely that teachers do more "off the clock" work than others. The perception that teachers do an unusual amount of work while not formally on the job is based on a very common but unfounded assumption: that teachers spend almost all of the school day teaching, leaving little time for grading papers and preparing lessons during regular school hours. One school superintendent, in an article praising teachers, opens with the statement, "teachers spend eight or more hours a day with our children."[21] But that isn't even close to true. In fact, teachers spend only about half the school day teaching, and it appears that even that amount may be declining over time. The average teacher in a departmentalized setting—that is, where students have different teachers for different subjects—taught almost 4.5 hours per day in 1982 and fewer than 3.9 hours per day in 2000 (data for nondepartmentalized teachers are not easily available).[22] This leaves plenty of time for grading and planning during the day.

What's more, in almost all other professions people make more money if they perform better. This creates a strong incentive to do more work on evenings and weekends. Teachers cannot earn a higher salary by performing better; they need only turn in a minimally acceptable performance in order to keep their jobs. This leaves them with little incentive to do great amounts of overtime work.

Drawing Appropriate Comparisons to Other Professions

Another, more complicated reason for the persistence of the Teacher Pay Myth is that people often draw improper comparisons when measuring whether teachers are paid better or worse than those in other professions. If the claim that teachers are "underpaid" is to have any meaning at all beyond mere sentiment, it must mean that teachers are paid less than some appropriate comparison group. Drawing the wrong comparisons can create a misleading impression.

Showing that teachers earn less than members of some other occupation is not sufficient to establish that they are underpaid. For example, it would not mean much to show that doctors make more than teachers. Students cannot even enter medical school without having passed through an unusually difficult undergraduate regimen of classes in biology and chemistry, and must then complete years of especially grueling graduate study followed by a period of residence before they can be licensed to practice medicine. All this ensures that only very bright and dedicated students can become doctors, so it is hardly surprising that doctors are very well paid. To establish that teachers are underpaid, one must show that they are paid less than members of other professions that require similar amounts of effort and academic ability to enter.

The American Federation of Teachers claims that "average teacher salary continues to fall well below the average wages of other white collar occupations," specifically citing higher salaries made by computer system analysts, engineers, and attorneys.[23] Even leaving aside teachers' shorter work years, it is simply wrong to imply that teachers should make as much money as workers in more demanding fields that require extraordinary talent and training. Even the broader comparison, drawn by Berliner and

Biddle, between teachers and "other professions requiring a college degree" is flawed.[24] This open-ended category includes many professions for which the criteria for entry are much higher and the work involved is far more demanding than those of teaching.

Relying on data from the U.S. Department of Labor for 2000, Richard Vedder of Ohio University has found that teachers' average hourly earnings are more than those of architects, civil engineers, mechanical engineers, statisticians, biological and life scientists, atmospheric and space scientists, registered nurses, university-level foreign-language teachers, editors and reporters, physical therapists, librarians, and technical writers. He also found that teachers' median household incomes—a measurement that does not take into account teachers' shorter work years—are about the same (within a margin of 10 percent) as those of accountants, biological and life scientists, registered nurses, and editors and reporters. While there is no such thing as a perfect comparison, since all professions have somewhat different requirements, these comparisons show that teachers are not underpaid relative to roughly comparable professionals and even relative to professionals in many fields that most would consider far more exclusive and demanding (such as architecture and engineering).

Vedder also draws some very broad comparisons similar to those drawn by the teachers' unions and Berliner and Biddle, but produces the opposite result. He finds that teachers' hourly earnings were greater than the average for all professional workers and greater than the average for the highest-paid major category of workers, those working in "executive, administrative, and managerial" positions.[25] So even comparing teachers to broad groups that include the highest-paid professions, Vedder finds they are well paid.

A look at more recent Department of Labor data confirms Vedder's findings. In 2002, elementary school teachers made $30.75 per hour and high school teachers made $31.01. The whole category of "professional specialty" workers made $29.34. Roughly comparable professions included architects ($26.64), economists ($27.83), biologists ($28.07), civil engineers ($29.45), mechanical engineers ($29.46), chemists ($30.68), physicists and astronomers ($32.17), and computer systems analysts and scientists ($32.86). Even electrical and electronic engineers, dentists, and nuclear engineers didn't make too much more than teachers ($34.97, $35.51, and $36.16, respectively). The category of "executives, administrators, and managers" makes an average of only $34.75. And teachers' earnings are much higher than those of registered nurses ($24.57), police officers ($22.64), editors and reporters ($22.38), firefighters ($17.91), social workers ($17.21), and secretaries ($14.77).[26] In light of these data, teachers don't look underpaid at all (see figure 6.1).

Allegretto, Corcoran, and Mishel question the Labor Department's measurement of the number of hours teachers and nonteachers work per year. They argue that the Labor Department data seem to indicate a roughly thirty-eight-week work year for teachers, while for nonteacher professionals the data seem to indicate a roughly fifty-two-week work year. They observe, correctly, that the fifty-two-week work year for nonteachers would obviously include paid vacation time as work time, so that the data are really measuring "time paid" rather than time actually worked. A thirty-eight-week work year for teachers would seem to exclude vacation days and holidays, counting them as time not worked. This would mean that the

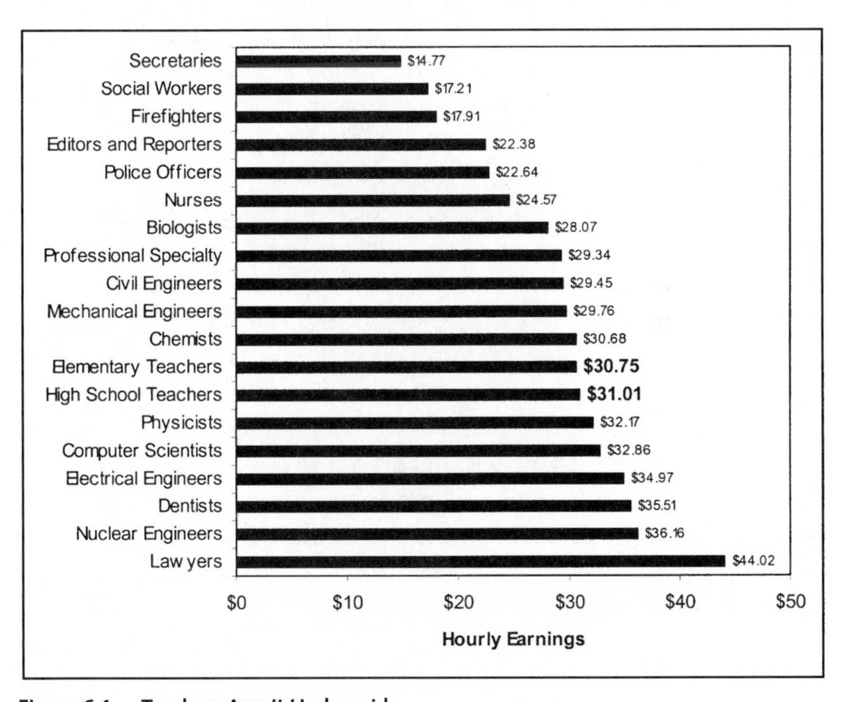

Figure 6.1. Teachers Aren't Underpaid
Source: National Compensation Survey: Occupational Wages in the United States, July 2002, Summary 03-02, U.S. Department of Labor.

Labor Department is overmeasuring the work time of nonteacher professionals relative to the work time of teachers.[27]

It would be premature to conclude that the way the Labor Department data count work time is truly biased against teachers. For example, the Labor Department data include sick days as time worked for both teachers and nonteachers. Podgursky cites data showing that teachers take much more sick time than nonteachers.[28] So a systematic correction of the Labor Department data to exclude all forms of time paid but not worked might not favor teachers as heavily as Allegretto, Corcoran, and Mishel contend.

But even if we ignore this possibility and correct the data only for vacation days and holidays, it turns out that the difference is not nearly large enough to justify the conclusion that teachers are underpaid. Allegretto, Corcoran, and Mishel propose that we correct the problem by subtracting four work weeks per year (twenty work days) from the work time of nonteacher professionals to account for their vacation days and holidays. This would increase our figures for the hourly earnings of nonteacher professionals by 8.3 percent. Making this adjustment, we find that elementary teachers ($30.75) and high school teachers ($31.01) are paid at about the same level as the overall figure for the category of "professional specialty" workers ($31.78 after the adjustment). Their pay is comparable to that of architects ($28.85), economists ($30.14), and biologists ($30.40).

Former *New York Times* education columnist Richard Rothstein draws another kind of inappropriate comparison when he compares trends in salaries over time in teaching and in other professions. He argues that schools have been unable "to maintain teacher quality in the face of greater competition from other professions" because from 1975 to 1995 starting salaries for teachers did not grow as fast as those for engineers, marketers, business administration graduates, mathematicians and statisticians, economists and finance personnel, and liberal arts graduates generally.[29] Rothstein is comparing annual salaries rather than hourly earnings, which masks the effects of teachers' unusually short work schedules, but there is a more fundamental problem here. Comparing the growth rates of salaries in different fields rather than their current salary levels is misleading. The required qualifications in these fields may well have increased over the period Rothstein is examining, or the number of hours worked by starting employees may have increased, or their employment benefits may have decreased, or other changes in working conditions may have made these occupations less attractive. For example, it is not hard to imagine that an entry-level engineer worked more hours in 1995 than in 1975. Conversely, it may also be that starting teachers' salaries did not grow as quickly because required entry qualifications for teachers decreased, or hours worked by starting employees decreased, or employment benefits increased, or other changes in working conditions made teaching more attractive. There may also have been changes in the labor pools of these fields—if, say, more people are becoming mathematicians and statisticians, salaries in those fields will go down due to the increased labor supply. Where any of the above conditions is true, the underlying economic value of a teaching career relative to careers in other professions may not have changed even though the salaries have grown at different rates.

A different kind of inappropriate comparison is that which measures U.S. teachers against their professional counterparts in other countries. Berliner and Biddle argue that U.S. teachers are underpaid because here "teachers make roughly 1.67 times the average per capita income of the nation," while "in Japan, teachers make 2.43 times the average per capita income of their country. The average teacher in Japan earns just about the same as the average engineer, while in our country the average teacher earns only about 60 percent as much."[30] But the school year is significantly longer in Japan, so teachers must be paid more there because they work longer. What's more, it is possible that the academic and training requirements for teaching in Japan are more demanding than those in the United States, in which case higher salaries would simply reflect the normal labor market realities rather than necessarily indicating any difference in society's underlying valuation of teachers.

Taking Account of Employment Benefits

Even these comparisons of salaries and hourly earnings do not tell the whole story, because they do not include the value of employment benefits. This category includes such valuable forms of compensation as medical coverage, retirement benefits, and life and disability insurance, so it can be quite important to getting an accurate picture of total compensation.

Data on employment benefits are less easily available than data on salaries and hourly earnings. Detailed field-by-field comparisons of employment benefits are not as feasible as the detailed comparisons of earnings examined above. Vedder writes that "typically, teachers' retirement and health insurance benefits are more generous than the average professional's, particularly those who work in the private sector." But the comparison group he uses to illustrate this appears to include all types of workers rather than just "professionals."[31]

However, it turns out that when it comes to employment benefits, teachers come out ahead even when we compare them to a broad category of professionals that includes the most highly skilled fields. U.S. Department of Labor statistics allow us to compare the rate at which teachers participate in employment benefits to the participation rates of "professional and technical" employees in the private sector. Vedder finds that half of all teachers pay nothing for single-person health coverage, while this is true for fewer than one-quarter of private-sector professional and technical employees.[32] Podgursky finds that health benefits amount to 7.1 percent of hourly compensation costs for teachers, compared to 5.1 percent for private-sector professionals.[33] A closer look at the data show that benefits are more broadly available to teachers than to private employees in that category. Teachers are more likely to qualify for medical coverage (86 v. 63 percent), outpatient drug coverage (82 v. 61 percent), dental coverage (62 v. 42 percent), vision coverage (40 v. 24 percent), retirement benefits (98 v. 65 percent), and life insurance (88 v. 75 percent). The only type of job benefit teachers are substantially less likely to participate in is paid vacation days and holidays, but given teachers' radically different work schedules this comparison is not meaningful.[34]

We should also take into account one very important employment benefit of teaching: job security. Because of the very strong tenure protections enjoyed by almost all teachers once they have served a certain number of years, teachers have a level of job security that is unparalleled in almost every other field. While it is difficult to put a specific dollar figure on the value of this benefit, it does have a substantial value.

Obviously this is incomplete information. For example, comparing the rate at which employees participate in retirement plans does not take into account the value of those plans. Information on the value of employee benefit plans is difficult to obtain so we must work with the evidence that is available. That evidence indicates teachers are not generally shortchanged on employment benefits.

Why Doesn't Teaching Attract the Best and Brightest?

A final aspect of the Teacher Pay Myth is that low teacher pay explains why the college graduates who go into teaching tend to be on the low end of the spectrum of academic performance. "Teachers are too often recruited from college graduates whose grades or ambitions are not high enough to win places in more remunerative professions," writes Rothstein. "Higher teacher salaries . . . will improve schools' ability to attract more highly qualified graduates."[35] Berliner and Biddle agree: "Thoughtful high school students surely know that teaching is not the royal road to high income and prestige. . . . At least in part as a result, teaching is *not* the chosen occupation for many of our most talented and ambitious students. . . . This is surely not desirable."[36]

But if the Teacher Pay Myth is false and teachers are paid about as well as employees in similar professions, how do we explain the generally low quality of the graduates attracted to teaching? No doubt, many factors are at work, but the most obvious one is the profession's truncated work year. Teachers are paid about as much per hour as those in similar professions, but work far fewer hours because schools are only open for about nine months per year. It seems likely that high-performing graduates are precisely the kind of ambitious people who would prefer to work more hours and make a higher total salary rather than work fewer hours and make a higher hourly rate but a lower total salary. That would make the teaching profession decisively unsuitable for them.

Another reason high-performing graduates might stay away from teaching is that the field's pay scales don't allow them to earn more money through better performance. Teacher pay is based almost entirely on credentials and years of experience, leaving no room to compensate excellent teachers for their better performance. Caroline Hoxby and Andrew Leigh of Harvard University find that since at least 1960 the inability of teachers to make more money by performing better has been the main cause of significant declines in the academic abilities of those who have entered the teaching profession.[37]

This is not to say that raising teacher pay would necessarily be undesirable. No doubt significantly raising teacher pay would attract higher-performing graduates into the field. Of course, a pay raise that wasn't accompanied by politically difficult reforms to the structure of teacher pay would also encourage the current low-achieving teacher workforce to remain in their jobs longer. What's more, any such plan must explain where the money would come from to provide significant raises for the very large number of teachers that our nation employs. In practice, any serious attempt to attract better teachers by raising teacher pay would probably have to be accompanied by a reduction in the number of teachers. This would result in some combination of larger class sizes and longer workdays for teachers, both of which are forcefully opposed by those who are currently working in the teaching field and their unions. So ultimately there are no easy answers to this problem—but then, that's how things usually look when you discard the myths and look at the facts.

PART II

Outcomes

CHAPTER 7

The Myth of Decline

"Schools are performing much worse than they used to."

The evidence in chapter 1 showed that increased spending is not producing improvements in student performance; despite large increases in education spending, test scores have not risen over the last three decades. But some critics of the public schools subscribe to the opposite myth—the Myth of Decline. They believe that public schools are not just failing to improve but that their performance is rapidly declining or even in free fall. Such critics claim that our once high-quality public schools have eroded to the point of mediocrity or even failure.

The popularity of the Myth of Decline can be traced to the U.S. Department of Education's landmark report *A Nation at Risk*.[1] The report warned that the quality of America's schools was eroding to such a degree that the decline posed both an economic crisis and a national security threat. The commission wrote of a "rising tide of mediocrity that threatens our very future as a Nation and a people." The warnings of *A Nation at Risk* shocked the nation and served as the kindling for what has become the modern school reform movement.

There was nothing novel about *A Nation at Risk*'s fear that America's education system was in decline. When it comes time to send the children to school, each generation of parents invariably longs for the bygone Golden Age of education when, as they remember it, schools were far more effective. Government officials often play a role in fueling the Myth of Decline. For example, when asked about a 1993 U.S. Department of Education report showing disturbingly low levels of adult literacy, then Secretary of

Education Richard Riley commented, "The numbers indicate that we have slipped to some degree."[2] The report only showed that things were currently bad, but Riley's comment suggests that things were once better, that at some time in the past our schools produced more literate citizens.

The evidence justifies neither parents' longing for the Golden Age nor the doomsday predictions of *A Nation at Risk*. Test scores, which are the best available measure of student proficiency, show that student performance has not changed much in the last thirty years. If today's schools are mediocre, they are no more so than the schools of a generation ago.

Like many other myths, the Myth of Decline survives because many people fail to consider the most relevant statistics. Though reasonable people can disagree about exactly where to draw the line between good test scores and mediocre test scores, a simple look at achievement on standardized tests shows that schools are performing just as well now as before. While it is true that schools are not improving on these tests, they are not losing ground either.

The National Assessment of Academic Progress

The National Assessment of Educational Progress (NAEP), often referred to as the Nation's Report Card, is a standardized test administered by the U.S. Department of Education to a nationally representative sample of fourth, eighth, and twelfth graders since the early 1970s. Both the quality and the longevity of the NAEP make it the best tool we have for measuring student proficiency over time.

Figure 7.1 shows that twelfth-grade scores on the NAEP have been stable. Scores have also been stable at the fourth- and eighth-grade levels as well. Between 1973 and 1999, math scores went up for fourth, eighth, and twelfth grade students by 13, 10, and 4 points, respectively. Between 1971 and 1999, twelfth graders improved 3 points on the NAEP reading test while fourth and eighth graders each gained 4 points. On the NAEP science test, fourth- and eighth-grade students made gains of 19 points while twelfth-grade students made a smaller gain of only 5 points between 1977 and 1999.[3]

Just as the national average scores on the NAEP have not declined, neither have the percentage of students reaching various proficiency levels. The percentage of students reaching the highest reading proficiency levels (a

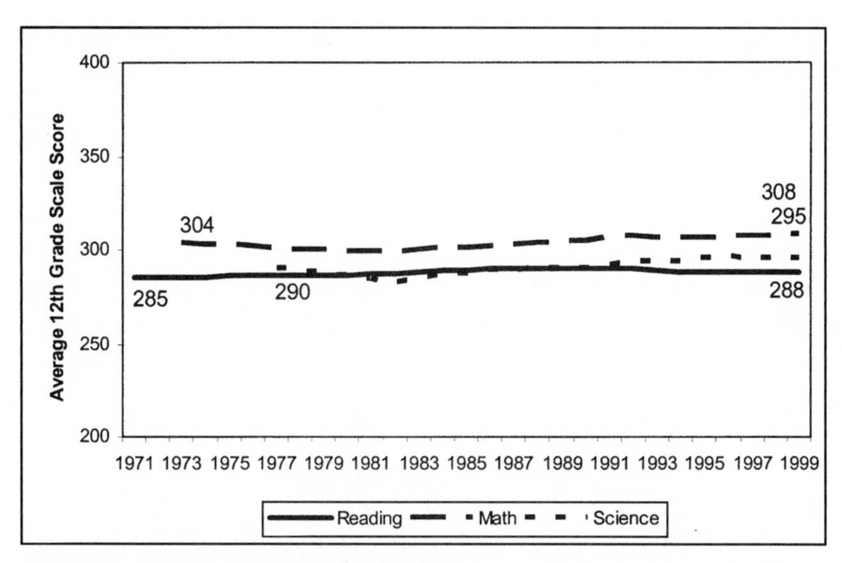

Figure 7.1. NAEP Scores Haven't Declined
Source: Campbell, Hombo, and Mazzeo, "NAEP 1999, Trends in Academic Progress: Three Decades of Student Performance," U.S. Department of Education.

score of 250 or higher for fourth graders and of 300 or higher for eighth and twelfth graders) increased by 0.3 percentage points for fourth graders, 4.7 percentage points for eighth graders and 0.6 points for twelfth graders. The math scores tell much the same story. The percentage of fourth graders reaching the highest proficiency level for that grade rose by 0.9 percentage points in this twenty-one-year period. Similarly, the percentage of students reaching the highest proficiency level in twelfth grade rose by 1.1 percentage points. There was a trivial decrease, 0.1 percentage points, in the percentage of students reaching the highest proficiency level among eighth graders. The percentage of students meeting the lower proficiency levels in both reading and math has increased moderately.

College Entrance Exams

Part of the Myth of Decline is the notion that students entering college are not as well prepared as they used to be. But the evidence seems to show that today's public schools are no worse at preparing students for college than the public schools of the previous generation. Just as scores on the NAEP have remained consistent, so have scores on college entrance exams.

Figure 7.2 shows that the nation's average scores on the Scholastic Assessment Test (SAT) have remained relatively flat over the last three decades.[4] While the nation's average score on the SAT verbal assessment did drop by 26 points between 1972 and 2002, scores on the math test rose by 7 points over the same thirty-year period.

Student performance on the American College Test (ACT) has also remained steady since 1990, the earliest year for which we have comparable information. National average test scores on the ACT remained the same in English and increased by 0.8 points in math. The story is much the same for scores in reading and science, which increased by 0.1 and 0.3 points, respectively.[5]

A Nation at Risk latched onto the relatively large drop on the SAT verbal test as proof that schools are getting worse. However, the absence of any similar decline in student performance on the NAEP reading test should give us pause. Furthermore, SAT verbal scores have remained flat for the two decades following the steep decline of the 1970s. Although college entrance exams are somewhat useful for comparing student performance over time, they are far from perfect in this regard.

Unlike the NAEP, which is given to a nationally representative sample of students, only students intending to enroll in college take the ACT and

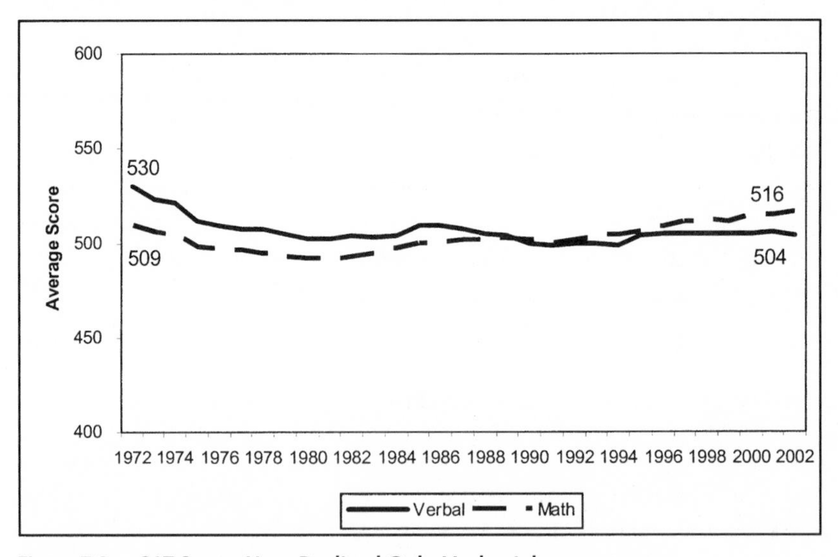

Figure 7.2. SAT Scores Have Declined Only Moderately
Source: Digest of Education Statistics 2002, U.S. Department of Education, Table 134.

SAT. Thus, the sample of students taking these exams changes over time and is not necessarily representative. In any given year, if a greater percentage of lower-performing students take college entrance exams than in previous years, we would expect the overall average score to decline. Such a decline could not be attributed to any change in the performance of the public schools. In fact, it might well be the case that more lower-performing students are taking these exams precisely because the public school system is doing a better job of preparing those students for college. In other words, it might be that students on the low end of the performance scale have improved their performance just enough to enter into the testing pool, even though they remain below the performance level of the average student taking the test. Thus, a decline in ACT or SAT scores can just as easily result from improvement in the public schools as from their deterioration.

Graduation Rates

There is evidence other than standardized test scores that public schools are not in decline. Since graduating as many students as possible is an important goal of our public schools, graduation rates also provide a reliable measure of school effectiveness.

Figure 7.3 shows high school graduation rates between 1971–1972 and 2001–2002, measured by taking high school graduates as a percentage of the seventeen-year-old population. This is the best available way to measure changes in the graduation rate over longer periods of time (see chapter 8 for a complete discussion of graduation rates).

Just as test scores have been consistent over the last thirty years, graduation rates have also not fallen dramatically. Between 1971–1972 and 1999–2000 the national high school graduation rate went from 75.6 to 70.3 percent. What's more, early estimates for the following two years indicate that the rate may have recovered a little—the estimate for 2001–2002 is 72.5 percent. While any drop in the graduation rate may be cause for at least some concern, such a small decrease cannot justify the Myth of Decline.[6]

Reality Check

The evidence is clear that our nation's public schools have not declined substantially. Appeals to a mythological Golden Age of education are misguided

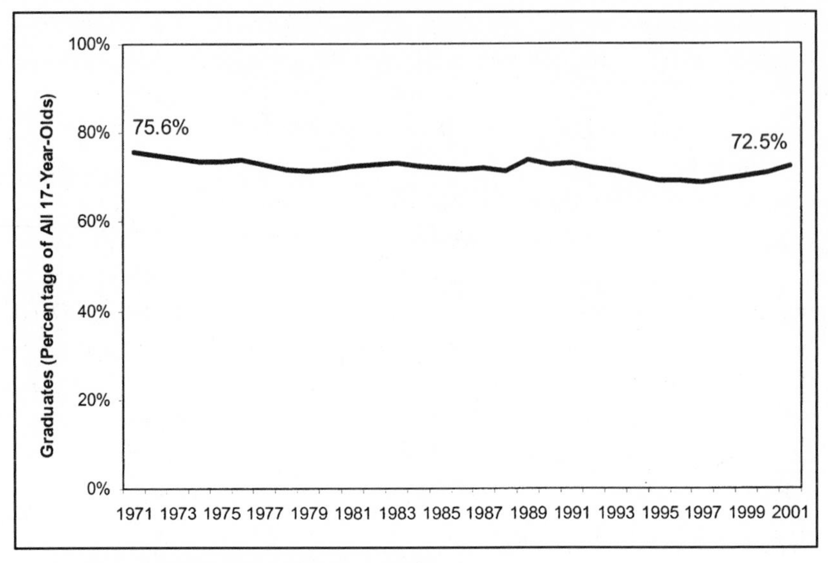

Figure 7.3. Graduation Rates Haven't Declined
Note: Data for 2000 and 2001 are estimates.
Source: *Digest of Education Statistics 2002*, U.S. Department of Education, Table 103.

at best. As New York University's Diane Ravitch points out in *Left Back*, in which she chronicles education reforms throughout the twentieth century, "those who seek the 'good old days' will be disappointed, for in fact there never was a Golden Age."[7]

Of course, it is one thing to say that our schools have not strayed from an earlier path of greatness, and quite another to ask whether the level of performance they have consistently displayed is a good or even acceptable level. Just as some education reformers are wrong to argue that our schools are getting worse, others are guilty of asserting that consistent test scores are proof that all must be well in American public education. David Berliner of Arizona State University and Bruce Biddle of the University of Missouri point to the absence of a decline in standardized test scores in accusing education reformers of creating a "manufactured crisis."[8] Former *New York Times* education columnist Richard Rothstein also relies on these consistent test scores in order to conclude that "we have been pretty successful, on the whole, with the educational improvements attempted in the past."[9] While *A Nation at Risk* was wrong to claim public schools were getting worse, consistent test scores alone also give us no reason to believe that reforms are unnecessary. Schools may not be producing lower test scores, but—as we saw in chapter 1—they have become astonishingly less productive. When a large influx of new resources produces only flat-lining test scores, that is just cause for concern.

Any reasonable debate about the ability of our public schools to produce knowledgeable and successful graduates must be based on the facts about their performance. Test scores and graduation rates over time show that the Myth of Decline is unfounded. Our judgments about whether we should be happy with the performance and productivity of our public schools should not be colored by any illusions of a lost Golden Age of education.

CHAPTER 8

The Graduation Myth

"Nearly all students graduate from high school."

Graduating from high school with a regular diploma is an important predictor of outcomes later in life. On average, those who drop out of high school earn lower salaries than those who graduate.[1] They are more likely to produce broken homes and more likely to depend upon welfare.[2] They are also more likely to spend time in prison.[3] Since graduating from high school is so important for our nation's youth, most people consider it a primary objective of the public schools to produce as many qualified graduates as possible.

It is generally thought that schools are living up to our expectations in this area. Many people believe in the Graduation Myth—that almost all students graduate from high school. Unlike many other myths, people have good reason to subscribe to the Graduation Myth because it is supported by what appears to be real evidence provided by a source they are accustomed to trusting: their government.

Government agencies with an interest in promoting the Graduation Myth are engaged in a sustained effort to inflate officially reported graduation rates. More often than not, government statistics claim that nearly all students attending public high schools graduate. The official U.S. public high school completion rate, as reported by the National Center for Education Statistics (NCES), a branch of the U.S. Department of Education, was 86.5 percent for the graduating class of 2000.[4] Individual states often report similar graduation rates or ones that are even higher.

But more reasonable estimates of graduation rates paint a much drearier picture. Officially reported graduation rates from the federal government and state governments mislead the public into believing that a much higher percentage of students graduate from high school than actually do receive a diploma. While a graduation rate of 86.5 percent is less than ideal, many would consider such performance to be at least acceptable and would be willing to commend the public schools for this relative success—if only it were true. But official graduation rate calculations such as this one are often misleading at best. The perception that almost all students graduate from high school is largely a state-sponsored myth.

Independent graduation measures indicate that out of all students who enter high school nationwide, about 30 percent leave without earning a diploma. Some states have graduation rates below 60 percent but claim to have much higher levels of success. Perhaps most startling, graduating high school with a regular diploma is little more than a 50/50 proposition for African American and Hispanic students nationwide.

Most people expect that calculating the percentage of students who graduate high school should be a simple and straightforward matter. However, there are actually competing methods for calculating graduation rates. To calculate official graduation rates, the federal government and many state governments use flawed methods that produce implausible results. As we will see, each of these methods has its own particular problems, but some methods are decidedly better than others. Unfortunately, the methods that most researchers agree produce the most reliable calculations of the graduation rate are rarely used for official calculations.

The NCES Method

Let us first examine the method NCES uses to calculate the nation's official high school "completion" rate. To compute this statistic, NCES relies on the Current Population Survey (CPS), a survey administered by the U.S. Census. NCES uses this survey to find the proportion of all eighteen-to-twenty-four-year-olds who "earned a high school diploma or the equivalent" and uses this percentage as the official high school completion rate.

The first problem with the NCES method is that people might lie about whether they graduated from high school. This problem is inherent in any survey that asks potentially embarrassing questions and collects answers that cannot be independently confirmed. We can reasonably expect that a nontrivial number of respondents might not be forthcoming about having dropped out of high school.

What's more, the CPS is administered to a population that is not a representative sample of all Americans. Any person living in an institutional setting is excluded from the survey sample. This includes those serving time in prison, which certainly inflates the apparent graduation rate because dropouts are disproportionately likely to be incarcerated. In fact, the same NCES report that disseminates the official graduation rate also cites a study estimating that 30 percent of federal and 40 percent of state prison inmates are high school dropouts. Since dropouts are more likely than other people to be overlooked by the CPS, they appear to be a smaller portion of the total population than they actually are.

The third problem with the NCES method, a problem that it shares with the methods many states use to calculate graduation rates, is that it counts GED recipients as though they were high school graduates. This is why NCES is always careful to refer to its calculation as a high school "completion" rate rather than as a high school "graduation" rate. GED recipients are classified as high school "completers" rather than as high school dropouts who went on to get alternative certification.

There are two major reasons why it is improper to treat GED recipients as though they were high school graduates. First, there is a large body of evidence showing that a GED is not comparable to a regular high school diploma. By almost every measure, the life outcomes of GED recipients are more like those of high school dropouts without GEDs than those of graduates. Research by Columbia University's Stephen Cameron and the University of Chicago's James Heckman has found that the earning and employment potential of GED recipients is indistinguishable from that of high school dropouts.[5] Other researchers have found that obtaining a GED does convey modest benefits, but these benefits are far too small to be comparable to those of a high school diploma.[6] A GED may well be better than nothing, but it is simply misleading to treat it as though it were the equivalent of a regular high school diploma. In fact, contrary to popular belief, the "E" in GED does not stand for "equivalency." The letters "GED" actually stand for "General Educational Development." The misconception that the "E" stands for "equivalency" is so widespread that even journalists for national news outlets are not immune to it.[7]

The other, perhaps more central, problem with treating GED recipients as though they were high school graduates is that doing so counts the failures of public schools as successes. The primary purpose of calculating a graduation rate is to determine how successful our public schools are at keeping students in school. GED recipients are students whom the public schools failed to keep in school. They are dropouts who took it upon themselves later in life to work hard and earn alternative certificates. Often they have to overcome the poor education they received in public school in order to do so. They earn their GEDs in spite of the performance of their schools, not because of it. Counting them as successes for the public school system rather than as failures is fundamentally misleading.

Tracking Students over Time

Many states promote the Graduation Myth by using methods for calculating their official graduation rates that are just as unreliable as that used by NCES. Many of them are flawed in part because, like the NCES method, they treat GED recipients as though they were high school graduates. However, individual states do not rely on survey instruments like the CPS. Instead, many states attempt to track each individual student over time, separating the ones who graduate, the ones who drop out, and the ones who move away or have other types of outcomes.

Tracking individual students may seem like an ideal method for determining student outcomes. But despite its initial attractiveness, this method is notorious for producing inflated graduation rates. The problem is not that tracking individual students over time is necessarily a bad idea, but that schools have neither the resources nor the incentives required to do so accurately.

The U.S. Census may make it look easy, but it is actually quite difficult to track the whereabouts, let alone the educational status, of large numbers of people over long periods of time. And this process is many times more difficult when it is performed by an institution whose primary function is something other than tracking individuals. The main objective of public schools is to educate the students who are still in the school system, not track students after they leave. Demanding that schools both teach the students within their walls and accurately keep track of all the students who leave is expecting a lot.

On top of the inherent difficulty of the task, there is also the problem of perverse incentives. Schools are under heavy pressure to report high graduation rates. School systems and state governments want to report as few dropouts as possible. Therefore, every time a student leaves a school, that school has a very strong incentive to attribute his departure to a benign reason—he moved, he went to a private school, etc.

Such distortions are even more likely because those outside the school system are unable to check whether schools are reporting student outcomes accurately. Because of privacy restrictions, it is impossible for researchers, reporters, or members of the community to obtain the information on individual students that is collected by the school system. While these privacy protections are certainly necessary, they leave us unable to determine whether schools are accurately tracking students. The public is expected to simply take the school system's numbers on faith, which is a little like depending on every taxpayer to audit his own income tax return.

A common way for states to inflate their graduation rates is to develop benign categories in which to place students who fail to graduate. For example, in Texas, students who leave school without a diploma but say that they intend to enter a GED program are not counted as dropouts. Until recently, the state of Washington only considered a student to be a dropout if he filled out official paperwork to declare that he was dropping out of high school.[8] Students who were no longer enrolled in school but did not bother to fill out the necessary paperwork were lumped into the category "other" and were not counted as dropouts in the official calculation.

Other states may not go to quite such extreme lengths, but these examples illustrate that states are under very intense pressure to inflate their graduation rates. Such perverse incentives, coupled with a real lack of the resources and expertise necessary to track students over time, has resulted in many states' reporting unrealistic figures as their official graduation rates.

A More Reliable Method

The Manhattan Institute's Jay Greene has developed a more reliable method for calculating the percentage of students who graduate from public schools. This method makes use of enrollment figures reported by each state to the U.S. Department of Education. Enrollment data are publicly available and highly reliable. While schools must go out of their way to track down dropouts, all they have to do in order to provide reliable enrollment data is simply take attendance. Schools also have an incentive to count every student in their classrooms because much of their funding is based on enrollment.

This method calculates the graduation rate by estimating the number of students who should have graduated in a given year if no student had dropped out. It does this in three steps. First, it uses enrollment data to estimate the number of students who entered ninth grade for the first time four years earlier. Then it makes adjustments to account for changes in the high school population over the ensuing four years. This produces an estimate of the number of students who should have graduated if none had dropped out. All that remains is to divide the actual number of diplomas awarded by this estimate.

It is necessary to estimate the number of students entering ninth grade for the first time because the actual ninth grade enrollment data are artificially high. In addition to students starting ninth grade for the first time, ninth-grade enrollment counts include students who were held back and are repeating the grade. First-time ninth-grade enrollment is estimated by averaging the enrollments of the same cohort of students as it passes through eighth, ninth, and tenth grades. That is, the estimate of first-time ninth-grade enrollment in a given year is the average of the eighth-grade enrollment from the year before, the ninth-grade enrollment from that year, and the tenth-grade enrollment from the following year.

Changes in population must also be factored in to account for changes in the student population that do not result from students graduating or dropping out. For example, if a large number of high-school-age students moved into the country between a given cohort's ninth-grade year and his twelfth-grade year, this would inflate the graduation rate because there would be a larger number of diplomas in his twelfth-grade year than there otherwise would have been. Population change is accounted for by measuring the percentage difference in the number of high schoolers during a cohort's ninth-grade year and the number of high schoolers during the cohort's twelfth-grade year.

To use this method to calculate the 2001 graduation rate, we would take the average of the eighth-grade enrollment in 1996–1997 (3,397,990), the ninth-grade enrollment in 1997–1998 (3,813,930), and the tenth-grade enrollment in 1998–1999 (3,378,348). This produces a first-time ninth-grade enrollment estimate of 3,530,089. The overall population of high school students in the United States grew by 2.99 percent over the ensuing four years. Applying this increase to our ninth-grade estimate, we get a cohort estimate of 3,635,689; this is an estimate of the number of students who should have graduated if no students had dropped out. Finally, we divide the number of high school diplomas actually awarded in 2000–2001 (2,566,148) by the number of students who could have graduated (3,635,689) to get the graduation rate (71 percent).[9]

Graduation rates calculated using this simple and highly reliable method often vary considerably from officially reported graduation rates. For example, this method produces a national graduation rate for the class of 2000 of about 69 percent, far below the 86.5 percent reported by NCES.[10] Many states fare no better when their official graduation rates are examined using this method. Table 8.1 shows that twenty-four states officially reported graduation rates that were at least 10 percentage points higher than those calculated using the method developed by Greene. For example, North Carolina reports a figure for the class of 2001 of 92.4 percent. Enrollment data for that class yield a graduation rate of only 63 percent.[11] Technically, North Carolina does not actually claim that the 92.4 percent figure is a "graduation rate" or "completion rate," but it is reported in a confusing way that will cause many people to mistake it for a graduation rate. Similar differences in graduation rate calculations are found in several other states.

Perhaps the most famous example of a state promoting the Graduation Myth through misleading statistics took place in Texas. When it was discovered that Houston—which had been hailed for its education "miracle"—was reporting wildly unrealistic graduation rates, a national scandal ensued.[12] However, the problem went far beyond just the city of Houston. Most recently, Texas has reported a graduation rate of 82.8 percent for the class of 2001, but in the past, the state had reported that only a little more than 1 percent of the students in the class of 2001 dropped out in each year of high school.[13] This would translate into a four-year graduation rate of about 95 percent. Enrollment data for that class yield a graduation rate of only 67 percent.[14] Clearly, Texas's official graduation statistics leave much to be desired.

Using the method developed by Greene to estimate graduation rates for students in different racial categories produces numbers that are downright shocking. Even those who promote the Graduation Myth are willing to

Table 8.1. Official Graduation Rates Are Often Inflated

	State Reported, percent	*Greene's Method, percent*
North Carolina	92	63
Alaska	85	64
South Carolina	78	57
California	87	67
Connecticut	87	70
Indiana	91	74
Texas	83	67
Tennessee	76	60
Colorado	82	68
Oregon	80	66
Delaware	83	70
Michigan	86	73
Washington	79	66
New Hampshire	85	72
Maine	87	74
South Dakota	97	85
Illinois	85	74
Virginia	85	74
Maryland	85	74
Arkansas	85	75
New York	75	65
Wisconsin	91	81
Kentucky	81	71
New Mexico	77	67

Note: Not all state-reported figures are labeled as graduation rates. State-reported figures are for 2001–2002; Greene's method figures are for 2000–2001.
Source: The Education Trust, "Telling the Whole Truth (or Not) about High School Graduation."

acknowledge that black and Hispanic students are less likely to graduate from high school than white students, but this method reveals that minority graduation rates are not just low, they are alarming. Only 51 percent of black students and 52 percent of Hispanic students graduated from high school with a regular diploma in the class of 2001.[15] Such low graduation rates for minority groups are highly disturbing given the importance of a high school diploma for achieving success.

While the federal and state governments continue to use faulty methods for calculating their graduation rates, many researchers have adopted the method developed by Greene, or other similar calculations, as a more reliable estimate of the graduation rate. For example, graduation rates using this method have been used in prestigious publications such as *Education*

Week's annual "Quality Counts" report,[16] and in a report on graduation rates by the Education Trust.[17]

The graduation rates produced by this method also are confirmed by those calculated using another reasonable method. In addition to its more widely publicized calculation of high school "completion" rates, NCES also estimates the high school graduation rate by dividing the number of graduates in a given year by the number of seventeen-year-olds in the population. Obviously not every graduate is seventeen years old, but the number of seventeen-year-olds provides a good estimate of the size of the population cohort for a given graduating class (using eighteen-year-olds instead provides almost identical results). This calculation finds that high school graduates were 70.3 percent of the seventeen-year-old population in 1999–2000.[18] This NCES calculation does not provide exactly the same information as Greene's method because it estimates the graduation rate for all students in both public and private schools, so unlike Greene's method it does not specifically measure the performance of public schools, but the NCES calculation does indicate that the figure produced by the Greene method is not far off the mark.

Hope for Raising Graduation Rates

Obviously, these findings raise the question of how we can improve these low graduation rates. Only a limited amount of empirical research exists on what kinds of reforms raise graduation rates, but some has been done. One study finds that smaller school districts have a strong positive relationship with higher graduation rates. For example, its results indicate that if Florida—a state with unusually large school districts—decreased the size of its districts to the national median, it could increase its graduation rate by 5 percentage points.[19] Smaller school districts create a greater degree of parental choice by making it easier for families to choose which school district they will live in, which in turn gives schools an incentive to perform better in order to attract students. Another study finds that students in Milwaukee using vouchers to attend private schools had a graduation rate of 64 percent, while students in Milwaukee public schools had a graduation rate of 36 percent.[20]

But before reforms to the education system can be successful, people must first recognize that there is a problem that must be rectified. The

Graduation Myth, fueled by badly inflated official graduation rates, falsely reassures the public that there is no major problem as far as keeping students in school is concerned. The evidence shows that far fewer students graduate from high school than many in the public believe, and this problem cannot be addressed until people come to understand the falsehood of the Graduation Myth.

CHAPTER 9

The College Access Myth

"Nonacademic barriers prevent a lot of minority students from attending college."

Just as earning a high school diploma leads to better life outcomes than dropping out of high school, going to college is also a good predictor of later economic success.[1] Because going to college opens doors that nothing else can, Americans have become increasingly concerned that minority students are less likely to enroll in college. Data from the U.S. Department of Education and U.S. Census show that only about 27 percent of black eighteen-year-olds and 14 percent of Hispanic eighteen-year-olds entered college in 2000, while about 40 percent of white eighteen-year-olds entered college.[2]

The racial gap in college attendance has led to the widespread adoption of the College Access Myth—that artificial barriers are preventing a significant number of academically qualified minority students from entering college. The evidence, however, shows that fewer minority students attend college because minority students are less likely to meet the bare minimum qualifications to apply to college. So, while it is true that minority students are less likely to attend college, the main barrier currently preventing more minorities from entering college is not money or race but the shoddy K-12 education many of them receive. Any attempt to address the problem of minority enrollment in higher education that does not focus on improving K-12 education will be ineffective.

Promoting the College Access Myth

Adherents of the College Access Myth routinely argue that more financial aid or stronger affirmative action policies are necessary to provide minority students with greater access to higher education. A report published by the NAACP argues that "discrimination against racial minorities in college admissions has been a longstanding problem."[3] The editorial board of the *Chicago Tribune* worries that "college is becoming a luxury only America's more well-off families can afford."[4] This sentiment was echoed by the *New York Times*, which argued that financial aid has not kept up with increasing college costs and that "this has increasingly discouraged the neediest students from applying to college at all."[5] And some opponents of affirmative action also promote the College Access Myth when they argue that affirmative action prevents qualified white students from attending college.

The arguments over college admission and financial aid programs typically take it for granted that there is a backlog of students who are academically ready to attend college but are shut out of higher education for other reasons. However, if no such backlog exists then the debate over what college admission policies would increase minority enrollment is misplaced. Changes in financial aid or affirmative action policies may be desirable for other reasons (such as the effect they have on which students are able to attend which particular colleges), but changes to these policies can only raise overall minority representation in college if there is currently a pool of minority students who are qualified to attend college but don't do so.

A report by the Advisory Committee on Student Financial Assistance (ACSFA), an agency of the U.S. Department of Education, claims that among high school graduates who are academically qualified for college 48 percent of low-income and 43 percent middle-income students are prevented from attending a four-year college by financial barriers.[6] They calculate that in all high school graduating classes there are a total of 400,000 students who are college ready but don't go to college because of insufficient financial aid. Since a much larger percentage of minorities than whites have low incomes, the vast majority of the students allegedly kept out of college by these financial barriers would probably be minorities.[7]

However, the study is misleading because it relies on an incorrect definition of what makes a student "college ready." The study's definition of college readiness is far too lax, counting many students as college-qualified when they do not possess the minimum qualifications that are actually necessary even to apply to four-year colleges. Thus, the study blames financial barriers for keeping out of college many thousands of students who could not enroll in four-year colleges no matter how much money they had.

Measuring College Readiness: The NCES Method

The ACSFA study uses a method developed by researchers at the National Center for Education Statistics (NCES), also part of the U.S. Department of Education, to measure the college readiness of high school graduates.[8] This method assesses students' performance on five academic indicators: grade point average, class rank, score on the NELS (an NCES aptitude test), SAT score, and ACT score. For each of these categories students are rated on a five-point scale ranging from "marginally or not qualified" to "very highly qualified."

Each student's highest-scoring indicator is then used as the measure of his overall college readiness. For example, a student whose NELS score rated him "somewhat qualified" but whose grade point average rated him "highly qualified" was considered to be "highly qualified." Students were then moved up a rank if they had taken "rigorous academic coursework," defined as four years of English; three years of each natural science, social science, and math; and two years of foreign language. Students in the top category of "very highly qualified" who lacked this level of coursework were moved down to the next lowest category.

The main problem with the NCES method is that using a student's highest-scoring indicator to determine his overall score sets the bar too low to measure real college readiness. For example, the NCES method considers a student with a GPA of 2.7 to be "minimally qualified" for college, regardless of his score on other measures. Even if such a student had a poor class rank and test scores, he would be considered qualified for college. No doubt, there are many high school graduates with 2.7 GPAs who could get into college, but it is equally certain that there are many who could not.

NCES uses this unrealistic rating system because it must cope with the problem of missing data. Many students, particularly low income and minority students, do not have information available on all five of the academic criteria NCES uses. This lack of available information on student academic outcomes is certainly not NCES's fault, but that does not make the study's results any less misleading.

The NCES method also produces an inflated college readiness rate because it fails to accurately reflect the importance of high school transcripts for college admission. Taking certain academic courses isn't simply an indicator of college readiness, it's an absolute requirement for it. Students who have not taken the necessary courses aren't just considered to be somewhat less well qualified for admission; at almost all four-year colleges they will be flatly ineligible to apply. (This is one reason it is important to distinguish between statistics on enrollment in "higher education" or "postsecondary education," which include minimally selective institutions like community college and trade school, and statistics on enrollment in four-year colleges.) The NCES definition of "rigorous academic coursework" is actually a higher standard than the transcript requirements at many four-year colleges, but almost all colleges at even the least selective, least prestigious level will not consider applications from students whose transcripts do not meet their standards. By not requiring that students take the necessary courses to be considered qualified for college, the NCES method seriously overestimates the percentage of students that is college ready.

A Better Method for Measuring College Readiness

We will need a more accurate way to measure how many college-ready high school students are in the population if we wish to find out whether artificial barriers are keeping college-ready students out of college. Manhattan Institute researchers Jay Greene and Greg Forster have developed a method for measuring college readiness that more accurately reflects the way colleges actually evaluate students.[9] By comparing the results of this more reliable method with the number of students who actually enroll in college, we can determine whether a significant number of students, or a significant number of minority students, are college ready but never enroll in college.

Three "Screens" of College Readiness

Under this method, to qualify as "college ready" students must pass three screens. Students must graduate from high school with a regular diploma, must have taken at least the minimum coursework that colleges require for admissions, and must demonstrate basic literacy. Students who fail to pass even one of these basic requirements are not only insufficiently prepared for college-level coursework; they are not qualified to apply to four-year colleges regardless of any other factor. This method more accurately accounts for the way colleges screen applicants, providing a clearer picture of the number of students who have been academically prepared for college by their local schools.

The first screen students must pass in order to be college ready requires that they graduate from high school. Enrollment data from the U.S. Department of Education are used to calculate a highly reliable estimate of the number of students who graduate high school (see chapter 8 for details). For the class of 2001, 70 percent of all students graduated from high school with a regular diploma. The graduation rates for minority students are far below the national average—only 52 percent of Hispanic students and 51 percent of black students graduate from high school. This tells us how many students pass screen one.

To determine how many students pass screens two and three, this method takes advantage of a large study of high school graduates conducted by NCES.[10] The study collected detailed information about students, including whether they graduated with a regular diploma, what courses they took, and their scores on the National Assessment of Educational Progress (NAEP), a nationally respected standardized test administered by the U.S. Department of Education.

The second screen students must pass in order to be college ready requires that they have the necessary classes on their high school transcripts. This screen is based on admission criteria at four-year colleges selected to be representative of the lowest level of prestige and selectivity. The least demanding admissions criteria out of all the colleges evaluated was four years of English, three years of math, and two years each of natural science, social science, and foreign language. This is the bare minimum standard a student must meet to pass the second "college-ready" screen.

Greene and Forster find that 36 percent of students pass both the first and second screens. That is, 36 percent had both received a regular high school diploma and taken the minimum coursework necessary to be considered eligible for college. The disparity in achievement between racial groups, already large in screen one, grew larger after screen two. Only 25 percent of black students and 21 percent of Hispanic students, compared to 39 percent of white students, passed both screens one and two.

In order to pass the third and final screen to be considered college ready, students must demonstrate basic literacy by performing at the "Basic" level of proficiency or higher on the NAEP reading test. After applying this screen, the researchers found that only 32 percent of all students leave high school eligible to apply to a four-year college. Racial disparities remained large in the final data: 16 percent of Hispanic students and 20 percent of black students are college ready, compared to 37 percent of white students.

Comparing the College-Ready and College-Entering Populations

To translate these percentages into useful enrollment numbers, Greene and Forster used Census data and multiplied the total number of eighteen-year-olds in the population by their estimated college readiness rates. They then compared the number of students who are college ready with the number of students actually entering college, in order to find out whether there is a significant pool of academically qualified students who do not go on to attend college.

The results of this comparison, reported in figure 9.1, show that the number of students who enroll in college is very similar to the number of students who are college ready. For the class of 2000 there were an estimated 1,298,920 students eligible for college admission, which is very close to the 1,341,000 students who actually enrolled in college that year. The similarities along racial lines are also striking. There were about 112,275 college-ready black graduates and 105,912 college-ready Hispanic graduates in the class of 2000, compared to actual college enrollments of 152,632 for black students and 91,466 for Hispanic students. The college-ready and college-entering populations were also very similar for Asian and American Indian students. It may seem curious that the number of students actually entering college is slightly greater than the estimated number of students minimally qualified to attend college, but we should bear in mind that these are estimates, not exact counts. Also, some students—though probably not a large number—become college qualified by alternative means outside the regular school system.

The similarity between the college-eligible and college-entering populations throws the College Access Myth into a considerable level of doubt. There

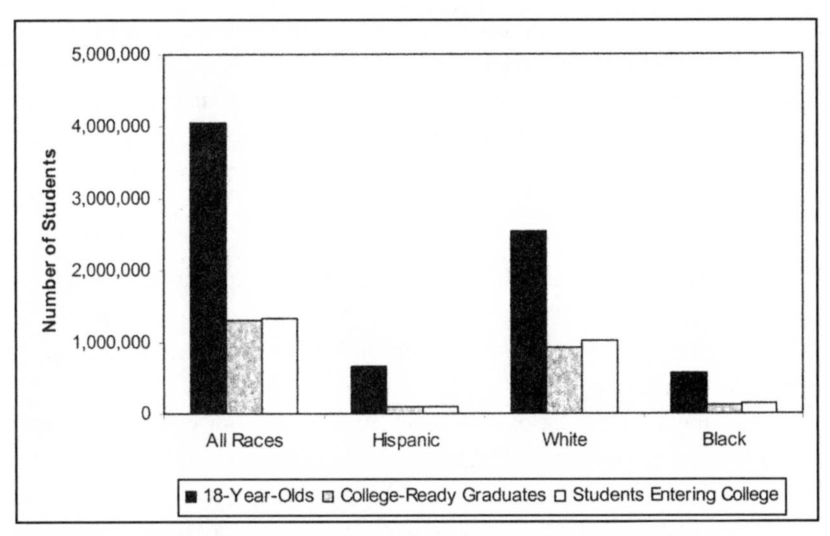

Figure 9.1. Nearly All College-Ready Students Enter College
Note: Figures are for the year 2000.
Source: Greene and Forster, "Public High School Graduation and College Readiness Rates in the United States," Manhattan Institute.

is not a large pool of students who are academically prepared for college but are failing to gain admission because of inadequate affirmative action or financial aid policies. We know this because the pool of college-ready students who do not enroll for *any* reason is very small. Almost all students who are eligible for college admission go on to actually attend college.

Blaming inadequate affirmative action or financial aid policies for the low minority enrollment in higher education is like saying that the reason an overweight, forty-year-old Monday morning quarterback doesn't play in the National Football League is because there aren't enough draft rounds for him to be selected. No matter how many rounds are added to the draft, it won't help that fan live up to the minimum standards that NFL teams require for their players.

Those who argue that affirmative action is keeping qualified white students out of college are similarly misguided. There were about 933,350 college-ready white graduates in the class of 2000, and in that year 1,018,025 white students entered college. Neither will strengthening affirmative action displace a significant number of white students from college, since there aren't enough college-ready minority students to displace them—just as throwing a bucketful of water into a river won't cause it to flood.

All of this does not necessarily mean that past efforts to increase minority participation in higher education through financial aid and affirmative action have been unsuccessful. It is certainly possible that such policies are the reason nearly all minority students who are eligible for college currently do enroll in college. But this analysis does indicate that strengthening such programs can have no more than a very limited effect on future minority enrollment.

Some may argue that colleges should stop requiring students to take a certain set of high school courses in order to be eligible to apply. Removing this condition for enrollment would certainly make more minority students eligible for higher education, but at a high cost. Colleges do not require students to take a certain set of classes simply because they enjoy tormenting young people, or because they're getting kickbacks from the nation's English and math teachers. They believe, quite reasonably, that these classes convey a set of basic knowledge and skills that students must possess to succeed in a four-year college. There's no point in allowing large numbers of students who haven't taken high school math courses to enter college if they're just going to flunk out because they don't have the necessary math skills.

Foundations of the College Access Myth

If it is not grounded in the facts, where does the College Access Myth come from? One culprit is the pervasiveness of the Graduation Myth. Many people believe that almost all students graduate from high school, and for them it is not too much of a stretch to infer that a large number of students are prepared to go on to the next academic level. But, as we saw in chapter 8, far fewer students graduate from high school than many believe, and the problem is particularly distressing for minorities. When nearly half of black and Hispanic students fail to graduate from high school, while we may be horrified, we should certainly not be surprised that so few are academically prepared for college.

Another reason the College Access Myth is so widespread is that, while a college education is certainly a sizeable investment, the financial barriers to attending college are not as high as many believe. An NCES report shows that many parents with college-bound children seriously overestimate the cost of college tuition. The report found that while the average yearly tuition of attending an in-state, four-year public university was $3,247, on average parents of college-bound high school juniors and seniors believed the cost to be $5,799. Nearly a quarter of parents surveyed believed the cost of tuition at an in-state public university to be $8,000 or more, while less than 1 percent of such schools actually charge such a large amount. Furthermore, when asked to add in the cost of room and board, on average parents thought the total cost of sending a child to college would be $9,148, when the actual average cost is about $7,789.[11]

Another factor is the large amount of financial aid that is available to families paying for college. The College Board, an association of colleges, found that a record $74 billion in financial aid was available to college students in 2001–2002. This amount is almost double what had been available ten years earlier (adjusting for inflation).[12]

Parents of children preparing to enroll in college are the very people who have the most incentive to correctly understand how much tuition will cost. If they overestimate the cost of college tuition by so much, it is likely that the general public also has a misconceived notion of the true expense of higher education. This misperception can only support the College Access Myth.

The Need to Reform K-12 Education

Since nearly all minority students who are qualified to go to college already do so, the blame for low minority participation in higher education should fall upon the K-12 schools that fail to prepare enough minority students for college. The evidence shows that the only reasonable prospect for increasing minority participation in higher education is increasing the supply of college-ready minority graduates. This cannot be achieved through any policy implemented at the college level; it must come through improvement in the education minority students receive from their K-12 schools.

Significantly increasing minority college readiness requires the improvement of notoriously underperforming urban school systems, in which minorities are highly overrepresented. While there is certainly room for reasonable disagreement over how to improve such schools, the evidence shows that focusing on any other policy area, such as strengthening affirmative action or financial aid, is simply a distraction that is unlikely to yield significant results.

At least the underlying premise of the College Access Myth is correct—far too few minority students enroll in college. The barriers such students face today, however, are neither racial nor financial, but rather academic. Improving minority participation in higher education requires more focused attention on improving the education such students receive before it's time for them to fill out a college application.

PART III

Accountability

CHAPTER 10

The High Stakes Myth

"The results of high-stakes tests are not credible because they're distorted by cheating and teaching to the test."

High-stakes testing, also known as accountability testing, has emerged over the last decade as one of the nation's most popular education reforms. These programs attach consequences, either positive or negative, to the results of standardized tests in order to make schools accountable for educating their students. The particular "stakes" attached to the tests vary from school system to school system. Some school systems require students to pass a test in order to be promoted to the next grade or to graduate from high school; others offer extra funding for schools that perform well. Depending on how one defines exactly what counts as a "high-stakes" test, somewhere between thirty and forty states as well as several individual school districts administered some form of high-stakes test even before implementation of the No Child Left Behind Act, which is now requiring all states to begin administering such exams.

These "make or break" exams have proven as controversial among experts as they are popular among the states. For the last several years, a debate has raged over the problems and benefits of high-stakes testing systems. Much of this debate has focused not on the educational benefits of measuring student proficiency, but rather on whether such measurement is even possible when the measuring device—the test—has consequences attached to its outcome. Critics of high-stakes testing argue that gains made on accountability tests are illusory because schools find artificial ways to improve their test scores. For example, the editorial board of the *Los Angeles Times* worries that "numbers-polishing has become a sad by-product of high-stakes accountability."[1]

However, the evidence indicates that high-stakes tests are reliable measurements of student proficiency. The track record of the nation's high-stakes testing programs shows that these tests are useful for making judgments about school achievement. The High Stakes Myth, which holds that various forms of test manipulation render these tests unreliable, does not square with the facts.

Different Forms of the High Stakes Myth

Defenders of the High Stakes Myth have identified at least three ways in which high-stakes test results are allegedly distorted. One is direct manipulation of the test results by outright cheating. There have been numerous reports throughout the nation, most prominently in Texas and Florida, of teachers coaching students during administration of the test, or obtaining test booklets before the test is administered and giving students the answers. There have even been reports of teachers and administrators physically changing students' answer sheets after they have taken the test. The University of North Carolina's Gregory Cizek chronicles several alleged incidents of cheating on high-stakes tests and questions whether we can make informed decisions about schools based upon the results of these exams. "By distorting test results," writes Cizek, "cheating can lead to ill-advised initiatives, improperly focused resources, and inaccurate conclusions about the course of education reform."[2]

A more common form of the High Stakes Myth is concern that teachers will indirectly manipulate test outcomes by "teaching to the test." Instead of improving test scores by better educating their students, this argument runs, teachers will tailor their curricula and teaching practices in a way that improves test scores without actually increasing students' learning. Thus, teachers may abandon useful subjects and material that are unlikely to appear on the test in favor of cramming rote facts (which their students will promptly forget after the test) and drilling students in test-taking strategies. Linda McNeil of Rice University writes that when it comes to high-stakes tests, "the real cheating is of a solid academic curriculum."[3]

The worry that high-stakes testing may cause teaching to the test is widespread among the public and is frequently cited by researchers and policymakers. The late Senator Paul Wellstone wrote that by implementing accountability testing "we force teachers to 'teach to the test,' an intellectually deadening experience for kids, whose curriculum becomes too focused on test-taking."[4] Joseph Renzulli of the University of Connecticut argues that high-stakes testing has led to a curriculum that focuses on a new version of the three R's: "ram, remember, regurgitate."[5] The airwaves and newspaper pages are also littered with personal anecdotes from teachers and parents claiming that the schools have been forced to abandon teaching useful skills in favor of drilling students on the material covered by standardized tests.

Finally, a third version of the High Stakes Myth holds that test scores don't accurately reflect students' capabilities because the seriousness of the consequences attached to high-stakes tests causes students so much stress that they perform more poorly than they otherwise would. As author Alfie Kohn, a notorious critic of standardized testing, puts it: "You think SARS is contagious, try stress."[6] In states and cities where schools use high-stakes tests, whenever the test is administered there is no shortage of newspaper reports on students who blanked on questions under the pressure of a test they had to pass in order to graduate or be promoted.

No doubt each of these problems—cheating, teaching to the test, and stress—does occur to some extent as a result of high-stakes testing. It is certainly true that some schools and their staffs respond in inappropriate ways to the consequences placed on high-stakes tests. This makes detecting and dealing with test manipulation a crucial element of any well-designed testing system.

But such manipulations would not invalidate the information we get from high-stakes tests unless they were so widespread that they systematically undermined the whole system. If one student in a class of thirty cheats on a pop quiz, the quiz scores of the other twenty-nine students are not invalidated. The appropriate course of action is to punish the one cheater, not to throw out the whole quiz, and certainly not to stop giving quizzes altogether. If the number of test manipulators is small, the integrity of a high-stakes testing system is not affected. The crucial question, then, is whether manipulations occur at high enough rates to invalidate the results of high-stakes tests.

Unreliable Evidence on the High Stakes Myth

A study by Audrey Amrein and David Berliner, researchers at Arizona State University, claimed to prove the High Stakes Myth as fact.[7] When its results were trumpeted on the front page of the *New York Times*, it quickly became the study of record on the question of the reliability of high-stakes tests.[8] Since making such a splash, however, its findings have been shown to be flawed due to fundamental errors in both the design and execution of the study.

Amrein and Berliner attempted to determine whether implementing a high-stakes test leads to improved performance on other tests. They did this by comparing state-level results on the SAT, ACT, Advanced Placement (AP), and National Assessment of Educational Progress (NAEP) tests before and after each state implemented a high-stakes test. They found that, on average, implementing a high-stakes test did not lead to higher scores on these other tests. From this they concluded that schools in these states had abandoned teaching the higher-order skills measured by their comparison tests in favor of less useful skills and rote drilling.

The most obvious problem with Amrein and Berliner's study is that the comparison tests they use are fundamentally different from those of state-mandated high-stakes tests, most importantly because they are administered to different populations. While high-stakes tests are administered to all, or nearly all, of a school system's students, the SAT, ACT, and AP exams are only administered to the cream of the academic crop. College entrance exams are only administered to students who intend to enroll in college; AP examinations are even more limited in that they are only taken by academically elite students in schools that offer AP curricula. Since these tests are administered to very different populations from those that take high-stakes tests, it is hardly surprising that the implementation of a high-stakes test does not necessarily lead to improvements on these highly selective tests.

In fact, if high-stakes testing is working as it should, we might even expect to see decreases in outcomes on these other tests. The purpose of high-stakes testing is to provide a better education to students at the lower end of the academic spectrum. If high-stakes testing is accomplishing this goal, we could reasonably expect to see a decline in overall scores on the elite SAT, ACT, and AP exams as high-stakes testing causes more historically underperforming students to apply to college or take on elite programs such as AP.

The other test Amrein and Berliner used to compare against high-stakes tests, the NAEP, is a more reasonable comparison, but their use of this test is also flawed. The NAEP is administered to a representative sample of all students rather than only to elite students. However, it is only administered intermittently in each subject—for example, the reading NAEP is not administered in the same years as the math NAEP. Thus, the NAEP does not lend itself to an accurate calculation of the effects of high-stakes testing, because it cannot track year-to-year changes in each subject.

Amrein and Berliner begin their analysis with scores on the 1990 administration of the NAEP, so they might have missed whatever gains were made in states that implemented a high-stakes test before this time. As for states that began testing after 1990, since the NAEP has only been given every four years in each subject, the years in which many of the states instituted high-stakes testing do not line up with a year for which the NAEP was administered. Amrein and Berliner try to make up for this limitation by assuming that NAEP scores increase or decrease smoothly over time—for example, if a state's score went up four points over a four-year period, they would assume that it increased one point in each year. But the whole objective of the study is to examine annual changes in test scores; it defeats the purpose to do this by imputing annual test score changes on the assumption that scores change gradually along a smooth line.

Even if we disregard these problems arising from Amrein and Berliner's selection of tests to compare against high-stakes tests, their study remains fundamentally misleading. Stanford University's Margaret Raymond and Eric Hanushek have exposed a series of devastating errors in Amrein and Berliner's study.[9]

The most fatal of these flaws is the study's point of comparison. The obvious method would have been to compare the gains made on the NAEP in states that administered high-stakes tests against those of states that did not administer such tests. Instead, Amrein and Berliner compared the gains made by states that give such tests to the average gains made in the nation. But given that most states give high-stakes tests, any educational improvements resulting from high-stakes testing will be contained within the national average. Thus if high-stakes tests cause SAT scores to go up, Amrein and Berliner's method may not discover this fact because scores will rise for both the high-stakes testing states and the national average; the scores for high-stakes states may rise faster than the national average, but this may not be enough to make the difference statistically visible. Raymond and Hanushek compare this method to "a medical trial where the treatment group receives the full dose of a medication while the control group receives a half-dose."[10]

Another major problem with Amrein and Berliner's analysis is that by using only the dichotomous measure of whether a state's change in test scores was above or below the national average they failed to measure the magnitude of the difference. For example, a state with test score gains that were 2 points below the national average on the NAEP would be counted the same as a state whose gains were 30 points below the nation. It would have been far more appropriate for Amrein and Berliner to use a simple regression model like those used by nearly all other researchers.

Raymond and Hanushek also point out that Amrein and Berliner did not adhere to some of the basic tenets of social science research. They administered no controls to their data, failed to perform any significance testing, removed some states from their sample in an arbitrary manner, and looked only at whether states made any test score gains without taking into account the magnitude of any such gains.

Raymond and Hanushek perform their own analysis of Amrein and Berliner's data using statistically sound methods and find the opposite result. That is, by applying sound methods to the same data, they show that states with high-stakes testing made greater gains on NAEP than states without high-stakes testing. They conclude that "Amrein and Berliner used scientifically inappropriate methods and applied them in an even shoddier manner. Simply taking Amrein and Berliner's approach and applying it correctly to all of the data on NAEP achievement reverses their conclusions."[11]

Other Evidence

There has been more research that is reliable on the reliability of high-stakes tests since the flawed Amrein and Berliner study. In a Manhattan Institute study, Jay Greene, Marcus Winters, and Greg Forster directly examined the evidence on the High Stakes Myth.[12] Unlike the Amrein and Berliner study, which compared state-level results on incomparable tests, the Manhattan

Institute study compared school-level results on high-stakes tests with results on other standardized tests administered to the same students in the same schools at around the same time. These comparison tests had little or no stakes tied to their results, so they might be called "low-stakes" tests. Since there is no incentive for schools to cheat on or "teach to" these low-stakes tests, we can reasonably expect the results on these tests to be accurate indicators of student proficiency. If high-stakes tests and low-stakes tests produce similar results, this would show that the scores on the high-stakes tests are not systematically tainted by manipulation.

The study covered nine school systems, including two states, comprising 9 percent of all U.S. public school students and a much greater percentage of all students who take high-stakes tests. Its results are a reasonable indication of the validity of high-stakes testing nationwide.

While the results varied from school system to school system, the analysis found strong overall correlations between results on high-stakes and low-stakes tests. This indicates that when standardized tests are properly designed and administered, students' test performance does not depend upon stakes tied to the exam. To the extent that cheating, teaching to the test, and negative effects due to student stress do occur, such distortions on high-stakes tests are scarce enough that the test results remain accurate measures of student ability.

The most interesting findings of the study were the results from Florida, home of perhaps the nation's most aggressive high-stakes testing program. Florida's A+ Accountability Program uses scores on the state's high-stakes test, the Florida Comprehensive Assessment Test (FCAT), for a variety of accountability measures. Students must pass the reading portion of the test in order to be promoted to the fourth grade and must pass the tenth-grade test to receive a regular high school diploma. Schools are also graded each year based upon their performance on the FCAT; if a school receives two Fs within any four-year period, the state offers vouchers to all of the school's students. Given that the stakes of the FCAT are among the highest in the nation, if there is any place we would expect to see an incentive for educators to manipulate scores or to see distortions from teaching to the test or student stress, it would be in Florida.

The study found impressively strong correlations between school-level results on the FCAT and a low-stakes test, the Stanford-9. The correlation of score levels on the high-stakes and low-stakes tests was an astonishing

0.96 (if the results on the two tests were perfectly correlated, the result would have been 1.00). The correlation of year-to-year changes in test scores on high-stakes and low-stakes tests was 0.71, a strong correlation. Both of these findings were the strongest of any school system in the study in their respective categories. These results show that there is little to no manipulation of scores on Florida's high-stakes test, despite the particularly high stakes of the FCAT. This suggests that high-stakes tests can be designed and administered in such a way that they produce reliable measures of student performance regardless of the importance of the test results.

Two Different Forms of "Teaching to the Test"

One reason that the High Stakes Myth is so widespread is that many people do not adequately distinguish test manipulation from other, legitimate responses that schools make when high-stakes testing is implemented. People find it plausible that schools are manipulating test scores because they correctly perceive that schools are reacting to the presence of high-stakes tests. However, not all of these changes are forms of test manipulation.

This is especially clear when we examine the oversimplified view many people have of the phenomenon that we have been referring to as "teaching to the test." Contrary to popular belief, teaching to the test is not always detrimental to education. There are actually two different senses in which a school can be said to "teach to" a particular test; one is harmful, but the other is not only harmless, it is actually quite beneficial.

One form of teaching to the test is to drill rote facts into students without conveying any genuine learning. This may allow students to "beat" the high-stakes test without transferring any useful knowledge to them. Clearly, this form of teaching to the test is detrimental.

The other form of teaching to the test is not only benign, it appears to be an effective method for improving school performance. Educators can respond to the presence of a high-stakes test by changing their curricula and teaching methods in a way that increases their effectiveness in the classroom and imparts more learning rather than less. Knowing that important consequences will follow from academic failure, schools have a strong incentive to improve their performance. Providing this healthy incentive is the main objective of high-stakes testing programs. Many parents and policymakers would be more than happy to accept this form of teaching to the test.

By showing that the increases in test scores occurring on high-stakes tests are matched by corresponding gains in scores on low-stakes tests, Greene, Winters, and Forster's study provides valuable evidence that if teachers are teaching to the test, they are doing so in a way that increases learning. Whatever changes educators are making to their curricula and classroom practices in response to high-stakes testing, if they result in higher scores on those tests it is because these changes are improving education, not because teachers are drilling students on useless information.

Educational Nihilism

Most adherents of the High Stakes Myth agree that standardized tests are not inherently unreliable; rather, they are concerned with the use of testing for accountability purposes. But there are some who disagree with the basic premise that anything meaningful at all can be learned from testing. They make no distinction between the results of high-stakes and low-stakes tests, claiming that both fail to produce reliable outcomes. Such critics argue that it is impossible to systematically measure education outcomes in a way that is independent of teachers' own evaluations of their students.

Respected educator Deborah Meier attacks those who seek to make educational improvements based on such "simpleminded" assessments as tests, "as though the purpose of schools were test scores based on schooling, not life scores based on living."[13] Alfie Kohn goes a step further, questioning the desirability of measuring student proficiency at all. Kohn writes, "Anyone trying to account for the popularity of standardized tests may also want to consider our cultural penchant for attaching numbers to things. One writer has called it a 'prosaic mentality': a preoccupation with that which can be seen and measured."[14]

The main problem with this line of thinking is that it leads to educational nihilism. If we are truly unable to measure student proficiency in an independent and objective way, rather than relying on teachers' own evaluations of their students, then we can never have any objective information about the effectiveness of reforms or the ability of schools in general to make a difference in their students' lives.

Standardized test scores are clearly not just random statistical "noise." The Greene, Winters, and Forster study found that scores on different standardized tests were strongly correlated. This not only shows that the stakes of a test do not dilute the significance of the test's results, it also shows that these tests are in fact effectively measuring something. Otherwise, we would expect to see randomness in the test results, and that would prevent a strong correlation in results on different test administrations. When multiple tests designed to measure the same set of skills produce very similar results, we can reasonably conclude that the tests in question are working properly. Furthermore, the thing these tests are measuring is not just a student's skill at test-taking, but something that has applications in the real world. Students who score well on basic skills tests go on to have better life outcomes such as income levels.[15] Whatever it is that enables students to score well on basic skills tests also enables them to earn more later in life. This suggests that the quality being measured by basic skills tests might just be basic skills.

Some critics argue that while the standardized tests used by accountability programs do measure something, they fail to measure what the critics call "real learning," such as critical thinking and other more sophisticated skills. But this thesis implies that basic literacy and numeracy do not count as real learning. While imparting more sophisticated knowledge and skills to students may be a desirable goal, it is not unreasonable to give greater priority to addressing the problem that many of our nation's youth—especially poor and minority students—do not possess even the most basic reading and math skills. Before we attempt to test students on advanced knowledge and analytical skills, it seems wise that we first teach them to read, write, and do basic math.

As high-stakes testing becomes a more prominent strategy of education reform, it is important that we have confidence that high-stakes tests produce useful information about student proficiency. While cheating and other forms of test manipulation do sometimes occur, an examination of the evidence shows that they do not fundamentally distort the information high-stakes tests provide. Research provides confidence that the High Stakes Myth is false. When properly implemented, high-stakes tests are accurate measures of student proficiency.

CHAPTER 11

The Push-Out Myth

"Exit exams cause more students to drop out of high school."

Many states require students to pass a standardized test in order to graduate from high school. States have adopted these high-school "exit exams" in response to concerns that the value of their diplomas has eroded due to insufficient academic standards. But many critics of exit exams think that they impose too high a price by making it too difficult to graduate from high school. These critics rely upon the Push-Out Myth—the idea that requiring students to pass exit exams forces more students to drop out of high school.

The purpose of exit exams is to use objective test scores to ensure that all students who graduate possess the basic skills that students should have to merit a diploma. Their proponents argue that they provide a form of quality control that is necessary to protect the value of high school diplomas in the labor force. If students can graduate from high school regardless of whether they have learned anything, employers will no longer consider high school diplomas valuable. Intel CEO Craig Barrett worries that "where Americans once viewed the diploma as a common national currency, its value has been so inflated that employers and postsecondary institutions all but ignore it in their hiring and admissions decisions today."[1] The Manhattan Institute's Marcus Winters and Greg Forster, pointing to U.S. Labor Department statistics, argue that employers are discounting diplomas held by certain minority groups. They found that among Hispanic students who did not go to college, recent high school completers are just as likely to be unemployed as recent high school dropouts. Whites who do not go to college, by contrast, have much lower rates of unemployment if they finish high school than if they do not. Winters and Forster argue that employers no longer believe diplomas held by Hispanic students indicate possession of any skills. They warn that if diplomas continue to lose their value in the marketplace, this phenomenon will likely spread across racial lines.[2]

Many people are concerned about the impact these exit exams have. Each year around testing time in states that have exit exams there is a flood of news accounts about students who will not graduate solely because they cannot pass the test. Typical of the genre is one *Miami Herald* profile of students who have been prevented by exit exams from attending college or entering the military.[3] In Florida such reports led minority leaders to call for a boycott of important Florida industries in protest against the state's exit exam.[4]

These accounts don't just show us students who can't pass the exam; sometimes they allege even more serious and widespread problems. A two-part series by the *New York Times* argued that New York's exit exam requirement had led several high schools to deliberately force low-achieving students to drop out before taking the exam. By taking advantage of bureaucratic loopholes, schools were able to process the pushed-out students in ways that would cause them not to be officially considered dropouts. The *Times* claimed that such students "represent the unintended consequence of the effort to hold schools accountable for raising standards."[5]

Like many other education myths, the Push-Out Myth makes intuitive sense. It would seem to many people that making it more difficult to graduate would necessarily lead to fewer students graduating. However, also like many other education myths, our first intuitions simply do not correspond to the evidence. The highest quality research available shows no relationship between adopting an exit exam and graduation rates.

The Evidence

There is a small but growing body of scientific studies evaluating the effects of exit exams on high school graduation. The evidence indicates that states can adopt exit exams without denying diplomas to any more students than before.

Arizona State researchers Audrey Amrein and David Berliner examined whether adopting an exit exam led to increases in dropout rates, declines in graduation rates, or increases in the percentage of students working to acquire GEDs instead of graduating. They declared that if a state with an exit exam saw undesirable changes on these measurements greater than those of the national average, the state was harmed by the test. Using this definition, Amrein and Berliner found that 66 percent of states with exit exams were harmed by the testing mandate.[6]

Amrein and Berliner's method for evaluating the effects of exit exams on high school graduation is similar to the method used in their study on the effects of accountability on test scores. Like that study, this analysis suffers from fundamental flaws. They compare states with exit exams to the national average instead of to states without exit exams, they adopt no controls for characteristics like race and poverty, they perform no significance testing, and they examine only the direction of changes in data rather than the magnitude of such changes (see chapter 10 for a complete discussion). These problems render their study untrustworthy.

John Warren and Krista Jenkins of the University of Minnesota studied the effects of exit exams in Florida and Texas.[7] The study analyzed data from the Current Population Survey (CPS), which is administered by the U.S. Census and collects a variety of economic and household data. The researchers were particularly interested in Florida and Texas because each of these states underwent two transitions related to exit exams: from not requiring students to pass any exam to requiring them to pass an easy basic skills test, and then to requiring them to pass a more difficult criterion-based exam. Warren and Jenkins found no relationship between high school graduation and the adoption of either the easier or the harder exit exams.

Warren and Jenkins's study is potentially problematic because people living in institutionalized settings, such as prisons, are excluded from CPS. A disproportionate number of high-school dropouts are in prison and thus are not included in CPS. However, while this does mean that overall graduation rates using CPS are of dubious value (see chapter 8), it may have less of an effect on Warren and Jenkins's study. Their analysis does not rely on overall calculations of graduation rates but rather on a comparison of students' chances of graduating with and without an exam requirement. Excluding people in institutionalized settings limits their pool of data, but may not cause a fundamental distortion in their analysis. What their results show is that among people who are not in institutionalized settings, exit exams did not have an effect on graduation rates. This pattern may also exist for those people excluded from the survey; it is a reasonable hypothesis that the dropouts who end up in prison are even more likely than other dropouts to be people who would have dropped out regardless of any exam requirement. Nevertheless, the exclusion of such a large percentage of dropouts from Warren and Jenkins's sample is less than ideal.

Some researchers have used data from the National Educational Longitudinal Survey (NELS), a widely respected survey that has followed a cohort of students since they were in the eighth grade in 1988. There have been five statistical studies analyzing this high-quality data set. Of these, four have found no overall link between having to pass an exit exam and dropping out of high school.[8]

The fifth study using NELS, a widely cited study conducted by Pennsylvania State researchers Sean Reardon and Claudia Galindo, reported that students who were required to pass an exit exam to enter the ninth grade were more likely to drop out of high school before reaching the tenth grade.[9] However, unlike other studies analyzing NELS that found more benign results, Reardon and Galindo relied upon the NELS survey of school administrators to determine whether students were required to pass a standardized test. Subsequent researchers have found that these data are flawed. For example, Warren and Edwards found a great deal of variability within each state in the survey's reports of the existence of a state-mandated standardized test. This data problem could explain why Reardon and Galindo's findings are so different from those of other researchers evaluating the same data set.

However, while the evidence from studies using NELS should be considered generally reliable, it has its limitations. Because NELS follows only a single cohort of students, studies using it are unable to evaluate whether graduation rates change over time with the adoption of an exit exam. As Warren and Jenkins write, "we can learn a lot from NELS:88 about the effects on high school exit examinations on the high school class of 1992, but absolutely nothing about their effects on subsequent (or preceding) high school classes."[10]

A study by Manhattan Institute researchers Jay Greene and Marcus Winters followed a decade's worth of high-school cohorts to evaluate the effect of adopting a high-school exit exam on graduation rates.[11] They calculated state-level graduation rates between 1991 and 2001 using two distinct but highly respected methods. They then performed an analysis that was able to measure changes in graduation rates before and after states implemented an exit exam. Their evaluation found that changes in graduation rates in states that adopt exit exams are not significantly different from the normal fluctuations in graduation rates that are present in states that do not adopt such exams.

But How Can Exit Exams Not Cause Dropouts?

To many it will seem implausible that adopting exit exams could fail to reduce the number of students who graduate. It certainly is counterintuitive. If we make it harder to obtain a diploma, shouldn't it follow that fewer students can meet these elevated standards? There are, however, explanations for why it might be that the Push-Out Myth is unwarranted.

First, exit exams as they exist today might test skills so basic that they disqualify very few students. The Fordham Foundation conducted an evaluation of state-mandated exams in thirty states and found that they are far easier than many expect.[12] No state received the study's highest rating in the category of Test Rigor and only one state earned its second-highest rating. Overall, the analysis gave a "poor" rating to test rigor nationally. Thus, the difficulty of passing an exit exam might be low enough that almost all students can clear the hurdle successfully. It is true that Warren and Jenkins found no increase in dropouts associated with increases in test difficulty in Florida and Texas; similarly, Greene and Winters find no increase in dropouts associated with more recent exit exams, which tend to be more difficult than older exams. However, even the new, more difficult exams may still be too easy to produce a significant effect on dropout rates. If exit exams become more difficult in the future, they could begin to hold more students back, but it may be that the tests as they exist today are not difficult enough to dramatically reduce the number of students who graduate.

Another reason exit exams' effect on graduation rates may be negligible is that students have several opportunities to pass the tests before they are finally denied a diploma. And not only are students typically given second, third, and even seventh chances to pass the exam, but between test administrations they are routinely provided with extra instruction specifically designed to help them pass the test. Given enough chances and additional preparation, the vast majority of students should eventually be able to pass high school exit exams, even if only by chance—just as most kids will eventually succeed in pinning the tail on the donkey if given enough tries.

Some even conclude that because most students eventually pass exit exams, their effectiveness at raising standards for graduates is actually limited. Exit exam proponents Michael Cohen, Chester Finn, and Kati Hayock argue that "most [exit exams] aren't nearly rigorous enough to ensure that those who pass them are prepared for postsecondary education or work."[13] However, we know from extensive media reporting that some number of students do not graduate solely because they fail exit exams. This indicates that despite their limitations exit exams do provide some level of diploma quality control. While the exams may not set standards high enough to satisfy some of their proponents, they certainly set a higher standard than was typically enforced in the past, when diplomas effectively served as little more than certificates of attendance.

Finally, the small number of students who are prevented from graduating by exit exams may be offset by a similar pool of students who would have dropped out but instead graduated because the exams forced their schools to educate them. One purpose of exit exams is to give schools an incentive to better serve low-performing students. The shift in resources and attention toward students in danger of dropping out could cause some number of students to receive diplomas when they otherwise would not have. However, the evidence suggests that if such a positive effect is taking place, it is only large enough to balance out the number of students who do not graduate only because they cannot pass the exams. Even over longer periods of time, they do not seem to increase levels of graduation.

Unable to find convincing evidence supporting the Push-Out Myth, some critics of exit exams have switched to complaining that they don't do enough. A report by the Center on Education Policy complains that even though exit exams may not decrease graduation rates, they are not increasing graduation rates either: "The research to date offers no evidence that exit exams decrease dropout rates—in other words, exit exams are clearly not helping to keep students in school."[14]

Complaints that exit exams do not increase graduation rates simply miss the point. While it would be very desirable if exit exams did decrease dropout rates, it is more than sufficient that they simply have no effect on dropout rates. Because exit exams require graduates to demonstrate a certain level of proficiency, they provide some level of quality control for high school diplomas. If, as the evidence indicates, these exams have no effect on dropout rates, it follows that with exit exams states can distribute higher quality diplomas to the same number of students. This is clearly a benefit.

The evidence shows that while exit exams eliminate a certain number of students from the graduation rolls, they also work to graduate a similar number of students who otherwise would have dropped out. Thus, while exit exams do not decrease the number of students who graduate, they do change the pool of graduates. Exit exams redistribute diplomas to those students who demonstrate that they possess the necessary skills and away from students who do not merit them.

Evidence versus Intuition

The Push-Out Myth is a particularly striking example of the important role evidence plays in testing common perceptions. At first glance, it not only seems plausible but necessary that by increasing the difficulty of obtaining a high school diploma, exit exams would decrease graduation rates. The evidence, however, consistently points in a direction different than our predispositions.

It is important for policymakers to give greater weight to evidence than to sentiment. While newspaper reports of students who are denied diplomas solely because they cannot pass the state test may be true, they only tell part of the story. The relevant evidence provides optimism that exit exams allow states to distribute more meaningful diplomas to the same number of students as before.

CHAPTER 12

The Accountability Burden Myth

"Accountability systems impose large financial burdens on schools."

Many critics claim that the costs of high-stakes testing outweigh their benefits. They insist that the cost of designing, administering, and fulfilling the mandates of accountability tests put an undue financial burden upon already strapped public schools. There have been varieties of competing cost estimates all claiming to show the "true" cost of accountability. When we evaluate the evidence, however, it becomes clear that those who portray testing as outrageously costly are subscribing to the Accountability Burden Myth. Accountability testing is actually relatively inexpensive, especially when compared to other popular reforms.

The most prominent accountability reform, and the one that has attracted the most complaints from advocates of the Accountability Burden Myth, is the federal No Child Left Behind Act (NCLB). Passed with strong bipartisan support in 2001, the law requires states to develop accountability goals and use a standardized test to measure whether students are reaching those goals. NCLB provides sanctions for schools that fail to make adequate gains for several years in a row. These include the diversion of a portion of schools' federal subsidies to tutoring for failing students, and allowing students to transfer to other public schools. States are also held accountable for their overall performance through the diversion of portions of their federal funding.

Among the many complaints about the law expressed by newspapers, educators, and politicians, the most common is that it is an "unfunded federal mandate." Though the law provided the largest-ever increase in federal education spending when it was passed, critics argue that the cost of the accountability testing and performance improvement required by the law far outweighs the additional dollars. Like the law itself, the complaints are bipartisan. For example, the Democratic-controlled Vermont legislature voted not to spend any local or state funds to comply with the mandates of NCLB, as did the Republican-controlled Utah House of Representatives.[1] Some have described the states' dissatisfaction with the law as a "rebellion" against NCLB and against the Bush administration more generally.[2]

The Cost of Meeting Accountability Goals

While NCLB contains provisions that do not directly relate to test scores, such as requiring that all classrooms eventually be headed by "highly qualified" teachers, most of the complaints about the burden allegedly imposed by the law concern the cost of administering tests and the cost of bringing up the test scores of the required percentage of students to a passing level. Estimates of the costs of meeting NCLB's test-related mandates range from very high to extraordinarily high. William Mathis, a school superintendent and fellow at the Vermont Society for the Study of Education, evaluated several studies that estimate the cost of meeting NCLB's test-related requirements in ten states. Based on these studies he estimated that national education spending would have to increase by somewhere between 24 and 46 percent to fulfill the test-related mandates of NCLB.[3]

Most of the studies Mathis evaluates calculate the cost of meeting NCLB's mandates using two distinct methods, both of which are flawed in ways that will cause them to greatly overestimate compliance costs. The "professional judgment" method designates a panel of experts who decide what qualities a school would need to adequately educate its students under NCLB, and then puts a price tag on achieving those qualities. The "successful school" method looks at a sample of well-performing schools and examines their resources and allocations.

In their evaluation of the costs of NCLB, James Peyser of the Massachusetts Board of Education and Robert Costrell of the University of

Massachusetts at Amherst show how each of these methods is inadequate.[4] They point out that the professional judgment method—relied upon by most of the studies Mathis evaluates—fails to ground the "expert" opinions on which it relies in any legitimate measurement of outcomes. We are expected to believe the panels' evaluations of what is required to meet NCLB's mandates not based on any evidence that their recommended changes are truly necessary to meet those mandates but simply on faith in the panel members' professionalism. No field other than education makes important financial decisions solely based on claims made by experts, even the most distinguished ones, without demanding empirical evidence to back up those claims. The reason for this is simple: expert professionals often have a large financial or political interest in the recommendations they make. This is certainly true for the panels relied upon by studies of NCLB costs, which are typically staffed by members of the public-school bureaucracy. When these experts find that NCLB's mandates can only be met by undertaking expensive reforms that put very large amounts of money into the public-school bureaucracy's budgets, we must take such findings with more than a grain of salt. In some cases the same public-school bureaucrats who serve on expert panels for NCLB cost estimates are also plaintiffs in lawsuits demanding more money for public schools.

The successful schools method is at least guided by test scores as a quantitative measure of performance. However, Peyser and Costrell show that schools are often designated as models of high educational performance based on the wrong criteria. It is well known that students' demographic characteristics are strong predictors of their test performance independent of the quality of their schools. Nonetheless, many analyses using the successful schools method simply choose the schools with the highest scores on standardized tests. To a large extent, what makes these schools "successful" is student demographics, not school quality. And since students who are demographically more likely to perform well on tests tend to live in communities that spend more money on schools, the successful schools method concludes that high spending levels improve schools. It is not at all clear that these schools' higher test scores were produced by higher spending rather than student demographics. Furthermore, even if the successful schools method were able to accurately identify which schools are truly of high quality, studies using this method often make the mistake of using average school spending at the designated schools as the minimum funding level necessary to meet NCLB's requirements. Peyser and Costrell point out that by definition half of the designated successful schools will have spent less than the average amount spent by all successful schools. Thus this method produces results that would designate half of all the "successful schools" as unable to meet NCLB mandates, even though the schools were chosen because they had in fact met those mandates.

Peyser and Costrell develop their own method for evaluating the cost of NCLB, which they call the "improvement" method. Like the successful schools method, the improvement method attempts to identify the best schools and calculate the cost of replicating those schools' successes. However, instead of taking the schools with the highest test scores, Peyser and Costrell identify the schools that make the greatest year-to-year test score improvements. This "value added" approach looks for schools that make more of a difference in students' lives regardless of student demographics, rather than schools whose students started out proficient.

After identifying the schools that made the largest gains on state tests, the improvement method calculates the cost of these schools' success. Recognizing that at least some schools making the highest gains on standardized tests might perform better with less money than other schools could be expected to, they develop a formula to calculate a level of spending somewhat lower than the average amount spent at these model schools. This amount is a much more reasonable estimate of the amount needed to meet NCLB's standards.

To put their theory to practice, Peyser and Costrell estimated the spending levels necessary for their home state of Massachusetts to comply with NCLB. They calculate that Massachusetts schools could be expected to meet NCLB's requirements by spending between $6,320 and $6,354 per student. This is less than what the state actually spends. It appears that Massachusetts schools already have more than enough money to meet NCLB requirements; the difference between the schools making the most test score improvements and other Massachusetts schools is not a lack of resources.

Peyser and Costrell's analysis confirms what we saw in chapter 1: schools are not inadequately funded, and there are no reasonable grounds for believing that simply spending more money would improve schools. It also suggests that most schools could be more successful than they currently are with the resources they already have. Certainly there may be some individual schools or school districts that are not adequately funded, but not the system as a whole.

The Unbearable Lightness of Accountability Mandates

Few laws are more misunderstood than NCLB. One important reason NCLB does not impose as much of a financial burden on schools as many believe is that, contrary to complaints from educators and state legislatures, its test-score mandates are quite modest. It is true that the higher we set the bar in terms of how well students have to be performing and how quickly schools need to get them there, the more costly compliance with the law would be. But that's a two-way street: the lower we set the bar, the less costly it is to comply. NCLB's short-term state goals are actually set surprisingly low.

The law requires states to test their students, and that adequate yearly improvements in test scores must be made both by the whole student body and by certain student subgroups (e.g., racial groups, low-income students, etc.). However, it is up to the states to decide what specific material is included on the tests, what score counts as a passing grade, and how much annual progress counts as "adequate" improvement. NCLB also requires states to measure graduation rates and improve them if they don't live up to a defined goal, but the states decide how to calculate the graduation rates and how much improvement is "adequate." As we saw in chapter 8, the method one uses to calculate graduation rates has a lot to do with the final graduation rate numbers.

The U.S. Department of Education does have to approve each state's NCLB plan. This is necessary to prevent states from setting ridiculously low goals. At least so far, the department has proven quite lenient in what it accepts as a sufficient accountability plan.

For example, one of California's goals under NCLB is to graduate 82.8 percent of its high school students. When it adopted this goal, it changed its method for calculating graduation rates; as a result, the official statewide graduation rate shot up from 69.6 percent to 86.9 percent overnight. What's more, those schools that still graduate fewer than 82.8

percent of their students under the new calculation method are deemed to be making adequate progress toward the goal if they increase their graduation rate by only 0.1 percentage points each year. At this lackadaisical pace, a California school starting out at a graduation rate of 69.6 percent (the state's more honest estimate of its true graduation rate) in 2005 would not reach the 82.8 percent goal until the year 2137. This is hardly a draconian mandate.

Critics of NCLB point to the law's mandate that all children have proficient test scores by 2014. They are right in criticizing this mandate. It's a little like requiring states to reduce traffic fatalities to zero—no matter what policy is imposed to get people to drive carefully, there will always be some traffic accidents. However, it is wrong to focus on this long-term mandate simply because it is so outlandish. Policymakers at the state and federal level are all working on the unspoken assumption that when the time comes this requirement will be quietly revised. The consequences for failure to meet the short-term mandates of NCLB are the truly appropriate yardstick for measuring the burden the law places on schools.

The Cost of Implementing Accountability Tests

The enormous estimates of the cost of implementing NCLB all make the fundamental mistake of assuming that improving performance costs extra dollars. For example, in an analysis of Indiana's accountability test cited by Mathis, the Center on Education Policy found that the most expensive part of accountability testing is the cost of improving student proficiency.[5] Of the $444 per pupil it calculated was the cost of the state's exit exam, only 18 percent was for actually administering the test. The rest of the estimated costs were divvied up between remediation (29 percent), prevention (28 percent), and professional development (25 percent), all of which they maintained would be necessary for a school to meet the average performance in the state.

The most appropriate way to evaluate the cost of accountability programs would be based solely on the cost of administering the exams, not on the cost of improving student scores. As we have seen from chapter 1 and from Peyser and Costrell's analysis, schools already have more than enough money for us to reasonably expect them to be able to produce test score gains by using their existing resources more effectively. If accountability mandates were so burdensome that even maximally efficient schools couldn't be reasonably expected to produce noticeable improvements with their present resources—say, a test measuring the ability of fifth graders to explain Einstein's theory of relativity—it might be appropriate to demand more funding. However, given that current accountability mandates are so moderate, the only real financial burden posed by accountability testing is the cost of designing and administering the tests.

NCLB requires states to administer a total of seventeen tests per year. Before NCLB, more than half the states had already implemented accountability testing (between thirty and forty states had it, depending on exactly how you define "accountability testing"). While NCLB requires many states with existing accountability programs to add tests, for these states the added financial burden of NCLB is mitigated by their previous investment.

However, even for those states that had no prior testing and were thus starting from scratch, the cost of designing and administering an accountability test to comply with NCLB is quite low. Caroline Hoxby of Harvard University calculated the average cost of state accountability testing. She found that the cost of testing varied from a low of $1.79 per pupil in South Carolina to a high of $34.02 per pupil in Delaware, depending upon how elaborate the testing regime was. In Delaware, the home of the most burdensome testing regime, the cost of testing represented only 0.35 percent of all per-pupil education spending in the state. If NCLB forced all states to either increase education spending by 0.35 percent or redirect that much of their existing spending, most people would not see this as very burdensome.

Hoxby puts the Accountability Burden Myth in perspective by comparing the cost of accountability testing to the cost of other popular education reforms. Figure 12.1 compares the cost of testing to that of reducing class sizes by 10 percent (a relatively small reduction) and the cost of increasing teacher compensation by 10 percent in the three states that Hoxby found had the most elaborate testing regimes: California, Kentucky, and Texas. The results of the comparison are striking. In California, testing costs about $19.93 per pupil. This is far smaller than the $557 and $400 per pupil necessary to reduce class sizes by 10 percent or increase teacher compensation by 10 percent, respectively. The comparison is similar in Kentucky and Texas.[6]

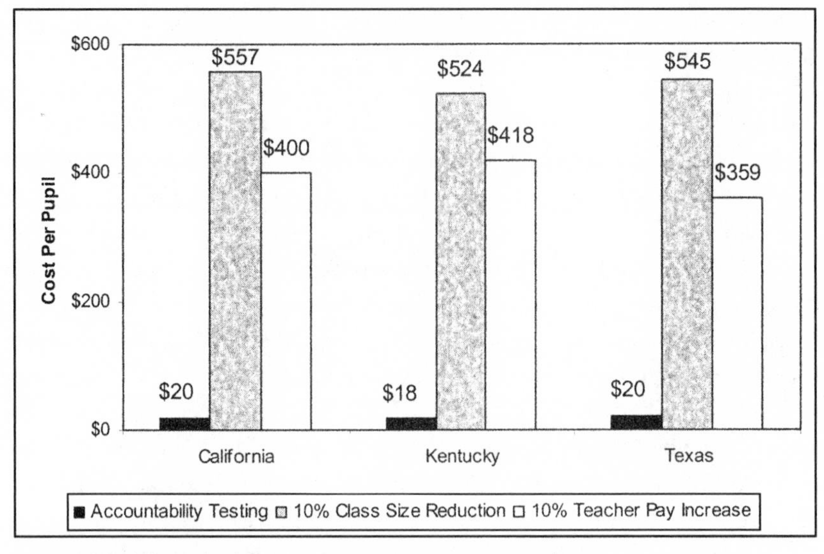

Figure 12.1. Accountability Testing Is an Inexpensive Reform
Source: Hoxby, "The Cost of Accountability," in *School Accountability*, Evers and Walberg, eds., Hoover Institution.

Accountability Testing Leads to Educational Gains

Though the dollar amount is small, we might consider any cost of accountability testing too high if it did not lead to real educational gains. However, there is evidence that accountability testing does lead to greater educational outcomes.

Eric Hanushek and Margaret Raymond of Stanford University evaluated the effect of states' accountability systems on their performance on the mathematics section of the National Assessment of Educational Progress (NAEP), a highly respected standardized test administered by the U.S. Department of Education. Because each subject of the NAEP is only administered every four years, Haunshek and Raymond follow the gains students made between taking the test in fourth grade and taking it four years later in eighth grade. They found that students in states that had no accountability measures made a 0.7 percentage point increase in their proficiency scores between the fourth and eighth grades. Students in states with tests that had explicit consequences for schools, however, made proficiency gains of 1.6 percentage points.[7]

Martin Carnoy and Susanna Loeb, also of Stanford University, conducted another evaluation of the relationship between accountability systems and NAEP scores. They developed an index that measured the strength of each state's accountability program. They found that stronger accountability systems lead to higher academic achievement on NAEP, particularly for minority students.[8]

The over-the-top cost estimates of accountability programs are unwarranted. It is clear from the evidence that the Accountability Burden Myth is a direct descendent of the Money Myth described in chapter 1. Those making the estimates simply assume that improving performance requires additional funds, but the evidence shows that more money is neither a necessary nor a sufficient condition for producing higher achievement. Peyser and Costrell show that many schools succeed with far fewer dollars than those that fail. Thus, we should be skeptical of any cost estimate of improving student performance. If we look simply at the cost of administering standardized tests, the only truly necessary financial cost of complying with accountability testing, we find that it is quite inexpensive. The benefits of accountability testing likely outweigh the minuscule cost of its implementation.

PART IV

Choice

CHAPTER 13

The Inconclusive Research Myth

"The evidence on the effectiveness of vouchers is mixed and inconclusive."

When reporting on school vouchers—programs that give parents money they can use to send their children to private schools—the media almost always describe the academic research on their effects as mixed and inconclusive. When the Supreme Court approved vouchers, the *New York Times* declared: "All this is happening without a clear answer to the fundamental question of whether school choice has improved American education. The debate about whether children in charter schools, voucher programs or schools run by for-profit companies show improved academic performance remains heated, defined more by conflicting studies than by real conclusions."[1] The *Washington Post*'s coverage of vouchers has a similar theme: "State-funded vouchers already are being used in some places, including Milwaukee and Cleveland, but the consensus among many education researchers is that studies of those programs have not yielded conclusive findings about the impact of vouchers on student achievement."[2] *Time* magazine repeats the mantra: "Do vouchers help boost the test scores of children who use them? Researchers are trying to find out, but the evidence so far is inconclusive."[3]

These reports perpetuate the Inconclusive Research Myth—that there is just as much evidence that vouchers don't provide students with a better education as there is that they do. In fact, media portrayals notwithstanding, the highest quality research produces remarkably consistent findings. The evidence on vouchers clearly shows that they are an effective education reform.

Foundations of the Inconclusive Research Myth

School vouchers expand families' educational options by giving them the choice of sending their children to private schools instead of public schools. Some voucher programs are publicly funded, others are funded by private donors. They set a fixed dollar amount—anywhere from a few thousand dollars to the full per-pupil funding available in the public system—up to which they will reimburse parents for private-school tuition. Maine and Vermont have done this through what they call "tuitioning" programs for a century. More recently, a publicly funded voucher program was started in Milwaukee in 1990, which has since grown to the point where students attending private schools with vouchers equal a full 15 percent of enrollment in the Milwaukee public system.[4] Ohio, Florida, Arizona, and Pennsylvania have also adopted various forms of publicly funded vouchers, and philanthropists have run private voucher programs in New York City, Washington, D.C., Charlotte, Dayton, and other cities. Congress recently created a federally funded voucher program in Washington, D.C.

Why do reporters promote the Inconclusive Research Myth? One reason is simply that they usually equivocate in this way when they summarize research on controversial and relatively technical questions. Claiming that the research is mixed and inconclusive spares reporters from the wrath of political advocates whom they might offend if they reported that the research favors one side of the debate. Reporters also describe results as inconclusive in order to minimize the danger of embracing the wrong conclusion on a technical question whose intricacies they may not fully grasp.

Repeating the Inconclusive Research Myth may be professionally safer for reporters, but that doesn't make it true. Even on highly controversial and technical questions, it can still be the case that the bulk of the evidence favors one conclusion over another. While not everyone is likely to be happy with this conclusion if the issue is politically contentious, nonetheless the research can still clearly support a conclusion.

Of course, the willingness of reporters to attribute a clear conclusion to voucher research is also influenced by the way in which that research is described by pundits, advocates, and experts. Here, too, there is a chorus of voices describing the research findings as mixed and inconclusive. Peter Beinart, writing in *The New Republic*, asserts that "school choice, then, offers something of a public policy 'veil of ignorance.' Neither proponents nor opponents really know if it works."[5] Ralph Neas of the People for the American Way similarly asserts that "there is no firm evidence . . . that vouchers offer low-income students a better education."[6] And researchers at the RAND Corporation summarize the research by saying: "Our evaluation of the existing evidence indicates that many of the important empirical questions about vouchers and charters have not yet been answered. Indeed, it would be fair to say that none of the important empirical questions has been answered definitively."[7]

Just like reporters, these pundits, advocates, and even professional researchers can have their own reasons for not wanting to admit that the research on vouchers supports a firm conclusion. Obviously ideology and financial interests play a role. If the research supports one side of a controversial question, those who are on the other side—either for ideological reasons or because they have a financial stake in the issue—would prefer to describe the research as inconclusive. Another problem is that professional researchers are no more eager than reporters to alienate people or put themselves in a position that will draw political fire. Doing so could jeopardize their academic credibility. Even if everything they say is accurate, they can expect to be forced into political controversy and attacked by advocates and ideologues, all of which will make them look like advocates themselves rather than objective social scientists. It's much safer for them to simply say that the research doesn't support any solid conclusions.

But the research on vouchers simply is not mixed or inconclusive. The highest quality research consistently shows that vouchers have positive effects for students who receive them. The results are only mixed with regard to the scope and magnitude of vouchers' benefits. The evidence for these benefits justifies a high level of confidence, especially when compared to the much weaker evidence supporting most major education policies. To be sure, there is still much that can be learned about the effects of school choice. But enough is known with sufficient certainty that the research on vouchers' effects cannot be accurately described as mixed or inconclusive.

High Quality Research

There have been eight "random-assignment" studies of five school voucher programs. Random assignment is the research design commonly employed in medical research. Subjects are assigned by random lottery to either a treatment group (which receives the treatment being studied) or a control group (which does not).

Random assignment is the gold standard of research designs. Since only chance determines who is in each group, the treatment and control groups are likely to be similar in terms of their background characteristics, such as race, family income, educational expectations, and motivation. By making the treatment and control groups very similar to one another, a random-assignment research design allows researchers to have much greater confidence that any observed effects are produced by the treatment being studied and not by the subjects' background characteristics. This is especially important in education research, because background characteristics have a strong influence over educational outcomes and are hard to observe and control statistically without a random-assignment design.

There are also some nonrandom-assignment studies of vouchers. However, their inability to control adequately for the influence of background characteristics makes their results significantly less reliable than studies using random assignment. Given that there are eight random-assignment studies, in whose results we can have much greater confidence, any evaluation of the research on vouchers should focus on the studies with this higher-quality research design.

Table 13.1. Statistically Significant Findings on Voucher Effects

City	*Voucher Effect*	*Subject*	*Time in Program*
Milwaukee	6 percentile point gain	Reading	Four years
	11 percentile point gain	Math	Four years
	8 percentile point gain	Math	Four years
Charlotte	6 percentile point gain	Combined	One year
Dayton	6.5 percentile point gain	Combined	Two years
New York City	9.2 percentile point gain	Combined	Three years
	4.7 percentile point gain	Math	One year
Washington, D.C.	9.2 percentile point gain	Combined	Two years

Every one of the eight random-assignment studies finds at least some positive academic effects for students using a voucher to attend a private school. In seven of the eight studies the benefits for voucher recipients are statistically significant, meaning that we can have high confidence that the academic gains observed are not merely the product of chance (see table 13.1). It is true that the studies differ on whether they find benefits for all students or only for African American students, whether the academic gains occur in both reading and math or only in math, whether the improvements are small or large in magnitude, and in the exact level of statistical certainty we can have in these effects. But to characterize the results of voucher research as "mixed" on account of these variations is simply inaccurate.

Milwaukee

The Milwaukee school choice program, the country's longest-running voucher program and one of its largest, has been the subject of two random-assignment studies. The Wisconsin law that created the program required that schools conduct lotteries to admit students if there were more applicants than spaces available at a school. Unfortunately, state-appointed program evaluator John Witte did not make use of this naturally occurring random-assignment research design, but two later studies have used it to provide higher-quality analyses.

The first study was conducted by Jay Greene, then of the University of Texas at Austin, and Paul Peterson and Jiangtao Du of Harvard University. It found that students who won lotteries and were able to attend private schools outperformed a control group of students who lost those lotteries and returned to Milwaukee public schools. After four years in the program, the treatment group produced standardized reading test results that were 6 percentile points higher than the control group and standardized math test results that were 11 percentile points higher than the control group.[8] Cecilia Rouse of Princeton University, using a slightly different set of test scores, found that students able to attend private schools with vouchers outperformed the control group by 8 percentile points on a standardized math test after four years in the program. She found no statistically significant effect on reading test scores.[9] In both of these random-assignment studies, all of the students were low-income and Hispanic or African American.

Charlotte and Dayton

Privately funded scholarship programs have also provided excellent opportunities for using random-assignment research designs to study the effect of school vouchers. These programs offer partial private-school scholarships that are like publicly funded voucher programs in that they enable low-income families to send their children to private schools. Because the demand for these scholarships has been far greater than the number of scholarships available, random lotteries have been used to determine which applicants receive them. These lotteries permit random-assignment studies of these voucher-like programs.

In a Manhattan Institute study of a program in Charlotte, North Carolina, Greene found that recipients of privately funded vouchers outperformed peers who did not receive a voucher by 6 percentile points on standardized tests after one year of participation in the program.[10] All of the students studied in Charlotte were from low-income households and the vast majority of the students were African American.

In a study of a similar privately funded voucher program in Dayton, Ohio, William Howell of the University of Wisconsin at Madison and Peterson found that African American voucher recipients outperformed African American students in the control group on standardized tests by 6.5 percentile points after two years in the program.[11] The study did not find significant effects for non-African American students. There were fewer non-African American students in the study than there were African American students, which may have made it harder for any voucher effects on their performance to be statistically visible; it may also be the case that non-African American students had previously been better served in public schools and thus had less to gain from vouchers.

New York City

A privately funded New York school choice program has been the subject of three random-assignment studies. One study, by Howell and Peterson, found that African American participants in the program outperformed the control group by 9.2 percentile points on a standardized test after three years in the program.[12] The study did not find statistically significant effects for non-African American students. As in Dayton, the number of non-African American students in the program was small, and these students may have been better served by their previous public schools, both of which might have made any voucher effects on their performance harder to see with high statistical confidence.

A reanalysis of these data by Alan Krueger and Pei Zhu of Princeton University altered the method by which students were classified by race and added into the study sample students for whom baseline test information was missing—that is, students for whom we do not have information on how they were doing before they entered the voucher program. Making these changes, Krueger and Zhu found that the estimated effect of the choice program for African American students remained positive (for example, one analysis they report found that the effect was 2.2 percentile points after three years) but fell short of statistical significance, meaning that one could not have high confidence that the results were distinguishable from there being no effect.[13]

Krueger and Zhu's changes are of dubious scientific validity. Adding students with missing data into the study sample reduces the quality of the study's data, just as adding water to soup dilutes its taste. When classifying students by race, Howell and Peterson used the method recommended by federal research guidelines; Krueger and Zhu adopted a different method that doesn't reflect the way most students really identify themselves by race and is not recommended by federal research guidelines. What's more, Howell and Peterson have shown that Krueger and Zhu were highly selective in choosing exactly how they set up their model of analysis; Howell and Peterson analyzed the data using 120 different statistical models and reported that all 120 find positive voucher effects, 108 of them finding statistically significant positive effects.[14]

A third analysis of the data from the New York program was performed by John Barnard of deCODE Genetics, Constantine E. Frangakis of Johns Hopkins University, Jennifer L. Hill of Columbia University, and Donald B. Rubin of Harvard University. This analysis examined only the first year of results. It found that students who left low-achieving public schools to attend a private school with the program's scholarships benefited by 4.7 percentile points on a standardized math test, a statistically significant finding.[15]

Washington, D.C.

Washington, D.C., was host to another privately funded voucher program that was studied using a random-assignment research design. According to Howell and Peterson, African American students participating in Washington's privately funded school choice program outperformed a control group by 9.2 percentile points on standardized tests after two years in the program.[16] They did not find statistically significant effects for non-African American students. As in their other analyses, this may have been due to insufficient numbers of such students or their not having stood to benefit as much from vouchers. Another complication in the Washington study is that after three years only 29 percent of the students who were offered a private-school scholarship were using them to attend a private school, so relatively few of the students in the treatment group were still actually receiving the treatment. This would have diluted the study's ability to detect any voucher effects statistically. Analyzing results after three years of participation, Howell and Peterson reported no statistically significant effects.

Positive Effects Other than Test Scores

In addition to producing improved test scores, every one of the voucher programs studied has resulted in enthusiastic support from parents. Parents of voucher recipients report substantially higher levels of satisfaction with the quality of the education their children receive in private schools. Parents also report that their private schools are safer, more responsive, and staffed with better teachers.

All of this is achieved in private schools that spend a fraction of the amount spent per student in public schools. The most generously funded of the five voucher programs studied by random assignment, the Milwaukee program, provides students with a maximum of only about 60 percent of the $10,112 spent per pupil in that city's public schools.[17] The privately funded voucher programs spend an average of less than half what public schools spend per pupil, even after adjusting for the differences in services offered by public and private schools.[18]

Imperfect But Not Inconclusive

In short, every random-assignment study of the effect of vouchers except one finds statistically significant benefits on test scores for at least some groups of students. Even the one other study still found positive effects from vouchers; it only failed to achieve statistical significance, and only after resorting to highly selective and questionable methods. Not one of these studies has claimed that student test scores are harmed when students use vouchers, and all the studies that look at what parents report about their voucher schools find that parents report that their children are benefiting by receiving vouchers.

So vouchers produce test scores that are at least as good as those produced in public schools, with happier parents, for about half of the cost. If similar results were produced for a method of fighting cancer or housing the homeless, we might expect reporters and analysts to be elated about such promise.

Of course, each of these studies has its limitations. The studies of Milwaukee's school choice program had a large amount of missing data, especially by the fourth year of the program. While there is nothing to suggest that the missing data seriously biases the findings in those studies, uncertainty about missing information does limit the confidence we can have in the findings of those studies. The Charlotte study does not have results beyond the first year of students' participation in the program, leaving us unable to determine whether the gains produced by vouchers were maintained or expanded in subsequent years. It also lacks test scores for students before they applied for a scholarship. Without being able to control for the academic achievement of students at baseline, the study is less precise in its estimate of learning gains for voucher students and is less capable of adjusting for students whose information is missing over time.

Voucher programs, like all programs serving poor families, suffer from relatively high turnover due to the high residential mobility of low-income populations. Also, privately funded voucher programs tend to provide families with less money, meaning families must usually pay some private-school tuition costs themselves, which further drives up attrition rates. This makes it difficult to continue random-assignment studies of voucher programs for long periods, because students who leave the voucher program also leave the study. The Dayton study suffered from a high amount of attrition of students from the study, causing the study to end after just two years. In Washington, D.C., the researchers chose to collect a third year of data despite high attrition from the treatment group, which resulted in the disintegration of the random-assignment research design and null findings. In

New York City the data collection and participation rates were the best among these studies, but even in New York there was some amount of missing information.

And reports of improved parental satisfaction are limited by the ability of parents to judge educational quality. People who are not already convinced that parents ought to be able to choose the best education for their children are not easily persuaded by evidence that shows that parents are happier with vouchers.

But to dwell on these limitations is like dwelling on emptiness in a glass that is three-quarters full. It is impressive that we have multiple studies on the effects of vouchers on participants using the highest quality research design. It is also impressive that all but one of these studies finds statistically significant benefits for voucher recipients, and that all the studies using sound methodology do so. It is impressive that vouchers satisfy parental demands for education quality at lower cost than public education.

Consider that, as we saw in chapter 4, one random-assignment study on class size reduction has been widely received as proof of the effectiveness and desirability of class size reduction despite uncertainty attending the study's results, the failure of large-scale class size reduction efforts to produce improvements, and the very high costs associated with this type of reform. It is puzzling that while one random-assignment study on class size reduction is so widely hailed as conclusive, eight random-assignment studies on vouchers are considered insufficient evidence. While future research might help resolve some of the questions that remain, existing voucher research is remarkably consistent and strong in finding positive effects from vouchers. Given the current level of resistance to recognizing the positive nature of existing research, one suspects that no amount of additional research, no matter what the quality, no matter how positive the results, will deter some people from perpetuating the Inconclusive Research Myth.

CHAPTER 14

The Exeter Myth

"Private schools have higher test scores because they have more money and recruit high-performing students while expelling low-performing students."

It is well known that private-school students outperform public-school students, and the reason for this gap is the subject of much debate. Some argue that private-school students experience these superior outcomes only because private schools have more money than public schools, and because private schools recruit high-performing students and expel low-performing students while public schools must accept everyone. This is the Exeter Myth—higher achievement in private schools is caused by their selectivity and resources.

In fact, far from having more money than the public school system, private schools on average spend substantially less money per student than public schools. Neither is it true that private schools are highly selective in admissions or expulsions; on average, private schools actually take almost all comers and expel few of their students. The practice of expelling students is also more common in public schools than is generally appreciated. The private schools for which we have data expel fewer of their students than the public school system does. What's more, research on voucher programs has shown that students randomly selected to attend private schools consistently outperform peers who applied for the same vouchers but were not randomly selected and thus remained in public schools. The evidence clearly establishes that private schools perform better independent of money or selectivity.

Foundations of the Exeter Myth

A number of political interest groups promote the Exeter Myth. Albert Shanker, the late head of the American Federation of Teachers, articulated the Exeter Myth clearly: "The critical factor [in higher outcomes for private schools] is that public schools are obliged to take all comers while private schools select their students, turn away applicants who do not meet their standards and are free to get rid of students who do not work out (and who generally end up in public schools)."[1] David Bernstein of the American Jewish Committee, a group that campaigns against school vouchers, repeats the argument: "The fundamental difference between public and private schools is that private schools select who attends, while public schools accept everyone."[2] These interest-group activists portray the typical private school as highly selective and expensive, like Exeter, Choate, or Georgetown Day, and attribute private schools' success to their selectivity and resources.

Belief in the Exeter Myth extends beyond interest-group activists to university professors and education pundits. For example, in *The Case Against School Choice: Politics, Markets, and Fools*, Kevin Smith and Kenneth Meier write that "private schools also do not admit all students who apply; they engage in an admissions process that screens out students who carry the risk of academic failure." They conclude that "while students at private schools unquestionably score higher on achievement measures . . . this is just as likely to reflect selective screening as the ability to provide superior education services."[3]

The tuition that private schools charge not only contributes to their selectivity, according to the Exeter Myth, but also generates resources that are another key to their success. In the imaginations of Exeter Myth advocates, the typical private school is as awash in money as the real Exeter. Private schools are portrayed in the media as resource-rich prep schools like those in *Dead Poets Society* or the TV series *The OC*. The common belief is that private schools are not only populated by rich students but are also able to spend huge sums to produce greater success.

This impression that most private schools, or at least all the good private schools, cost an arm and a leg prompts some to complain that even very generous voucher plans are insufficient to be of any real help. Marc Fisher complains in the *Washington Post* that "The vouchers funded by this new program [in Washington, D.C.] would provide up to $7,500 each for 1,300 children. That wouldn't come close to the $22,000 some politicians spend to send their children to elite schools."[4] And editorial writers at the *Michigan Daily* warn that "a voucher system would force penniless public schools to shut down while channeling more and more money into wealthy private schools."[5]

People are willing to believe the Exeter Myth for a variety of reasons. One is that defenders of the status quo in public education repeatedly chalk up the better results at private schools to those schools' alleged special advantages. If private schools perform better than public schools because they're all copies of Exeter with highly selective admissions policies and big stacks of gold bullion secreted away in their basement vaults, then their superior performance doesn't reflect poorly on public schools. But if the reality is that private schools aren't highly selective and spend less money than public schools, their superior performance sends a strong message about the public school system's failure to perform adequately.

Another reason some people are inclined to believe the Exeter Myth is that the private schools with which they are familiar are more likely to be the exceptional private institutions. The wealthy and exclusive elite prep school captures the cultural imagination in a way that the more pedestrian reality of private schooling never could. Whether in news reports or in popular fiction, wealth and glamour will always make for a more fascinating story than plain old everyday normalcy.

In particular, policy discussions and political decision making are mainly the province of elites. Often these elites are the same people who attended exceptional private schools themselves, send their children to those schools, and are friends with others who attended and send their children to elite academies. Policy elites live in rarified circles and are just as prone as everyone else to generalize from their immediate experiences. Almost every city has at least one or two elite private schools that policy elites know well, but those cities also have scores of ordinary private schools with which politicians, journalists, and academics may be much less familiar.

The only way to escape the prejudices of personal experience is to examine the evidence. The typical private school is not particularly resource-rich, nor does it exercise much academic selection in admissions and expulsions. The success of the students in those schools cannot be explained by their selectivity or resources.

Private Schools Don't Have More Money

There is no question that on average students in private schools demonstrate significantly greater achievement than students in public schools. For example, on the eighth-grade reading portion of the National Assessment of Educational Progress (NAEP) eighth-grade reading test, 53 percent of private-school students perform at or above the level that the U.S. Department of Education defines as "proficient," compared to only 30 percent of public-school students.[6] On the NAEP eighth-grade math portion of the NAEP test only 27 percent of public-school students perform at the "proficient" level, compared to 43 percent of private-school students.[7] According to the U.S. Department of Education's National Education Longitudinal Study, 45.6 percent of private-school eighth graders will go on to earn a bachelor's degree, compared to only 23.2 percent of their public-school counterparts.[8]

But it isn't true that public schools are penniless while private schools are wealthy—in fact, as figure 14.1 shows, the opposite is closer to the truth. According to the U.S. Department of Education, the average private school charged $4,689 per student in tuition for the 1999–2000 school year.[9] That same year, the average public school spent $8,032 per pupil.[10] Among Catholic schools, which educate 48.6 percent of all private-school students, the average tuition was only $3,236. Among other religious private schools, which account for another 35.7 percent of private-school students, the average tuition was $4,063.[11] The vast majority of private-school students attend schools whose tuition is less than half the per-pupil spending of public schools.

It is true that most private schools receive donations to supplement revenue from tuition. However, they also offer scholarships, reducing the revenue they receive from tuition. Specific figures on donations and scholarships are not easily available. But given that private schools are starting from a tuition baseline of about half what public schools spend, it would strain cred-

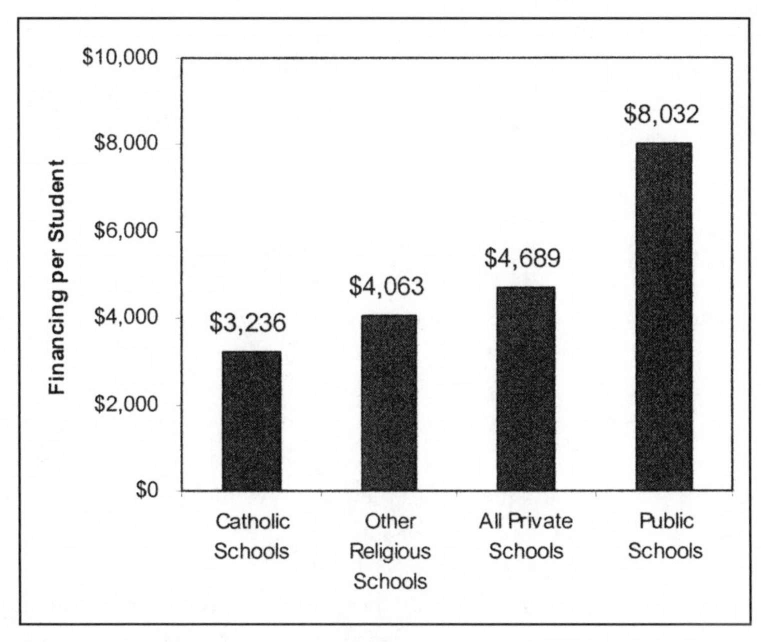

Figure 14.1. Private Schools Don't Have More Money
Source: Digest of Education Statistics 2002, U.S. Department of Education, Tables 61 and 166.

ibility to speculate that the difference between what private schools make from donations and what they spend in scholarships even comes close to eliminating the financial gap between public and private schools.

It is also true that private schools do not always provide the same set of services that public schools provide. For example, private schools are less likely to provide transportation, segregated special education classes, lunch, and counseling. But in an analysis comparing public-school and Catholic-school costs in New York, Washington, D.C., Dayton, and San Antonio, Paul Peterson and William Howell find that excluding all of these services as well as all central administration costs from the public-school ledger still left public schools with significantly more resources to spend per pupil than Catholic schools had.[12] Furthermore, if public schools provide additional services then those services should contribute to their students' educational outcomes. Excluding these costs from the public school ledger, as though for some reason spending isn't really spending when it's spent on services that private schools don't always provide, doesn't make sense. All spending is ultimately relevant to the question of a school's cost-effectiveness. Given that on average private schools actually spend considerably less per pupil than public schools, their students' better outcomes cannot be explained by differences in resources.

Private Schools Aren't Highly Selective

The better outcomes achieved by private-school students also cannot be fully explained by the selectivity of private schools. Private schools are not nearly as selective as most people think, and they expel very few students. The private schools for which we have data actually expel fewer of their students than the public school system. While the mild selectivity of private schools may play some small role in their students' higher performance, the evidence does not allow us to dismiss all or even most of the test score gap as merely the product of exclusivity.

Surprising as it may be to many people, most private schools are not very selective. Anthony Bryk, Valerie Lee, and Peter Holland studied Catholic schools nationwide, which educate about half of all private-school students. They conclude that "in general, Catholic high schools are not highly selective in their admissions. The typical school reports accepting 88 percent of the students who apply. . . . Indeed, the school does not operate as the principal selection mechanism; the real control rests with the students and their families through the decision to apply for admission."[13] Howell and Peterson's study of voucher programs in Washington, D.C., Dayton, and New York also found that private schools participating in those programs were not very selective—only 1 percent of parents reported that their children were denied admission to a private school because they failed an admissions test. In addition, their comparison of the academic and demographic backgrounds of students who used vouchers to attend private school with those who declined to do so showed that the two groups were very similar, further suggesting that private schools were not using subtle techniques to select more desirable students.[14] Evaluations of private-school scholarship programs in Charlotte, San Antonio, and nationwide similarly found small or no differences in the academic and demographic characteristics of students who gained admission to private school with scholarships and those who did not.[15] While there certainly are some private schools that are selective in their admissions, the Exeter Myth greatly exaggerates the selectivity of the typical private school and leads people to wrongly attribute the success of private-school students primarily or even solely to that selectivity.

Private schools also do not significantly alter their student population by expelling low-achieving or troublesome students. Bryk, Lee, and Holland find that "contrary to widespread belief, very few students are expelled from Catholic high schools for either academic or disciplinary reasons. On average, Catholic high schools dismiss fewer than two students per year."[16] In their evaluations of school choice programs in Washington, Dayton, and New York, Howell and Peterson find that "very few parents—less than 1 percent—said that they changed schools because their child had been expelled."[17] John Witte observed private schools participating in Milwaukee's voucher program and found that although participating private schools had the right to expel students, in practice "it was seldom used."[18] Similarly, examinations of private schools participating in voucher programs in Charlotte, San Antonio, Cleveland, and elsewhere found no indication that expulsion was a common practice among private schools. This evidence is limited to Catholic schools and urban schools that agree to participate in voucher programs, but we must evaluate the evidence we have available. There is no other body of evidence supporting the Exeter Myth's claim that private schools produce success by expelling low performing or troublesome students.

Adherents of the Exeter Myth are also incorrect when they assert that public schools accept all students. While it is true that every student is entitled to an education funded by the public, not all students receive that education in a public school, and students in the public school system are regularly expelled from school altogether. According to the U.S. Department of Education there were 1,163,000 serious disciplinary actions taken in public schools in 1999–2000, of which "11 percent were removals with no services [expulsions], and 7 percent were transfers to specialized schools."[19] So about 127,930 students were expelled from public school and about 81,410 were removed from their regular public schools and sent to separate schools. There were 13,368,771 students enrolled in secondary public schools in that year.[20] This means roughly 1 percent of public high school students were expelled and roughly 0.6 percent were segregated into specialized schools. This 1 percent expulsion rate in public schools is greater than the expulsion rates in Catholic and other private schools reported by the studies mentioned above.

In fact, students expelled from public school sometimes find their way to private schools. As Bryk, Lee, and Holland relate, "nearly one-fifth of Catholic high school principals reported having accepted students during the previous year who had been expelled from public schools for either disciplinary or academic reasons."[21] In addition, public schools regularly contract with specialized private schools when the public schools do not believe they are able to handle a student's disciplinary or disability needs. While figures on the frequency of students with disciplinary problems being sent by public schools to private schools are not easily available, the U.S. Department of Education does report that the public school system sends 1.3 percent of its students with disabilities to private schools for their education. Among students diagnosed as emotionally disturbed, 7.5 percent are sent to private schools; 7.6 percent of students who are both blind and deaf are sent to private schools; 8.2 percent of students with multiple disabilities (not counting blind-deaf students) are sent to private schools; and 6.5 percent of autistic students and 5.5 percent of students with traumatic brain injuries are sent to private schools.[22]

Clearly public schools do not actually accept the burden of educating "all" students. They expel about 1 percent of students, send another 0.6 percent to specialized schools, and contract out to private schools 1.3 percent of disabled students and also some students with disciplinary problems. Meanwhile, private schools are not highly selective in their admissions, and the ones for which we have data are actually less likely than public schools to expel students.

Students' Family Backgrounds

Even though private schools are not highly selective, they do have somewhat more advantaged student populations than public schools. For example, 77.4 percent of private-school students are non-Hispanic whites, compared to 61.2 percent of public-school students.[23] Given even the modest tuition required to attend private schools, private-school families are likely to have more income than public-school families. And the willingness of these families to make the financial sacrifice to send their children to private schools may indicate that on average they are families that place a higher value on their children's education than public-school families do. This might lead us to attribute the superior performance of private school students to their favorable family backgrounds rather than to any quality of their schools.

But private schools have been put to the test in high-quality studies examining this very question. As we saw in chapter 13, numerous studies have confirmed that students selected at random to attend private schools with a voucher consistently outperform peers who applied for the same vouchers but didn't get them and remained in public schools. One of the main benefits of random-assignment research is to help ensure that observed differences in achievement are not just the result of differences in student or family characteristics. Only random chance distinguishes between the students who do and do not receive the voucher, making the two groups nearly identical. Higher achievement demonstrated by private-school students in those experiments is therefore attributable to their having attended a private school.

The superior academic outcomes for private school students are not the result of policies that shape the student bodies in public and private schools. Nor is it the case that private schools produce better outcomes because they have more money to spend. In short, private schools' success is not caused by their all being Exeter.

CHAPTER 15

The Draining Myth

"School choice harms public schools."

How voucher programs and charter schools affect the students who remain in public schools is the most important political and research question in the debate over school choice. Even if these programs benefit the students who use them to attend private or charter schools, everyone recognizes that the vast majority of students will continue to attend regular public schools for the foreseeable future. The effect of school choice on the larger pool of students who remain in public schools could be the decisive factor in determining whether or not school choice policies are ultimately desirable.

Both sides in this debate make superficially plausible arguments, but only one side is supported by the evidence. Voucher opponents argue that expanding educational choice drains money and talent from public schools, harming their performance. Voucher supporters argue that choice increases competitive pressures on public schools, providing them with incentives to improve in order to retain students. Belief in either of these arguments without reference to the evidence is educational myth-making. When we look at the evidence, we find that school choice improves the academic performance of public schools. The claim that choice harms public schools is the Draining Myth.

Foundations of the Draining Myth

That a plausible story can be told to support the Draining Myth does not justify adopting it without checking to see whether it is supported or contradicted by the facts. Just because it is possible that school choice might theoretically harm public-school students by taking talent and money away from public schools does not mean that school choice does in fact harm public-school students by taking talent and money away from public schools. Storytelling is not the same as providing evidence.

Unfortunately, the slide down the slippery slope from plausible story to confirmed fact is a remarkably fast one in most discussions of school choice. The *New York Times* has editorialized that "vouchers do nothing to improve education for those remaining in the public system. In theory, they are supposed to cause bad schools to reform themselves by threatening them with market competition. In fact, they make reform harder, if not impossible, by siphoning away meager resources and skimming off good students, leaving the most troubled children and the most apathetic families behind."[1] Note the editorial's prominent use of the words "in fact." The *Times* has not actually provided any facts to support its claims; the words "in fact" are followed not by facts, but by storytelling. The *Times* may prefer to believe its own story rather than the alternative story to which it alludes—that school choice helps public school students by providing public schools with positive incentives—but the mere words "in fact" cannot change a story into a fact.

The *Boston Globe* has similarly claimed that "vouchers by definition can help only a handful of needy students."[2] Here the effects of school choice on public school students are determined not by examining the evidence but "by definition." The *Globe* does not say why it is impossible "by definition" that school choice might help public-school students. Like the *Times*, it simply prefers to believe the story of the Draining Myth: "When the public dollars contained in vouchers follow a student to a private school, the public system is slowly impoverished and those who are left behind are doubly disadvantaged."[3]

The "fact" that school choice makes public schools worse would only be true if a lack of resources were a major problem for public schools. For example, the *Times* casually refers to public schools' allegedly "meager resources." The meagerness of public schools' resources is taken so much for granted by the *Times* and most of its readers that for them it need only be asserted; supporting evidence is unnecessary. But as we saw in some detail in chapter 1, public schools' resources are actually far from meager, and large increases in resources have produced no improvement in the system's performance. Inflation-adjusted per-pupil public school spending has doubled in the past thirty years, but test scores and graduation rates are flat.

Clearly, many people will believe something as a proven fact on the basis of little more than a plausible story that reinforces their worldview. However, important policy decisions should be based upon evidence, not intuition. The actual facts strongly suggest that, far from harming public education, vouchers work to improve public schools.

Studies of Voucher Programs

Research on U.S. voucher programs consistently finds that public school performance improves in response to voucher competition. Some of the eleven voucher or tax-credit scholarship programs existing as of this writing are difficult to study because their size and scope make it hard to measure the effect they have on public schools.[4] Programs are sometimes too tiny, too new, or too diffuse (with a limited number of participants spread out over many schools) for any impact at all on public schools to be visible. Nonetheless, those programs that are in a position to affect the public school system have been studied, and the evidence always indicates that vouchers improve public schools. There has not been a single study of which the authors are aware showing that U.S. public-school student performance has been harmed by a voucher program.

Some researchers have studied educational programs in foreign countries and drawn conclusions from them about the likely effects of school choice in the United States.[5] But foreign education systems are fundamentally different from the U.S. education system. Assigning students to government-operated schools based on residence is not the norm in industrialized democracies.[6] Other countries have a variety of arrangements involving public funds for private schools, choices among public schools, and varying combinations of centralized and decentralized control over school curricula, teacher compensation practices, work rules, credentialing, and so on. What's more, sometimes the details of foreign programs that are described as "vouchers" bear little resemblance to the important programmatic features of U.S. voucher programs. Because of these differences, studies of school choice in other countries have little application to the United States.

Florida's A-Plus Voucher Program

The Manhattan Institute's Jay Greene and Marcus Winters conducted a study of Florida's "A-Plus" choice and accountability program. The program assigns grades to public schools based on a formula involving the percentage of students achieving above certain thresholds on the state's test, the amount of improvement students exhibit on the test, and other achievement indicators. If a school receives two failing grades in a four-year period, the state offers vouchers to that school's students, with which they can attend a private school or a different public school.

The study examined whether public schools whose students had been offered vouchers made academic progress that was significantly different from similar Florida public schools not facing voucher competition. The researchers found that public schools whose students were offered vouchers produced significantly greater year-to-year test score gains than other Florida public schools. On the Stanford-9 math test, for example, schools whose students were offered vouchers made year-to-year gains that were 5.9 percentile points larger than Florida public schools not facing voucher competition. Voucher-eligible schools also made significantly larger gains on the state's achievement test, although the reading improvements were smaller and sometimes fell short of statistical significance.

Even schools facing only the prospect of possible future competition from vouchers, because they had received one failing grade, made exceptional gains. These voucher-threatened schools improved in one year's time by 3.5 percentile points on the Stanford-9 math test and 1.7 points on the reading test greater than Florida public schools not in danger of having vouchers offered to their students.[7] These schools had incentives to improve in order to avoid having vouchers offered to their students. They made smaller gains than the schools already facing vouchers, but even the prospect of future competition produced significant public-school improvement.

It is possible that failing schools in Florida might exhibit exceptional improvement because of a statistical phenomenon known as regression to the mean, because their scores may have already been so low that they had nowhere to go but up. To examine this possibility, Greene and Winters compared voucher-eligible and voucher-threatened public schools to public schools with similarly low test scores that had escaped the voucher threat. A number of schools had average test scores as low as or even lower than the schools designated as failing, but were not themselves designated as failing because they had slightly different distributions of scores within their student populations. When the study compared the improvement of voucher-eligible and voucher-threatened schools against this control group of similarly low-performing schools not facing the prospect of vouchers, they still found exceptional improvement from voucher competition. This shows that the positive effect from vouchers was not caused by regression to the mean.

Critics, such as Martin Carnoy of Stanford University, have suggested that voucher-eligible and voucher-threatened schools in Florida might exhibit exceptional improvement not because of voucher competition, but simply because "being branded an F school may itself carry sufficient stigma to cause F schools to raise their test scores, whether or not there is a voucher threat."[8] To address this concern, Greene and Winters identified a group of schools in Florida that had received a failing grade but were no longer facing any threat from voucher competition. Because students were only eligible for vouchers if schools had failed twice in a four-year period, schools that had failed in one year and then gone three years without failing would have the failing stigma without the voucher threat (because the four-year window had closed). Not only did these schools fail to match the test score gains produced by voucher-eligible and voucher-threatened schools, but they actually slipped academically relative to all other Florida schools. Once the voucher threat was lifted from these schools, their rate of academic progress fell despite the stigma of their failing grade.

Of course, this does not prove that the failing stigma had no positive effect at all, and for vouchers to have a positive effect it need not be the case that voucher competition is the only force that can inspire improvement in failing public schools. This point has been lost on some researchers. Helen Ladd and Elizabeth Glennie of Duke University found that schools designated as failing in North Carolina made exceptional gains in the following year even though that state has no voucher program. From this they conclude that "if vouchers were the explanation for the gains in the F-rated schools in Florida, it is unlikely we would have found comparable patterns of gains in the low-performing schools in North Carolina."[9] Ladd and Glennie ignore the obvious possibility that both the stigma of failure and voucher competition could be driving improvement in Florida. As we have already seen, the stigma of failure cannot completely explain the exceptional gains achieved in Florida, since voucher-threatened schools made exceptional gains but schools once threatened by vouchers actually lost ground when the threat was removed. Just because something else may help improve public schools doesn't mean that vouchers don't also improve public schools.

A more recent analysis of Florida's A-Plus voucher program by Rajashri Chakrabarti of Cornell University confirms Greene and Winters's finding of a significant improvement in Florida public schools in response to voucher competition. Unlike Greene and Winters, who looked at academic progress over a one-year period, Chakrabarti examined academic gains between 1999, when the A-Plus program began, and 2002. She found that schools that had failed in 1999 and faced the threat of vouchers made significantly greater academic improvements during this period than schools that had received D grades in 1999.[10] Chakrabarti ruled out regression to the mean as an explanation for the superior performance of voucher-threatened schools by examining the gains made by low-performing schools between 1998 and 1999, before the A-Plus program was adopted. Low-performing schools did not make reading or math gains nearly as large as those they made after the voucher threat was introduced, suggesting that the threat of competition and not simply low initial scores account for the improvement. Chakrabarti also ruled out the stigma of failure as a sufficient explanation. Schools that received a low grade from the state in 1997, before vouchers were introduced, did not experience gains comparable to those achieved by failing schools facing competition after 1999. In short, Chakrabarti's analysis provides independent confirmation of Greene and Winters's conclusions and rejects the alternative hypotheses of critics.

Milwaukee's Voucher Program

Harvard economist Caroline Hoxby studied the effect of Milwaukee's voucher program on the academic performance of public schools. Because students had to come from families with incomes at or below 175 percent of the poverty line to receive vouchers, some public schools in Milwaukee had more students eligible for vouchers than others. Hoxby compared those Milwaukee public schools that were more exposed to voucher competition because at least 66 percent of their students were eligible for vouchers to schools that were less exposed to voucher competition. She found that

Milwaukee public schools exposed to greater voucher competition made significantly larger test score gains than schools less exposed to voucher competition.

Because all Milwaukee public schools faced at least some voucher competition, Hoxby also identified a control group of demographically similar schools in Wisconsin that were unaffected by the Milwaukee voucher program. Milwaukee public schools facing both high and low levels of voucher competition made academic gains significantly greater than the control group of demographically similar schools outside the city. Milwaukee public schools facing a high level of voucher competition made annual test score gains that were 3.4 percentile points greater than those of the control group in math, 5.4 percentile points greater in science, 3.1 percentile point greater in language, and 2.7 percentile points greater in social studies.[11] These are average annual gains in excess of the gains produced by the control group over a three-year period, meaning that over the entire three-year period schools facing a high level of competition from vouchers made roughly 10 to 15 percentile points greater improvement than similar schools facing no voucher competition.

Hoxby's analysis of the effects of voucher competition in Milwaukee is confirmed by a similar study conducted for the Manhattan Institute by Greene and Greg Forster. Rather than dichotomizing Milwaukee public schools into high and low voucher competition groups, this study treats exposure to competition as a continuous variable. The study also differs from Hoxby's in that it includes an additional year of test score results. The results, however, are very similar. Exposure to vouchers had a statistically significant positive effect on Milwaukee public schools such that a school with all of its students eligible for vouchers would have exceeded the academic gains of a school with only half of its students eligible by roughly 15 percentile points over a four-year period.[12]

Maine and Vermont's Voucher Programs

Although they are less well known than Florida and Milwaukee's voucher programs, Maine and Vermont have vouchers known as "tuitioning" programs. At more than a century old, they are the country's oldest existing voucher programs. They provide vouchers to residents of towns that have decided not to build their own high schools. Students can use those vouchers to attend other towns' public high schools or to attend private high schools. Christopher Hammons of Houston Baptist University analyzed the effects of those programs on the academic performance of neighboring public high schools. He found that the closer public high schools were to towns with vouchers, the better their academic performance was. Schools closer to tuitioning towns had stronger incentives to perform better in order to attract students who could use vouchers to choose them over other schools. Hammons found that "if a town one mile away from a school decided to tuition its students, we would expect that the percentage of students passing the state test at that school would increase by 3.4 points—a gain of 12 percent over existing scores."[13]

Studies of Charter Programs

Vouchers are not the only form of school choice that provides positive incentives to public schools through competition. As the charter school movement grows, regular public schools increasingly have to compete with charter schools for their students and the resources they generate. It is possible to learn about the effects of school choice and competition on public schools by examining how public schools react to charter schools as well as voucher competition.

But the effects of charter and voucher competition may not be exactly the same. Charter schools are public schools. While they are less heavily regulated than the regular public schools with which they compete for students, they are still subject to a greater amount of regulation than the private schools that participate in voucher programs. Those regulations may hinder their ability to compete effectively with regular public schools, reducing the competitive effect they might have on regular public schools.

In addition, in a number of states charter school authorizers—agencies that must approve charter schools before they can open and may subsequently close them—are either the local public school district or some other entity closely allied with the interests of the traditional public school system. In those circumstances, charter schools that pose a low level of competitive threat to regular public schools are more likely to be approved. For example, charter schools designed for dropouts, students in prison, or at-risk youth do not provide regular public schools with much competition because they are targeted toward student populations that regular schools may not mind losing. A recent Manhattan Institute study found that the rate at which charters were given to schools targeting disadvantaged populations was very high in some states, reaching as high as 79 percent of all charter schools in Wisconsin for which information was available, and 67 percent of all charter schools in Illinois for which information was available.[14]

Despite these limitations on charter schools' ability to compete with regular public schools, a number of studies have found regular public schools improving their academic performance in response to competition from nearby charter schools. For example, Hoxby has studied the effects of charter schools on student achievement at regular public schools in Arizona and Michigan. In both states she found that regular public school students produced significantly greater test score gains when they went to school in an area with a critical mass of charter schools than if they attended a regular public school without many charter schools nearby. The benefit was large enough that if the regular public schools' faster rate of improvement continued, urban public school students would catch up to the academic performance of their suburban counterparts in ten years in Arizona and twenty years in Michigan.[15]

Greene and Forster examined the effects of charter school competition on regular public schools' performance in Milwaukee. They examined whether regular public schools located closer to charter schools experienced greater academic gains than public schools further from charter schools. In theory, closer proximity to charter schools should expose regular public schools to greater competition because students could more easily exercise the choice to leave for the nearby charter school. The study found that Milwaukee's regular public high schools made significantly larger test score improvements if they were located closer to charter schools. The analysis showed that if a new charter school opened one kilometer from a regular public high school, student test scores could be expected to improve by 9 percentile points over a four-year period. If the charter were located five kilometers away, the expected gain would be 3.5 percentile points.[16] Greater exposure to competition from charter schools caused regular public high schools to make greater academic progress.

Studies of Residential and Existing Private School Choice

Debates over the effects of school choice often forget that some amount of school choice already exists virtually everywhere. Families unhappy with their assigned public schools can consider changing their residence to obtain access to a more desirable school. Families can consider sending their children to private schools. Sometimes school districts allow families to transfer their children to other public schools without having to change residences, such as with magnet programs.

Of course, all of these existing choices face serious constraints. Families wishing to move to areas with better schools have to have the resources to afford to buy homes in those areas. Those families may also face racial barriers to residential choice. And moving may separate families from friends, relatives, and convenient access to work. Choosing a private school is similarly only an option for the families with the money to exercise that choice. The option of transferring to another public school is limited by the availability of spots in desired schools, testing requirements for admission to selective public schools, and access to affordable transportation to the desired school. In short, school choice already exists but it is fairly limited in its availability.

But these existing forms of school choice and competition are more accessible in some areas than in others. For example, in some places there are more schools and school districts within a single metropolitan area, making choice relatively more accessible and increasing the level of competition those schools face. A family in Boston need not move a great distance to cross into a new school district, since the greater Boston area has a very large number of school districts. By contrast, a family in Hawaii cannot change school districts without crossing the Pacific Ocean, since the entire state is consolidated under a single school district. Because existing school choice is more available in some places than others, researchers have been able to compare the performance of public schools under higher and lower levels of existing competition.

Drawing inferences from the results of these studies for the effects of voucher and charter school competition is imperfect but still helpful. Expanding school choice and competition through vouchers or charters may have effects that are different from the effects of existing choice arrangements. There are constraints on existing choice that may hinder their impact relative to that of vouchers, and to a lesser extent charter schools. Existing choice arrangements may not alter the flow of funds into schools in the same way as voucher programs, perhaps altering the reactions of the schools. But while this evidence is imperfect as a guide to the effects of school choice reforms, it is still useful to examine it. If competition produces positive incentives that improve schools even under the highly constrained circumstances that apply to existing forms of choice, we can reasonably expect that school choice reforms would have an even stronger impact.

Clive Belfield and Henry Levin of Teachers College, the education school of Columbia University, have conducted a review of studies on the effects of existing choice and competition. They conclude that "a sizable majority of these studies report beneficial effects of competition across all outcomes, with many reporting statistically significant correlations."[17] In particular, they review 206 analyses from twenty-five studies of the effects of existing choice and competition on academic outcomes. They find that 38 percent of these analyses produce statistically significant positive results for the effects of competition. If there were no relationship between competition and student achievement we would expect only about 5 percent of these analyses to produce statistically significant results by chance. Only a trivial number of analyses found significant negative results.[18] The average effect across all 206 analyses suggests only a modest increase in public school student achievement, but the high percentage of statistically significant positive results and the trivial number of negative results suggests that competition does improve public schools.

Belfield and Levin also found significant benefits when they examined the effects of existing choice and competition on graduation rates. Of the fifty-two analyses they reviewed from six studies, 42 percent produced statistically significant positive results. And when they examined the effect of choice and competition on public school efficiency—that is, student outcomes relative to spending—they found that 66 percent of the sixty-four analyses from thirteen studies produced statistically significant positive results. As Belfield and Levin conclude: "The above evidence shows reasonably consistent evidence of a link between competition (choice) and education quality. Increased competition and higher educational quality are positively correlated."[19]

While more could be learned about the effects of school choice on academic achievement for students who remain in public schools, there is already a fairly large body of evidence on the question. Rather than draining public schools of resources and talent, harming their academic performance as advocates of the Draining Myth claim, school choice improves public schools' performance. The evidence from existing voucher programs consistently shows public schools improving in response to the challenge of vouchers. The authors are not aware of any study that shows U.S. public-school test scores declining in response to vouchers. In addition, three studies of charter school competition and the body of research on existing choice arrangements support the conclusion that increased choice and competition lead to better public schools. Other than a plausible story, the Draining Myth has very little to support it.

CHAPTER 16

The Disabled Need Not Apply Myth

"Private schools won't serve disabled students."

A common indictment against voucher programs is that they leave disabled students behind. Critics assert that private schools will not offer appropriate services to disabled students, who make up almost 13 percent of all students in public schools. If it were true, the claim that voucher programs have an implicit "disabled students need not apply" policy would raise serious questions about the equity of those programs. But the evidence shows that when vouchers offer private schools the same resources as public schools, those schools provide disabled students not only with appropriate services, but on average with a superior education. And even vouchers that don't provide equal funding have expanded the range of quality options available to disabled students.

Foundations of the Disabled Need Not Apply Myth

Advocates of the Disabled Need Not Apply Myth justify their argument by pointing out that private schools are not required by law to provide the same specific services that public schools do. For example, Sandra Feldman, the former president of the American Federation of Teachers, writes that "private schools are not required to accept special education students, so nearly all of them . . . are educated in the public schools."[1] Barbara Miner, a teacher-union researcher, writes in *The Nation* that "voucher schools do not necessarily serve all children. . . . By law, the private schools are not required to provide the same level of special-education services as public schools."[2] A report from People for the American Way and the Disability Rights and Education Defense Fund (PFAW/DREDF) asserts that vouchers "shortchange the needs of students with disabilities" because "once parents use a voucher to transfer their children to private schools, they have effectively opted out of the legal rights and educational services" guaranteed under federal disability rights law.[3]

The assumption behind these criticisms is that schools do not provide services for disabled students unless they are required to do so. This assumption is not entirely unreasonable in light of the public school system's track record. Prior to the adoption of a federal law now known as the Individuals with Disabilities in Education Act (IDEA) in the mid-1970s, public schools regularly denied appropriate services to disabled students. In the absence of a federal mandate to serve disabled students and additional funds to subsidize those services, public schools were reluctant to provide services for disabled students, particularly for students with severe disabilities that would be more expensive to accommodate.

IDEA changed this by imposing a legal process-compliance model of accountability. It requires schools, in consultation with the families of disabled students, to develop an Individual Education Plan (IEP) specifying the services it is required to provide to each student. The IEP is similar to a contract in some ways: schools promise certain services to address a student's disability. If the school fails to provide those services, or if the services the school is promising don't live up to its full obligations under IDEA, families can take their schools to court to protect the interests of their disabled children.

There is no doubt that the quality of services provided to disabled students has improved greatly over the last thirty years with the introduction of IEPs. The question is not whether this legal process-compliance model has benefited students. The question is whether this is the only model of accountability under which disabled students can expect to receive appropriate services, and if not, which accountability model works best.

Advocates of the Disabled Need Not Apply Myth believe that unless disabled students have IEPs, legal documents defining the services to which they are entitled, they cannot be assured of appropriate services. Since private schools are not required to use IEPs, their reasoning goes, disabled students are not served by voucher programs. The Disabled Need Not Apply Myth overstates the effectiveness of the IEP process at protecting the rights of disabled students and dismisses the ability of private schools to provide quality services to disabled students.

The legal process-compliance model is neither a necessary nor a sufficient condition for ensuring that disabled students receive appropriate services. The evidence indicates that a substantial number of disabled students are denied adequate services in their public schools despite the formal process provided by IEPs. And the evidence further shows that disabled students using vouchers have obtained better services in private schools even without IEPs.

Vouchers do not leave students without any way of holding schools accountable. Rather, vouchers provide a choice model of accountability to replace the process-compliance model. When dissatisfied parents are able to withdraw their children from a school and seek better services elsewhere, schools have a powerful incentive to provide adequate services. This makes schools accountable to parents through a more direct, less adversarial, and less costly method.

Problems with the IEP System

There are several large problems with the legal process-compliance model that limit its effectiveness in ensuring that disabled students receive adequate services. First, families have to be aware that they have access to this legal process if their children's disabilities are not properly addressed by public schools. Lower-income and less well-educated parents are less likely to be aware of their procedural rights under this model and therefore can more easily be taken advantage of. Recognizing this problem, states often make subsidized legal services available, but their resources are limited and in any event parents need to be aware of this legal assistance before it can do them any good.

Second, schools have significantly greater experience and sophistication in writing IEPs than most parents of disabled students. The IEP is created by a bargaining process between parents and schools that determines the services disabled students require. As in any bargaining process, one side's incentives and interests differ from the other's. Parents want to maximize the services their children receive, while schools have an incentive to limit their obligations to provide services. Schools have the advantage in this bargaining process. They know how to write IEPs that impose minimal obligations on them and how to get parents to agree to these provisions. That doesn't mean parents always get a raw deal; many parents are satisfied with their IEPs. And schools' advantages are somewhat mitigated by the networks of parental advocates that have been developed to assist parents of disabled students during the IEP process. But, as before, lower-income and less well-educated parents are less likely to be aware of or have access to these networks.

Schools' desire to minimize their IEP obligations is exemplified by a satirical skit presented at a 2003 national conference for public-school disability lawyers making fun of parents' IEP demands. According to the *Washington Post*, the skit's mock newscast "was greeted by abundant laughter" as the anchorman "joked that Cuisinart has come up with the Due Processor, which 'shreds, dices, cuts, blends, frappes and otherwise destroys' unwanted applications for due process hearings, where schooling disputes are resolved. Showing a photo of elated children, he said, 'In Boulder, Colorado, a group of students took to the streets in celebration of their due process victory, where the judges awarded them new sets of parents.'" Perhaps most striking was the skit's frank depiction of public-school manipulation of the IEP process: "With a John Madden display of arrows and circles, he gave a play-by-play of how a school system used its skill to deny a family the placement sought for a child." This attack against parents for seeking their IEP rights was so well received that the conference organizers invited the performer—himself a senior special-education attorney for a school district—to deliver it again at the next year's conference.[4]

The third problem is that enforcing compliance with an IEP when the school fails to provide the services it requires is costly and difficult. Using the legal system to compel public schools to fulfill the terms of an IEP can impose significant legal expenses as well as consume a large amount of time and energy for families that may also be struggling just to raise a child with a disability. Perhaps even more important, parents of disabled students may be particularly reluctant to engage in a legal struggle with the same people who care for their children every day. Public schools can sometimes get away with providing less than all required services without triggering any legal consequences because the cost of holding them accountable is so high.

A 2004 state report on academic outcomes among special-education students in New York City provides evidence of the school failures that can develop in spite of IEP guarantees. The state found that only 3.5 percent of special-education eighth graders pass its reading exam and 5 percent pass its math exam.[5] This even though most special-education students have relatively mild diagnoses, and even though New York spends more than any other state on special education—$13,000 per student in 1999, the most recent year for which data are available, on top of regular education spending that is now well over $12,000.[6]

A survey of parents of disabled students conducted by Jay Greene and Greg Forster of the Manhattan Institute found considerable evidence that the IEP process does not ensure appropriate services for all disabled students. They surveyed a sample of parents who participated in a Florida voucher program for students with disabilities. More than two-thirds of those parents reported that the public schools their children were in before they used vouchers failed to provide all of the services required by their IEPs. In addition, half of those parents reported having conflicts with their public schools over their IEPs, and only one-third were satisfied with the process for developing the IEP.[7]

Of course, these responses are representative of the experiences of the parents of the 12,000 disabled students who left the public school system under Florida's special-education voucher program, about 3 percent of all special-education students in the state. It is possible that the large portion of families with disabled students who remain in public schools may be satisfied with the services they receive under their IEPs. However, even if we make the unlikely assumption that all disabled students in the state who were dissatisfied with the IEP process left using a voucher, this represents a nontrivial number of students who reported the failure of their public schools to fulfill their IEP obligations—a stark contrast to the Disabled Need Not Apply Myth, which insists that public schools educate all disabled students. But it strains credibility to assume that these voucher-using students are in fact the only students being shortchanged by their public schools. If two-thirds of parents participating in a voucher program report that their public schools didn't live up to their IEP obligations, it is likely that a substantial portion of parents remaining in public schools are also receiving inadequate services. That would make the total number of under-served students quite large.

Private Schools Serve Disabled Students Better

If public schools do not always provide appropriate services for disabled students even when legally required to do so by an IEP, can disabled students hope to find appropriate services in private schools that aren't required to follow IEPs? Advocates of the Disabled Need Not Apply Myth don't think so. But the evidence shows they are mistaken about both the absence of disabled students from private schools and the quality of the services private schools provide to them.

Private Schools Do Serve Disabled Students

To a large extent, the Disabled Need Not Apply Myth relies on suggestions that there are almost no disabled students in private schools. Feldman claims that "nearly all" disabled students "are educated in the public schools," and Miner writes that because they aren't covered under IDEA "voucher schools do not necessarily serve all children." But it simply isn't true that private schools don't admit disabled students. Public schools regularly contract with private schools to educate disabled students, particularly students with severe disabilities such as deaf-blindness, emotional disturbance, and autism. There exist private schools eager to accept disabled students, even severely disabled students, when those schools are provided with sufficient funds to address those disabilities.

Even when they don't receive additional funding, private schools often serve students with special needs. Determining the exact percentage of students in private schools who have disabilities is difficult because those schools often do not assign students disability labels. Public schools assign labels because these labels are required by the IEP process, and additional resources are provided to schools to address the identified disabilities. Private schools that do not receive additional funds and are not bound by the legal process-compliance model have no reason to label students as disabled. That does not mean disabled students are absent from private schools, or that they aren't receiving services that address their disabilities. It only means that private schools don't put the same labels on students.

The labeling of disabilities is not the same thing as the existence of disabilities. We saw in chapter 2 that public schools have responded to the financial incentives of the special-education funding system by identifying low-performing students as disabled without regard to whether their academic difficulties are truly caused by disabilities. Because students who are behind academically are found in large numbers in private as well as public schools, it is certain that some of those private-school students would have been identified as disabled had they been in public schools. Conversely, some students in private schools also have disabilities that are not just a matter of being academically behind—blindness, orthopedic impairments, etc.—but schools do not necessarily use a labeling system to track them.

Evidence from Milwaukee's Voucher Program

The experience of Milwaukee's voucher program illustrates how private schools serve disabled students even without IEPs or additional funds. The program in Milwaukee does not require private schools accepting voucher students to provide any specific services for disabilities. The absence of this mandate leads the People for the American Way to condemn the program for failing to serve disabled students: "It's deeply troubling to see that the schools in the [Milwaukee] voucher program are being permitted to turn their backs on children with special needs."[8]

But the Wisconsin Legislative Audit Bureau, a state agency that was charged with reviewing the voucher program, noted that there were at least 171 students in the voucher program who had previously been identified by the public school system as disabled.[9] An additional unknown number of Milwaukee voucher students were disabled but did not have labels because private schools had no need to formally label them. For example, Brother Bob Smith—head of Messmer High School, which accepts voucher students in Milwaukee—estimated that between 15 and 20 percent of his students had special needs. The Lutheran Special School, another Milwaukee private school accepting vouchers, had twenty-eight elementary school students with disabilities ranging from cognitive disability to emotional disturbance. The Milwaukee Lutheran High School employed two special education teachers who served between twenty-eight and thirty students with special needs. Pius XI High School had fifty students with disabilities.[10] While there is no comprehensive catalogue of students with disabilities in Milwaukee's voucher program, it is clear that the program does not turn its back on students with special needs.

Since private schools in Milwaukee do not receive additional funds to serve disabled students, as public schools do, it is remarkable that we see as many special needs students as we do using vouchers. But this is even more remarkable given that the vouchers are only worth approximately half the amount of money that is spent on the average Milwaukee public school student. So Milwaukee private schools are willing to take on disabled students, who are more expensive to educate, for significantly less money than the city requires to educate regular students.

Evidence from Florida's McKay Scholarship Program

In addition to claiming that private schools don't accept disabled students, the Disabled Need Not Apply Myth also claims that private schools don't provide adequate services to the disabled students they do accept. But the evidence shows that when private schools are provided with the same funding public schools get, they actually provide disabled students with better services. Under Florida's McKay Scholarship Program, every disabled student in public school is eligible to receive a voucher worth as much money as the school system spends on that student. In its fourth year of operation more than 12,000 of the state's 375,000 students labeled as special-education students had chosen to use the voucher to attend a private school.

Some claim that private schools only admit disabled students with the mildest disabilities. The PFAW/DREDF report asserts that "many private schools that claim to welcome students with disabilities frequently pick and choose, denying admission to students with more severe or specific kinds of disabilities."[11] The evidence does not support this depiction of private-school behavior. Florida rates the severity of students' disabilities based on a scale of five categories and determines school funding based on these categories. Greene and Forster found that 54 percent of students in the special-education voucher program are in the least severe category, while the state estimates that 60 percent of its "exceptional" public-school students are in that same category. If gifted students are removed from the "exceptional" category, leaving only disabled students, approximately 50 percent of Florida public schools' disabled students are in the least severe category. Meanwhile, about 7.5 percent of Florida's disabled public-school students are in the two most severe categories, while 7.4 percent of disabled students attending private school with the voucher program are in those categories. Thus the voucher program roughly mirrors the state's disabled student population in terms of severity of disabilities.[12]

The distribution of the types of disabilities found in the special-education voucher program also roughly reflect the Florida special-education student population. Half (51.4 percent) of all voucher students have been identified as having a specific learning disability, roughly the same as the proportion of specific learning disabilities among disabled students in public schools in Florida (45.4 percent). Just under a fifth (17.4 percent) of voucher students had a speech or language impairment, not far from the roughly one-quarter (24.0 percent) of Florida public-school students with such impairments; 9.4 percent of voucher students were mentally handicapped, compared to 11.1 percent of public-school disabled students; 10.7 percent of voucher students were emotionally disturbed, compared to 10.0 percent of public-school disabled students; 3.0 percent of voucher students were autistic, blind, or deaf, compared to 2.5 percent of public-school disabled students.[13]

The distribution of types and severities of disabilities in Florida is also similar to the distribution of disabilities nationwide. This means that there is no unusual skewing of disability types or severities in the Florida population that might have an effect on participation in the program that would prevent these data from having implications for special-education services elsewhere.

Disabled students using the special-education voucher program to attend private schools were also roughly representative of Florida's income distribution. It is not true, as the *New York Times*' then-education columnist Richard Rothstein once claimed, that "only better-off families can afford schools offering special education" in the program.[14] Half of all participating families reported household incomes under $40,000 in 2002–2003; the median family income in Florida was $45,625 in 1999.[15]

Most importantly, figure 16.1 shows that the program empirically disproves the Disabled Need Not Apply Myth by offering disabled students better services, on average, than they had been receiving in public schools. While two-thirds expressed dissatisfaction with their previous public schools, only 7.2 percent expressed dissatisfaction with their voucher schools. More than 90 percent of participating parents reported being satisfied with the services they received at their voucher schools, compared to fewer than a third reporting satisfaction with their previous public school experience.

Participating families had good reasons to be more satisfied. The average class size in their voucher schools was 12.8 students, compared to 25.1 in their previous public schools. While 63.2 percent of participants had experienced average class sizes of over twenty-five students in their previous public schools, only 6.0 percent had that experience in voucher schools. The service that many students in special education need—particularly the half of all students who have specific learning disabilities—is simply the greater individual attention and customized instruction that is only possible in a smaller group setting. Even though many of the private schools did not have IEPs mandating this service, they were more likely to provide it than public schools.

Another service that many parents of disabled students seek from private schools is the protection of their children from bullying and harassment. Students with special needs are particularly vulnerable to this kind of

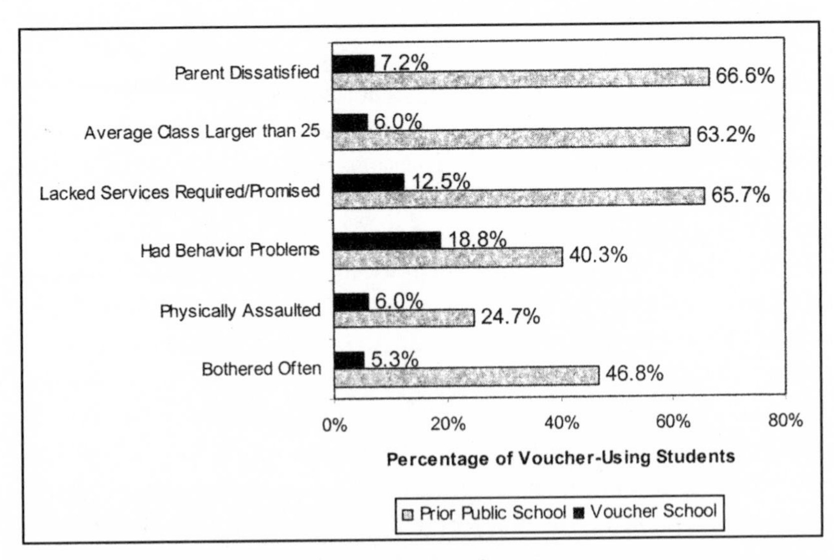

Figure 16.1. Private Schools Serve Disabled Students Better
Source: Greene and Forster, "Vouchers for Special Education Students," Manhattan Institute.

predatory behavior, which can seriously disrupt their educational progress. Greene and Forster found that 46.8 percent of participating students were bothered often at their prior public schools, and 24.7 percent physically assaulted, because of their disabilities. The rate of being bothered often dropped to 5.3 percent and that of physical assaults to 6.0 percent in voucher schools. Again, public-school IEPs provided no protection against this kind of educationally disruptive predation, while private schools without legal mandates provided students with significantly safer learning environments.

One more service private schools can provide is that of helping students learn appropriate behavior. This is as much a part of education as academics, and for many disabled students it is a very important educational need. In their previous public schools 40.3 percent of participating students had behavior problems, compared to 18.8 percent in their voucher schools.

Voucher schools held accountable through choice were more likely to provide all the services they promised to parents than were public schools to provide all the services they were required to provide under the legal process-compliance model. While only 30.2 percent of participating parents reported that their previous public schools provided all of the services legally required under the IEP system, 86.0 percent reported that their voucher schools provided everything that they promised to provide, though they were not legally required to do so. The provision of all required services is what the process-compliance model of accountability needs in order to function; the provision of all promised services is what the choice model of accountability requires. Clearly parents are getting what they expect to get from voucher schools, which is what is necessary for them to effectively hold schools accountable through choice.

Even the roughly 10 percent of families that had left the voucher program since the previous year reported receiving better services in their voucher schools. If anyone were going to report having a worse experience in voucher schools, it should be the parents who had exited the program. But 62.3 percent reported being satisfied with their voucher schools, compared to 45.2 percent with their previous public schools. Former participants also reported receiving better services on virtually every measure, including class sizes, victimization by other students, behavior problems, and the provision of promised or required services. A full 91 percent of former participants said the program should continue to be available for others.

Process Accountability and Choice Accountability

The Disabled Need Not Apply Myth is based on the assumption that schools only provide services to disabled students if they are required to do so. But the evidence shows that even when public schools are required to provide services they sometimes fail to deliver. Process-compliance requirements are only as good as people's ability to enforce them. Given that the process for forcing public schools to provide appropriate services to disabled students is difficult, it is inevitable that many public schools will fall short of their legal mandates. The evidence shows that these shortcomings exist and are not trivial.

Choice is another accountability mechanism that can help ensure that schools provide disabled students with appropriate services. Private schools participating in voucher programs in Milwaukee and Florida provide disabled students with appropriate services because they want to attract those students and the revenues they generate. Of course, when the funds available to private schools are comparable to what is offered to educate disabled students in public schools, as is the case in Florida, it is easier for private schools to offer a wider array of appropriate services. But even with only a fraction of the money, as in Milwaukee, private schools still seek to educate disabled students. Disabled students do have a reason to apply for vouchers: the evidence suggests they will usually find better services.

CHAPTER 17

The Democratic Values Myth

"Private schools are less effective at promoting tolerance and civic participation."

We rightly expect schools to do more than teach academic skills. In addition to preparing students for participation in the economy, schools have the responsibility of preparing students for participation in the nation's civic life. Democratic values like toleration, political participation, and volunteerism are as central to the proper functioning of our nation as academic skills are to the proper functioning of our economy.

Advocates of the Democratic Values Myth believe that only government-operated schools can ensure that students are inculcated with these civic values. Private schools, whatever their academic benefits, simply can't be trusted to adequately prepare students for their future role as tolerant democratic citizens. And proponents of the Democratic Values Myth fear that vouchers further undermine civic values not only by increasing the proportion of students enrolled in private schools but also by encouraging public schools to abandon their civic purposes in order to compete more effectively.

The evidence, however, does not support any of these claims. Studies consistently show that private schools are actually better at conveying the democratic values of tolerance, participation, and volunteerism than public schools. Rather than undermining students' adherence to democratic values, private schools and vouchers actually enhance it.

Foundations of the Democratic Values Myth

The Democratic Values Myth is based on the notion that the public purposes of education can only be reliably accomplished by public operation of schools. If a school is government-operated, it will teach tolerance and democratic participation; if it is privately operated, and particularly if it is operated by a religious group, it probably will not. Private schools are specifically alleged to undermine democratic values in two broad ways.

First, advocates of the Democratic Values Myth allege that private schools are more likely to segregate students by race, religion, and values, undermining the teaching of tolerance and respect for democratic processes that flows from managing those differences in a shared school environment. As Richard Riley, the Secretary of Education during the Clinton Administration, put it: "The 'common school'—the concept upon which our public school system was built—teaches children important lessons about both the commonality and diversity of American culture. These lessons are conveyed not only through what is taught in the classroom, but by the very experience of attending school with a diverse mix of students."[1] Private schools, however, may cater to particular religious or ethnic tastes, undermining this common school experience.

With vouchers this subversion of democratic values will allegedly become more widespread. After the Supreme Court upheld Cleveland's voucher program, the *New York Times* declared that "in public schools, Americans of many backgrounds learn together. In the religious schools that Cleveland taxpayers are being forced to sponsor, Catholics are free to teach that their way is best, and Jews, Muslims and those of other faiths can teach their coreligionists that they have truth on their side."[2] In the extreme case, advocates of the Democratic Values Myth fear that this erosion of the common school experience will lead to such widespread promotion of intolerance that a breakdown of political order followed by mass violence might result. David Berliner of Arizona State University testified to the New Mexico state legislature that "voucher programs would allow for splintering along ethnic and racial lines. Our primary concern is that voucher programs could end up resembling the ethnic cleansing now occurring in Kosovo."[3]

Second, advocates of the Democratic Values Myth believe that the market for education found in private schools and expanded by vouchers encourages a consumerist mentality that is antithetical to democratic values. Dorothy Shipps, of Teachers College at Columbia University, writes in the *Los Angeles Times* that "Americans ask schools to turn out citizens who vote, pay taxes, join organizations and actively engage in civic life. Yet, the corporate model of reform encourages students (and their parents) to focus on immediate individual rewards at the expense of cooperation, collaboration and other shared experiences that build social cohesion and strong communities." Shipps sees dire consequences from allowing parents to choose schools, and from allowing schools (rather than teachers) to control what goes on in the classroom: "Fostering extreme individualism through competition and strict management accountability exacerbates a pattern of civic disengagement that researchers are finding more widespread today than at any time in the last century."[4]

The underlying premise of this charge is that there is an inherent tension between parents' desire to promote the welfare of their own children and the public purposes of education. Social theorist Benjamin Barber, then of Rutgers University, argued that "the voucher system would mobilize individuals, but it would mobilize them via private incentives; it speaks exclusively to their private interests as parents and thus as consumers of parental goods (such as education)." Barber asserts that it is impossible for people to want both what is best for themselves and what is best for the community: "Incentives privatize: vouchers transform what ought to be a public question ('What is a good system of public education for *our* children?') into a personal question ('What kind of school do I want for *my* children?'). It permits citizens to think of education as a matter of private preference."[5] The only way to get people to take an interest in other people's well-being is to get them to stop taking a particular interest in their own.

Both these charges ultimately rest on factual assumptions that can be empirically tested. Is it the case, as the advocates of the Democratic Values Myth suggest, that government-operated schools are better at promoting the public goals of education as opposed to people's own personal goals? Do private schools really exacerbate racial segregation? Is it really true that the pursuit of private interests in education is incompatible with the public goals of students learning tolerance, political participation, and public-spiritedness?

Unfortunately, proponents of the Democratic Values Myth offer little or no empirical support of their claims. For example, Barber simply declares point blank that "public schools are not merely schools *for* the public, but schools of publicness: institutions where we learn what it means to *be* a public and start down the road toward common national and civic identity. As forges of our citizenship, they are the bedrock of our democracy."[6] On the basis of what evidence does he believe that public schools succeed in teaching "publicness" and in being forges of citizenship, and on the basis of what evidence does he believe that private schools do not teach "publicness" and are not forges of citizenship? He doesn't say.

People do not address other policy questions in this way. Advocates of "single-payer" health care plans do not simply take it for granted that government-run health care systems will succeed in making health care available to all; they bring evidence from countries with single-payer plans to support that conclusion. Opponents of single-payer plans similarly bring evidence to back their claims that single-payer plans don't work or have unacceptable costs. But when it comes to education and the promotion of democratic values, too many people allow emphatic statements ("I believe in public education") to substitute for examination of the evidence.

Why Private Schools Might Be Better at Promoting Democratic Values

The threat allegedly posed to democratic values by private education and vouchers is not self-evident. In fact, there are good reasons to believe that private schools and vouchers would actually enhance the teaching of democratic values rather than undermining it.

First, one might expect private schools to do a better job of teaching democratic values simply because the evidence shows that they are better at teaching things generally (see chapters 13 and 14 for a discussion of this evidence). Whatever qualities make private schools better able to teach math and reading may also make them better able to teach tolerance and civic participation. By providing access to higher-quality education, vouchers may be providing access to higher-quality democratic education as well as to higher-quality academic education.

Second, the sorting of students by religion and belief systems in private schools, which advocates of the Democratic Values Myth fear is harmful, may actually help promote the values of tolerance, participation, and public-spiritedness. A considerable body of research suggests that the greater self-esteem produced by a strong sense of one's own identity is associated with greater tolerance for others.[7] A Catholic (for example) who is secure in his own identity as a Catholic will find it easier to accept that others are not Catholic, and thus to accept their right not to be Catholic, whereas a Catholic who is not secure in his own Catholicness may seek to prove (to others and himself) that he really is Catholic by denigrating non-Catholics and refusing to respect their rights. In light of this research, it is reasonable to expect that students who learn more about their own religious and ideological backgrounds may have improved self-esteem and a greater sense of security in their own identities, which can make it easier for them to be tolerant and respectful toward others.

Democratic values may actually be more threatened by culturally rootless individuals than by individuals with strong cultural identities. Children who do not have a secure sense of their own identities may be more vulnerable to hatred's seductive promise to provide that security. People who are grounded in the institutions of their religions and communities have a set of social, cultural, and moral norms that help them make sense of the world and restrain their behavior. Children without these firm psychological roots can be expected to seek something to fill that void, making some of them easy prey for hatred's recruiters.

Segregation of students by race is fundamentally different from segregation by religion or belief system and is definitely not desirable. However, it doesn't appear to be exacerbated by private schools. Difficult as it may be for some to believe, it simply isn't the case that private schools are more racially segregated than public schools. The evidence establishing this fact, and the reasons for it, are discussed at length in chapter 18. For our present purposes, it is enough to point out that Berliner's concern that more private schooling may make New York look like Sarajevo is not consistent with the evidence.

The third reason private schools may promote democratic values better than public schools is the greater singularity of mission more commonly found in private schools. Terry Moe of Stanford University argues that because public schools are politically controlled, they cannot have the unified sense of community and purpose that often prevails in private schools. Responding to adherents of the Democratic Values Myth, he argues that "the schools they want are ideal training grounds for democracy—small, flexible, participatory communities that encourage active involvement, information exchange, debate, deliberation, and self governance." But public schools don't provide this type of "participatory community" because it is politically necessary that they be governed by rigidly neutral bureaucratic rules rather than by a common mission. "A bureaucratic 'community' is artificial, built on formally specified relationships, rights, and responsibilities that literally obstruct the development of a true community."[8] Charles Glenn of Boston University makes a similar argument, writing that "we might have set ourselves an impossible task in seeking to provide a single model of education that is to be at once capable of nurturing character and civic virtue and yet inoffensive to the convictions of any parent."[9]

The shared sense of purpose among school staff may also help private schools to better handle the controversial nature of civic value instruction. The political governance of public schools, which have diverse constituencies and must constantly struggle not to alienate any of them, may hinder their willingness to take on contentious discussions. For example, teaching students tolerance requires teaching them to respect the rights of groups that they intensely dislike, but public schools may find it politically difficult to engage students in a discussion where an intensely disliked group is specifically identified. Without specific examples of groups to be tolerated and a willingness to dive into a contentious discussion, public schools may be left providing students with nothing but gaseous affirmations of the abstract generality that people ought to tolerate other people—a lesson so vague that it may have little effect on students. Private schools, on the other hand, have a better idea of what they think is good and bad. This clarity may enable them to address controversial issues more comfortably and to illustrate lessons with specific examples.

Studies of Democratic Values in Private Schools

Whether we should believe any of these arguments for or against the efficacy of private schools in teaching democratic values ultimately depends on the weight of the evidence. Democratic values may seem like something too abstract to be studied empirically, but this isn't the case. Social scientists have developed valid methods for measuring the extent to which people are tolerant of the political rights of others, participate in the democratic process, and volunteer to help achieve common goals. Whether private schools and vouchers undermine democratic values is an issue that can be addressed with evidence.

The evidence on this point is unambiguous. Empirical investigations of the effects of public and private schooling, including private schooling under voucher programs, consistently find that democratic values are better taught in private schools.

Political Tolerance

Most studies of tolerance use a method refined by social scientists over the last few decades in which subjects are asked to identify their least liked group, sometimes from a list of groups provided by the researchers. People often pick groups like the Ku Klux Klan, Nazis, Communists, pro-life or pro-choice groups, or gay activists or the religious right. Subjects are then asked whether they would be willing to let members of this least liked group engage in political activities such as marching in their town, running for elected office, or having a book in the library. Subjects are said to have a higher level of tolerance if they are more willing to let members of their least liked group engage in these political activities.

Patrick Wolf of Georgetown University conducted a systematic review of the research on democratic values. The studies overwhelmingly found more effective teaching of democratic values in private schools. Wolf identified twelve studies providing eighteen analyses of the effects of private schooling on tolerance. Ten of the analyses showed statistically significant benefits to private education on levels of tolerance, seven showed inconclusive results, and one showed significant benefits to public schools.[10] The benefits of attending private school on students' levels of tolerance occurred both when students were still enrolled in school and later on in their adult lives.

For example, in a large random-assignment designed study David Campbell of Notre Dame University examined levels of tolerance among students who used privately funded vouchers to attend private schools, comparing them to a control group of students who remained in public school after losing a lottery for the voucher. Random-assignment studies help ensure valid comparisons between treatment and control groups because only chance determines which students receive the treatment (in this case, a voucher) and which students do not. Any difference in levels of tolerance observed over time between the two groups can be attributed to the type of school they attended, since the two groups of students were otherwise identical on average. Campbell found that "one year in a private school leads to a considerable increase in students' average level of political tolerance" as compared to the control group that remained in public schools. Using a voucher to switch to a private school increased students' tolerance after only one year by as much as 33 percent on the index Campbell used.[11]

Other studies find that the increased level of tolerance caused by attending a private school endures well after students leave school and enter adulthood. For example, Jay Greene, Joseph Giammo, and Nicole Mellow of the University of Texas at Austin examined levels of tolerance among a nationally representative sample of 3,400 adult Latinos who participated in the Latino National Political Survey. Controlling for a broad set of background characteristics, they found that adult Latinos who attended private school for more years displayed significantly higher levels of political tolerance than Latinos with less or no private school education. The benefit of private-school attendance was modest, suggesting that the effect does attenuate over time.[12]

Political Participation

Studies of the effects of public and private schools on political participation have focused on the rates at which people vote in elections. Wolf's review of the evidence shows that there have been three studies of the effects of private schools on political participation, providing four analyses. Three of the four analyses found a statistically significant increase in political participation resulting from private schooling, while the fourth analysis was inconclusive. The Greene, Giammo, and Mellow study of adult Latinos found that years of private schooling increased voting rates to such a degree that a subject who received all his education from private schools would be 16 percent more likely to report that he voted in the most recent election. In another study, Greene, Mellow, and Giammo surveyed a representative sample of adults in Texas. Controlling for background characteristics, they found that people who received some of their education in a private school were 9 percent more likely to report having voted in the most recent election. They did not find a significant result for those who received all of their education in private schools, but this may be because the relatively small size of this group makes it difficult for any effects of private schooling to be statistically visible.[13]

Private schools not only increase the political participation of their students, they also have more politically involved parents, even after demographic factors are taken into account. Christian Smith and David Sikkink of the University of South Carolina examined a large national sample from the National Education Household Survey. They found that "private schooling is absolutely *not* privatizing" in its effects.[14] For example, they found that parents of Catholic-school students were 11 percent more likely to report that they had voted in the last five years; parents of other Christian-school students were 15 percent more likely; and parents of home-schoolers were 3 percent more likely.[15] Private-school parents were also more likely to have engaged in other forms of political participation.

Volunteerism

Wolf's review of the evidence shows that there have been eight studies, providing twelve analyses, of the effects of private schools on the rate of volunteering for charitable activities. Wolf reports that eight of these twelve analyses find statistically significant benefits from private schools on volunteerism, three find no significant effect, and one finds a significant benefit from public schools. The bulk of the evidence suggests that private education does not encourage selfish, consumerist behaviors, as advocates of the Democratic Values Myth have suggested.

Greene examined the volunteering behavior of a nationally representative sample of public-school and private-school twelfth graders from the National Education Longitudinal Study. He found that private-school students were 20 percent more likely than public-school students to report that they had volunteered in the previous two years. Private-school students were also significantly more likely to report that they volunteer every week and that they consider it very important to volunteer in one's community.[16]

Some might argue that people who are already inclined toward volunteering are more likely to be attracted to private schools. Such a hypothesis would not be a concern for random-assignment studies, where only chance separates students in the treatment and control groups, but in the absence of random assignment it can be significant. While this hypothesis does not fit the description of private education advanced by proponents of the Democratic Values Myth, it is worth considering. If it is true, and if the initial propensity of private-school families to volunteer is not fully captured by statistical controls for demographic differences, studies such as Greene's would be unable to determine if private education actually caused greater rates of volunteering. Perhaps private-school students are 20 percent more likely to report that they volunteered in the past two years, even after controlling for demographic differences, because people already interested in volunteering are more likely to seek out private schools.

Another study reviewed by Wolf employs a statistical technique designed to correct for this possible "self selection" into private schools of people who volunteer frequently. Applying what statisticians call "instrumental variable" analysis, the study uses a variety of factors to predict which students will be enrolled in private schools and then examines those predicted private-school attendees to determine the effects of private school on volunteering. In this study, Kenneth Godwin and Frank Kemerer of the University of North Texas surveyed a sample of two thousand eighth graders in New York City and Dallas/Ft. Worth.[17] Controlling for demographic differences, they found that private-school students were 21 percent more likely to report volunteering than were comparable public-school students, virtually the same as what Greene found without an instrumental variable analysis. Apparently private schools do not attract students who are already more likely to volunteer; rather, private schools make students more likely to volunteer than they were when they first walked in the schoolhouse door.

While faith in the Democratic Values Myth is remarkably strong and widespread, the evidence clearly shows that there is no reasonable basis for believing it. Of the forty-four analyses of democratic values compiled by Wolf's review of the research, twenty-one find that private schools do a better job of promoting democratic values than public schools, while only two find the opposite. Far from undermining students' commitment to democratic values, private schools generally and school vouchers in particular promote and strengthen students' commitment to tolerance, political participation, and volunteerism.

CHAPTER 18

The Segregation Myth

"Private schools are more racially segregated than public schools."

Advocates of the Segregation Myth portray private schools as havens for white students fleeing racial integration in the public schools. They argue that introducing vouchers would only worsen segregation by enabling larger numbers of whites to flee. But the research on school segregation demonstrates that on average private schools are actually more racially integrated than public schools. If access to private schools were expanded with vouchers, racial integration would be likely to improve, not worsen.

Foundations of the Segregation Myth

Perhaps the simplest form of the Segregation Myth is the belief that private schools are currently more racially segregated than public schools. For example, the American Federation of Teachers' website claims that "private schools are . . . less racially diverse" than public schools.[1] The belief that private schools are racially segregated often accompanies a stereotype of private schools as protected bastions of privilege where longstanding forms of social domination, including white racial privilege, are maintained. As Michael Hout of the University of California at Berkeley put it: "White parents use wealth to send their children to private schools. . . . They do not see how such practices hand today's inequalities on to the next generation."[2]

Closely associated with this view of private schools as racially segregated is the belief that segregation would worsen if vouchers were available. David Bositis of the Joint Center for Political and Economic Studies wrote in the *New York Times* that "many white Americans today seem to be comfortable with segregation in schools (and elsewhere), though a line is drawn at intentional or explicit discrimination. Vouchers may be well suited to reinforcing this pattern."[3] This fear that vouchers will exacerbate segregation is widely and deeply held among the civil rights establishment. Kweisi Mfume, former president of the NAACP, was described in *Newsweek* as warning that "Vouchers don't educate, they segregate."[4] Hugh Price of the Urban League declared that he opposed vouchers because "we will wind up subsidizing segregation."[5] Rep. Jesse Jackson Jr. argued that "the underlying political foundation and dynamic of the [voucher] movement is avoidance of racial integration."[6] The education establishment is similarly certain that vouchers will lead to greater segregation. David Berliner of Arizona State University wrote that "vouchers add another means to segregate our citizens, this time using public money."[7] The National Education Association declared on its website: "A pure voucher system would only encourage economic, racial, ethnic, and religious stratification in our society."[8]

The implicit assumption made by advocates of the Segregation Myth seems to be that most people, or at least most white people, have racist impulses that make them prefer segregated schools over integrated ones. Private schools are thought to be more segregated than public schools because private-school families have used their resources to realize more fully their racist preferences, even if those racist preferences are often only subconscious. Certainly Hout and Bositis seem to endorse this view. And Jackson and Berliner are both more or less explicit in attributing to white parents a desire to use vouchers to separate their children from children of other races.

This fear of potentially segregating consequences from school vouchers is understandable in historical context. It is true that segregationists pushed voucher plans as part of their effort to avoid court-ordered racial integration, contributing to this negative association between vouchers and segregation. Memories of this history no doubt make many people wary of vouchers.

But leaders of the civil rights and education establishments seem not to remember the similarly shameful role that the public school system played in the history of segregation. Public schools were segregated by law in much of America during most of their existence, and even where schools were not officially segregated by law they were frequently kept segregated by unofficial practices. It would be wrong to remember the painful history of segregation only in association with vouchers and not with public schools.

Vouchers were only briefly hijacked by segregationists. Vouchers have surprisingly deep roots on the political left, having first been proposed by Thomas Paine as a progressive idea for relieving poverty and empowering the powerless. They are currently supported by a substantial number of progressive leaders, even in spite of an interest-group political environment that punishes them for doing so. If we're going to reject vouchers on the basis of their historically fleeting association with segregationists, then we might just as well stop building highways because Hitler built the autobahn.

But the real question is not which policy was more associated with segregation in the past; it's which policy is likely to promote integration in the future. We should not judge policies based on their pedigrees but on their likely effects. Ultimately, the only way to judge the merits of vouchers with regards to integration is to review the empirical research on the question.

Inadequate Measures of Integration

There is a large volume of research on integration in private schools and the relationship between school choice and segregation. The amount of research specifically examining vouchers is smaller. This is because there are not very many voucher programs and those that do exist are relatively recent.

Unfortunately, much of the research on this question is plagued by improper understandings of what we mean by "integration" and how to measure it. In particular, there are four conceptual errors commonly found in research on choice and integration: 1) confusing a greater number of minority students with greater integration, 2) confusing evenness of racial distribution within a given school system with greater integration, 3) adopting the racial composition of regular public schools as the normative benchmark for measuring levels of integration, and 4) comparing choice program participants to nonparticipants rather than examining whether choice programs lead to greater or lesser levels of school integration.

The first of these common errors, and the one heard most often in popular discussion of school integration, is to confuse a higher proportion of minority students with better integration. Journalists, interest group advocates, and politicians sometimes argue that private schools or schools of choice are less well integrated if they educate a lower percentage of minority students than other schools. For example, the American Federation of Teachers backs up its claim that "private schools are . . . less racially diverse" by pointing out that "the share of white students attending private school (11 percent) is double that of Hispanic and black students (5 and 6 percent, respectively)."[9]

More minority students, however, is not the same as more integration. If it were, then many Southern schools during the era of Jim Crow would have been wonderfully integrated due to their very high proportion of minority students. By this standard, *Brown v. Board of Education* was a terrible defeat for integration since it broke up an educational system explicitly designed to maximize the number of minority students in many schools. Clearly, what we really mean by integration is having a balanced mix of different racial groups rather than just greater numbers of certain groups.

The second mistaken way of examining school integration is to measure how evenly distributed racial and ethnic groups are within a school system. Measures like the Index of Dissimilarity, the Index of Exposure, and the Gini Index are examples of this approach. The difficulty is that this takes the racial composition of a school system as a given, looking only at how evenly this given population of racial groups is distributed among particular schools. School systems themselves, whether public or private, are frequently segregated, but this approach has no way to detect segregation at that level. If a school system is racially homogeneous compared to the broader community, it does not seem sensible to identify it as well integrated simply because it distributes its racial homogeneity evenly.

For example, a school district that was 98 percent white would receive the highest possible score on the Index of Dissimilarity if every school within that district had a 98 percent white student body. This is not "integration" as we normally understand it. The school district may not have done anything to deliberately segregate students, but it certainly cannot be reasonably described as integrated—especially if the 98 percent white school district were in the same metropolitan area as an adjoining school district that was 98 percent minority. The Gini Index is a variant of the same method.

The Index of Exposure measures the percentage of one racial group in the same school as the average member of another group. In the hypothetical district described above, the average white student is in a school with 2 percent nonwhite students, producing a very low score on the Index of Exposure. But the average nonwhite student is in school with 98 percent white students, producing a very high score on the Index of Exposure. That is, the Index of Exposure would tell us that our hypothetical district was very well integrated for nonwhite students but horribly integrated for white students. So the Index of Exposure does not give us a straight answer on whether the district is or is not well integrated, since the score depends on which group is the focus of our analysis.[10]

These approaches to measuring integration have been used by a number of researchers to assess levels of integration in public and private schools, including several of the landmark studies on this question. In the early 1980s James Coleman of the University of Chicago and his colleagues employed a measure similar to the Index of Exposure to determine whether public or private schools were better racially integrated. Their conclusion was that private schools were better integrated because their distribution of racial groups was more even than that of public schools.[11] Similarly, in 1984 Robert Crain of Stanford University employed the Index of Exposure in a comparison of Catholic and public schools in Cleveland and Chicago; he concluded that Catholic high schools were better racially integrated than their public school counterparts.[12] More recent research has also used this approach. Critics of these studies have responded that because private schools have a lower percentage of minority students, on average, than do public schools, they should not be described as contributing to integration.[13] These critics have a point: private schools may have a more even distribution of minorities, but if they have a general lack of minority students that could make them relatively racially homogenous, not integrated.

The third error is adopting the racial distribution in regular public schools as the normative standard to which schools of choice should be compared. For example, Casey Cobb and Gene Glass of Arizona State University observed the racial composition of a group of charter schools in Arizona as well as the racial composition in nearby traditional public schools. Cobb and Glass labeled charter schools as segregated if they deviated by too much from the racial composition of the nearby traditional public school: "Judgments were made as to the presence and degree of ethnic separation primarily on the basis of the magnitude of difference in the proportion of White students enrolled [in charters and nearby traditional public schools]. Typically, occurrences of ethnic separation were documented in instances where the magnitude of difference was 15 percent or greater."[14]

In this analysis, the standard against which charter schools were being judged was the proportion of minority students in the closest public school. But what if the charter schools were better integrated than the public schools? How could the study ever discover this, since it considered any difference between the racial compositions of public schools and charter schools as being by definition proof that the charter schools were more segregated? The public schools were adopted as the ideal, and to the extent that charters deviated from this ideal they were labeled as segregated. This comparison is clearly not appropriate. We must have an objective standard to which both public schools and schools of choice can be compared. Reanalysis of the Cobb and Glass data using an objective standard shows that the charter schools were actually better integrated.[15]

A study of charter schools in California by Amy Stuart Wells of the University of California at Los Angeles makes a similar error. Wells compared the racial composition of seventeen charter schools to the racial composition of the school districts in which they were located. She found that "in ten of the seventeen schools . . . at least one racial or ethnic group was over- or underrepresented by 15 percent or more in comparison to their district's racial make up."[16] But why are the school districts the appropriate basis for comparison? If the districts themselves were more racially segregated than the charter schools, then racial groups would by definition be "over- or underrepresented" in charter schools as compared to the districts.

In many metropolitan areas, school districts are racially homogenous because of where the boundaries are drawn or how people have moved. Given how common the racial homogeneity of public school districts is, those districts are not an appropriate standard for judging levels of integration in schools. Adopting such a standard and working to achieve it would only reproduce and reinforce the high levels of racial segregation that already exist in school districts.

Wells also does not examine whether the charter schools are any better or worse at reflecting the racial composition of their school districts than are the regular public schools in those districts. In fact, she acknowledges that "having student populations that are less diverse racially/ethnically than the surrounding district student population is not unique to charters. In many, but not all, of the school districts studied this was the norm for public schools." Nevertheless, she criticizes integration levels in charter schools even if they are doing a better job at integration than the traditional public schools.[17]

The fourth error that is common in studies of the relationship between parental choice and integration is comparing the demographic characteristics of the families that participate in choice programs to the demographic characteristics of eligible families that do not participate. If "choosers" (those who select their schools through choice programs) appear to be more advantaged or are more likely to be white than nonchoosers, some studies conclude from this that choice exacerbates segregation. But the level of integration produced by school choice is an outcome arising from the introduction of choice into the status quo, not just a description of the choosers. The important question is not whether choosers are different from nonchoosers. The important question is whether offering choices produces more integration of students.

This point can best be illustrated by considering choice and integration in another policy realm: housing. Imagine a program where low-income families are offered housing vouchers to subsidize rent payments in the housing that those families choose. If we observed that the participants in this program were more likely to be white and otherwise advantaged than nonparticipants who were also eligible to participate, should we conclude that the housing voucher program contributes to housing segregation? No. We would look instead at how housing patterns changed as a result of the housing voucher program. If choosers differ from eligible nonchoosers, this does not tell us anything about the relationship between choice and integration.

Comparing the characteristics of choosers to nonchoosers is a very common approach in academic research. In a widely cited study published by the Economic Policy Institute, J. Douglas Willms and Frank Echols use this approach to examine the effect of choice on integration in Scotland. They find that "parents who exercise their right to choose a school other than the designated school tended to be more highly educated and have more prestigious occupations than those who did not." They also find that parents tend to choose schools whose students have a higher average socioeconomic status. From these findings they conclude that "parental choice will result in increased segregation."[18] But they do not examine whether schools have become more or less homogeneous in their make-up as a result of the choice program, so they do not actually provide any evidence on whether choice increases, decreases, or has no effect on school segregation. Similarly, Jeffrey Henig of George Washington University criticized a public-school choice program on grounds that "while many minorities participated, their rate of participation was not as great as that of whites."[19] However, a reanalysis of the data by Jay Greene of the Manhattan Institute shows that the program actually produced more integrated schools—the white parents whose greater participation rates Henig found so troubling were using the program to choose magnet schools located in heavily minority areas, ultimately resulting in greater racial mixing of students.[20]

Adequate Measures of Integration

What we mean by "integration" is the mixing of white and nonwhite students in schools as best as can be done given the number of white and nonwhite residents in the broader community. An appropriate measure of integration would compare the racial composition of schools, or of each school in a school system, to the racial composition of the broader community from which students could reasonably be transported to the school. The more closely schools approximate the racial composition of the broader community, the better integrated they are. The "broader community" should not be defined in terms of political boundaries such as school district or city lines, because these boundaries may themselves reflect or encourage racial segregation. Instead, for most urban schools the appropriate broader community to examine is the whole metropolitan area in which the schools are located. And since the primary type of segregation with which we are concerned is white/nonwhite segregation, in measuring how well urban schools approximate the racial composition of the metropolitan area we should focus on the extent to which the proportion of nonwhite students in each school resembles the nonwhite proportion in the metropolitan area.

Ideally, an appropriate measure of integration would look at the extent of racial mixing within schools, such as in classrooms and lunchrooms, and not just within the walls of school buildings. As considerable research has demonstrated, students are often resegregated within schools by being assigned to different classes, tracking, or other forms of separation.[21] It is not uncommon to find public schools that have complied with desegregation requirements by housing predominately white magnet programs inside predominantly minority schools. Those students may be integrated in the eyes of the courts or the school systems, but when students experience racial mixing primarily as something that happens when they walk through the hallways, we should not accept this as "integration." If we look at the racial composition of students within classrooms or lunchrooms we have a clearer picture of the experiences of racial mixing that students actually have.

A less ideal but still acceptable measure of racial integration is to examine the absence of racial segregation. Schools that are overwhelmingly composed of white or nonwhite students cannot offer their students a racially mixed or integrated experience. And those schools are very unlikely to reflect the racial composition of the broader community very well because there are very few sizable metropolitan areas with overwhelmingly white or nonwhite residents. Schools could reasonably be described as segregated or racially homogenous if more than 90 percent of their student bodies were white or more than 90 percent were nonwhite.

These appropriate methods for assessing integration avoid the common errors described above. They do not assert that schools are more integrated by having more minority students or focus on how evenly students are distributed by race within school systems that may themselves be racially homogenous. They compare the integration in choice schools against an objective benchmark, such as the broader community, rather than against the racial composition of potentially segregated nearby public schools or school districts. And they do not compare the racial or other characteristics of choosers versus nonchoosers, instead focusing on whether students attend better integrated schools when they have greater choices. The appropriate approaches described here conform to our common understanding of integration as an experience of mixing white and nonwhite students in shared environments.

The Evidence

There are several studies that have examined the effect of private schools, vouchers, and other forms of school choice on integration. The bulk of those studies find that parental choice in education contributes to racial integration rather than promoting segregation. The few studies that find otherwise, although they use appropriate measurements of integration, suffer from other research design problems. The studies that have been conducted on vouchers have all found that vouchers improve integration. There has not been a single study of which the authors are aware showing that any U.S. voucher program has increased school segregation.

Unfortunately, studies of charter schools and other public-school choice programs have not been able to overcome the methodological difficulty arising from the regulations imposed on these programs. The existence or absence of racial segregation in heavily regulated school choice programs could be a function of the regulations under which they operate rather than of choice itself. For example, many public-school choice programs have limits on participation whose purpose is to ensure racial integration. This may produce integrated schools, but that sheds no light on how school choice would affect integration in the absence of these regulatory controls. Conversely, many charter schools are created for the purpose of targeting students from at-risk or other disadvantaged populations.[22] This produces overwhelmingly minority student bodies, but this is the result of regulatory design rather than parental choice.

Studies of Existing Levels of Integration in Private Schools

In one study, Greene (then of the University of Texas at Austin) analyzed the racial composition of a national sample of public-school and private-school classrooms. In 1992 the National Education Longitudinal Study (NELS) surveyed a national sample of twelfth graders in public and private schools, as well as their teachers. NELS asked the teachers how many total students and how many minority students (defined as Asian, black, or Hispanic) they had in their classes. This allowed Greene to calculate the percentage of minority students in each classroom. More than half of public-school students (54.5 percent) were in racially homogenous classrooms—that is, classrooms that were more than 90 percent white or more than 90 percent minority. Fewer private-school students, 41.1 percent, were in similarly segregated classrooms. Private-school students were also more likely to be in classrooms whose racial composition was similar to that of the national student population, which according to NELS was 25.6 percent minority.

More than a third (36.6 percent) of private-school students were in classes whose racial composition was between 15 percent and 35 percent minority, while only 18.3 percent of public school students were in similarly integrated classrooms.[23] It would have been better to compare the racial compositions of those classrooms to the racial compositions of the communities in which they were located, but NELS does not permit that type of analysis. Nevertheless, the lower level of segregation and the greater approximation of the national racial composition in private-school twelfth-grade classrooms suggest that when families choose private schools, their children are in classrooms that are better racially integrated.

In another study Greene and Nicole Mellow of the University of Texas at Austin observed a random sample of public-school and private-school lunchrooms in Austin and San Antonio. They recorded where students sat by race and then calculated how often public-school and private-school students sat in racially mixed groups during lunch.[24] They found that 63.5 percent of private-school students sat in a group where at least one student was of a different racial group, compared to 49.7 percent of public-school students. With statistical adjustments for the city, the existence of seating restrictions, the size of the school, and student grade level, the rate at which private-school students sat in racially mixed groups increased to 78.9 percent while the rate for public-school students dropped to 42.5 percent.[25] This study does have limitations. It reports observations from thirty-eight schools in two cities, and it is possible that these schools or these cities are somehow different from other places in the country.

Two other studies find that private schools tend to be more segregated than public schools. In one study, Sean Reardon of Pennsylvania State University and John Yun of the Harvard Civil Rights Project examine U.S. Department of Education data to compare the extent of racial segregation in the public and private sectors. They conclude "that segregation levels are quite high among private schools, particularly among Catholic and other religious private schools, where the levels of segregation are often equal or greater than levels of segregation among public schools."[26] While their analyses rely upon the Index of Exposure and Index of Dissimilarity, which are inadequate measures of integration, the data provided by the study's appendix tables make it possible to reproduce their analysis using an adequate measure. If we define segregated classrooms as those that are over 90 percent white or over 90 percent minority, their data tables indicate that nationwide 43.2 percent of public-school students attend schools that are segregated, compared to 58.6 percent of private-school students.[27]

There are two important reasons that might explain why this study found such a different result from that of Greene's analysis of the NELS data. First, Greene's analysis examines levels of integration in classrooms, while Reardon and Yun's examines only the student populations of whole schools. Racial resegregation within schools, which can arise from ability tracking and classroom assignments, is much more common in public schools than in private schools.[28] This means that public schools could appear to be less segregated when we examine them at the school level when they are actually much more segregated at the classroom level, which is the level that counts for student experiences. Second, Reardon and Yun combine student enrollments across all grades, while Greene compares twelfth graders to twelfth graders in each sector. Combining enrollments across all grades is inappropriate because private schools disproportionately educate students in the primary grades while public schools disproportionately educate students in the secondary grades. Secondary schools tend to be better integrated (in both the public and private sectors) simply because they draw students from larger geographic areas than primary schools. Lumping all student grades together makes private schools appear to be more segregated than they truly are because they are more likely to be primary rather than secondary schools.

The other study was conducted by Gary Ritter, Alison Rush, and Joel Rush of the University of Arkansas. It replicates the method used in Greene's study of twelfth graders but uses a more recent national sample of kindergarten students. It finds that 47.0 percent of public-school kindergarteners are in segregated classrooms (which they define as those that are over 90 percent white or over 90 percent minority), compared to 57.3 percent of private-school kindergarteners.[29] Unlike Reardon and Yun, Ritter and his colleagues focus on segregation in classrooms and compare students in the same grade level.

The problem here is the choice of kindergarten as the grade level to be examined. Not every school district offers universal, full-day public kindergarten. In those areas without full-day public kindergarten, wealthier families (which are disproportionately white) may be more likely to send their children to private schools with full-day programs and then send them to public schools starting in first grade. This artificial inflow of white families into private schools just for the one year of kindergarten may make private-school kindergarten classrooms more segregated. Kindergarten is also an inappropriate choice for comparison because the problem of resegregation from ability tracking, which is more common in public schools, has not arisen yet in kindergarten. Ritter and his colleagues have not published any subsequent studies finding higher levels of private-school segregation in higher grades.

Studies of the Effects of Vouchers on Integration

Studies on existing levels of integration in private schools are limited because they involve only the currently existing private-school system, not private schools as they might evolve under a system of expanded school choice. It is possible that beneficiaries of school choice programs might behave in a way that produces less integration than is produced by those who currently have access to private schools. On the other hand, private schools may well be less well integrated in the absence of vouchers because the financial barrier to attendance prevents a higher proportion of minority students from attending. If access were expanded by vouchers, private schools might be able to offer even better integrated experiences.

The two studies that have been conducted on vouchers and segregation show that vouchers have promoted racial integration because voucher recipients attend better integrated schools than do their public-school counterparts. In Milwaukee, Howard Fuller of Marquette University and Deborah Greiveldinger of the American Education Reform Council examined the extent of racial segregation at private schools attended by voucher students as compared to Milwaukee public schools. Defining racial segregation as attending a school that was more than 90 percent white or 90 percent non-white, they found that 54.4 percent of Milwaukee public-school students attended racially segregated schools, compared to 49.8 percent of students at private schools receiving voucher students. Among religiously affiliated private schools receiving voucher students, the proportion of students attending segregated schools dropped to 41.8 percent.[30]

The Cleveland study, conducted by Greene, found that nearly a fifth (19 percent) of voucher recipients attended private schools whose proportion of white students fell within 10 percent of the average proportion of white elementary students in metropolitan Cleveland. Only 5.2 percent of public-school students in metropolitan Cleveland were in similarly integrated schools. Meanwhile, more than three-fifths (60.7 percent) of public-school students attended schools that were more than 90 percent white or more than 90 percent minority, while only half of voucher recipients attend similarly segregated schools.[31] A family moving to the Cleveland area would have better odds of finding an integrated school experience for their children if they enrolled in the choice program than if they were randomly assigned to a public school.

Why Private Schooling and Vouchers Can Contribute to Integration

While these studies do not tell us why private schooling and vouchers promote integration, two explanations are consistent with the results. First, they may promote integration by reducing the connection between where students live and what schools they attend. Most public-school students are assigned to schools based on where they live. Housing patterns tend to be strongly segregated by both race and class, and public schools reproduce racial and class segregation in housing.

This pattern probably works both ways—that is, public-school attendance zones and district boundaries not only reproduce existing racially segregated housing patterns, but probably also encourage segregation in housing, thus producing a vicious circle. Families are averse to risking a substantial loss of value in their homes, which are usually their largest and most highly leveraged asset. Home values are affected by school quality. Thus many families find it prudent to move into a house on the "right side" of school district and attendance zone lines. What's more, attendance zones and district boundaries were historically drawn to intentionally separate racial and ethnic groups. The enormous impact of that segregation has not been fully eliminated.

Freely chosen private schools, however, are not constrained by housing patterns. Private schools can and typically do draw students from across neighborhood lines and public-school boundaries. Obviously there are some constraints arising from physical distance between home and school, such as the expense of transportation. But racially segregated neighborhoods are usually far more separated by psychological and political distance than by physical distance.

Families may be particularly willing to cross the invisible barriers between segregated neighborhoods when they are drawn to a private school for some common purpose. People from different neighborhoods may be drawn to the same private school because they share its educational philosophy or its emphasis on academic quality. They may also be drawn because of a shared desire for religious or cultural instruction. These various overarching goals can help private schools transcend racial segregation in housing.

Of course, many urban public school districts have at least some schools, such as magnet schools, whose composition is not determined by where students live. But those schools are only a small portion of all schools in the United States. In addition, even if public schools draw students from outside their attendance zones, they almost never draw students from across school district boundaries. For example, Cleveland has tried numerous magnet school, busing, and other programs where students attend schools outside their attendance zones. But all of these programs are seriously compromised in their ability to produce integrated schools because the school districts themselves are very racially homogenous, and students rarely cross district lines. There are simply too few white students in Cleveland to facilitate racial integration. Cleveland's private schools, however, do not face this constraint. Downtown schools can attract students not only from all over the downtown school district but also from the suburbs outside it to produce more racially heterogeneous schools. Being free from school district as well as attendance zone constraints is an important advantage for private schools in producing racially integrated schools.

The second reason that freely chosen private schools may promote integration is because families are more likely to trust those schools to manage integration successfully. Racial integration raises various concerns in some parents' minds, mostly concerning safety and discipline. Some of these concerns are reasonable and some are not, but regardless of their validity the existence of these anxieties is a serious barrier to racial integration. Parents who don't trust public schools to handle integration well can take steps to avoid integration, most importantly by moving into racially homogenous school districts. Milwaukee, for example, has attempted to produce integration through an interdistrict public-school choice program that allows parents to cross school district lines, but this has not prevented high levels of segregation in the city's schools. Just because parents are able to cross district lines doesn't mean they will.

Parents are more willing to cross attendance zone and district boundaries to send their children to racially mixed schools when they have confidence that the integration will be managed successfully. Private schools have achieved a higher level of parental confidence in this area. Various surveys have shown that parents, students, teachers, and administrators report much higher confidence in the safety and discipline offered by private schools. In particular, despite the greater level of racial diversity found in private-school classrooms, there are reports of significantly fewer racial conflicts in private schools.[32]

Once we have a proper approach to measuring integration, we see that the evidence clearly contradicts the Segregation Myth. When families are able to choose their private schools, either with their own funds or with vouchers, they are more likely to enroll their children in racially mixed schools. The proponents of the Segregation Myth are mistaken in believing that choice only allows families to realize their racist preferences. By removing barriers to racial integration in schools and by increasing parental confidence that integration will be successful, vouchers may actually hold the greatest promise for racial integration of schools.

Conclusion

What approach to education policy is vindicated by the evidence?

Myths dominate education policy. Over the past thirty years, our education system came to be based more and more heavily on beliefs about education that the evidence shows to be false. These myths have distorted virtually every area of education policy. Disentangling them from the education system and establishing policy based on facts supported by systematic evidence will be the work of at least a generation.

These myths fall into four major clusters. The first and most prominent cluster of myths claim that the performance of the education system is hindered by a lack of resources, and that policies seeking to improve education by redirecting more resources to the classroom (through class size reduction and personnel policies) are effective. The second cluster is a set of myths about the outcomes produced by the current system—about whether those outcomes have changed in the past thirty years, about how many students successfully complete K-12 education, and about how qualified those who graduate are. The third cluster of myths claims that policies seeking to hold schools and students accountable for their performance will be undermined by test manipulation and lack of resources, and to the extent that they aren't thus undermined will end up pushing too many kids out of school altogether. The fourth cluster claims that choice does not improve education. Private schools only appear to do better because they have tons of money and they "cream" in admissions; allowing students to leave public schools for private ones would only cripple the public schools; private schools are racially segregated and produce closed-mindedness and hate.

Surveying these myths, we can see a pattern emerging across most of them. One might call it a "meta-myth." It is the belief that education is different from other policy areas in that the types of incentives that normally shape human behavior do not shape educational behavior. In most areas of life, people respond to the presence of economic incentives and other, similar kinds of incentives. Businesses know that they will lose business if they treat customers badly, so they strive to treat customers well. Parents reward their children for good behavior and punish them for bad behavior, with the expectation that these rewards and punishments will create incentives for better behavior. But when it comes to education, people seem to believe that incentives just don't apply. For example, in any other area of life, if someone is never rewarded for doing a job well and never punished for doing it badly, we would naturally expect them to do it badly. Yet this is exactly the way we run our education system—schools, teachers, and administrators get almost no reward for good performance and no penalty for bad performance—and still we believe that any failures must be the result of inadequate resources. Even after doubling education spending without seeing any improvements, we continue to think that pouring in more money will produce better results. It would never occur to most people that schools will not make better use of the money they get until they have some incentive to do so. Reform policies that promise to harness incentives, such as accountability and school choice, are rejected as counterproductive.

It is not hard to see why people believe in this meta-myth. Because education involves the well-being of children, it naturally engages strong emotions. We want to believe that the classroom doesn't work the same way other human activities work. We want to believe that the people to whom we entrust the education of our children are not affected by incentives. We do know that teachers are generally good people who go into teaching because they want to help children, and from this fact we think it necessarily follows that teachers will teach just as well without having to be given incentives to do so. We want to believe that it would be wrong for incentives to affect the education system, that no one would stand for it if a teacher or a school acted in ways that were shaped by incentives. We think that it would be odd if we treated the education of children the same way we treated all the other departments of social activity.

People also believe in the meta-myth because powerful interest groups promote it. For example, teachers' unions promote the idea that teachers will teach just as well even if we don't hold them responsible for their job performance. They promote this myth because they have an incentive to do so—it serves the interests of their membership if teachers are not held accountable for the quality of their teaching. Ironically, people believe the meta-myth that incentives don't work in education largely because interest groups are driven by powerful incentives to promote the idea that incentives don't work in education.

The Evidence versus the Meta-Myth

Hard as it may be to accept, a full reading of the evidence supports the importance of incentives and refutes the meta-myth. The evidence shows that attempts to improve education by increasing resources have not worked, and provides some direct instances where incentives have strong effects on education. A very large increase in educational resources has not produced any improvement in educational outcomes. This failure cannot be blamed on disabled children, social problems, or other factors outside of schools' control. The evidence also shows a powerful effect from incentives—disability diagnoses are growing 62 percent faster in states whose funding systems create perverse incentives in favor of diagnosis than in states where such incentives are absent. Specific policies that seek to improve education by relying on increased resources are also not supported by the evidence. While there is some reason to believe that major reductions in class size can produce moderate improvements, there is also reason to doubt this conclusion, and even if the policy does work the expense required to implement it is grossly disproportionate to the benefits. It is not much of a vindication to say that a resource-based policy can work if you are willing to invest tons of resources for a small benefit; to be truly effective, a policy must produce benefits that justify its costs. Requiring teachers to be certified, and paying them more for accumulating certificates, advanced degrees, and years of experience, does not improve education outcomes. And here the evidence uncovers another way in which incentives shape the education field. People who go into teaching tend to have low academic abilities not because teachers are underpaid—they aren't—but because teacher pay does not reward academic aptitude.

We also find that the evidence shows accountability policies work. In states that have adopted accountability testing, students achieve a higher level of basic skills than those in other states. And these gains have not been bought at the expense of pushing more students out of school; the same percentage of students graduate as before. When schools and students know that there are immediate consequences for failure, they become less likely to fail. These policies are not defeated by problems like cheating and teaching to the test or a lack of necessary resources for compliance. The incentives imposed on the education system by accountability are effective.

The evidence also vindicates school choice. Students attending private schools with vouchers do better than comparable control groups who remain in public schools. This effect cannot be attributed to superior resources or creaming in admissions at private schools. Vouchers not only improve general education outcomes, they also improve the teaching of democratic values, racial integration, and services to disabled students. Most importantly for examining the role of incentives, public schools improve when exposed to higher levels of school choice, whether in the form of vouchers, charter schools, or smaller school districts (which create greater choice through residential mobility). When students can more easily leave a school, that school does a better job of serving those students. So incentives created by choice mechanisms are also effective.

The power of incentives to change behavior, and therefore to improve outcomes when properly harnessed and to harm outcomes when improperly aligned, is a pattern that emerges across the whole body of evidence in education. Adding resources without changing incentives doesn't work. Imposing accountability incentives through positive and negative consequences for performance works. Providing incentives through choice, ensuring that schools cannot take students for granted and forcing them to compete for students by offering more effective (and therefore more attractive) services, also works. Against the education myths that dominate current policy, the importance of incentives is a scientifically established fact.

Do Incentives Belong in Education?

It's natural for people to be unsettled when they first begin to perceive the falsehood of the meta-myth that education is somehow protected from the incentives that shape human behavior in every other area. Having been led to believe that it would be wrong for incentives to shape education, it's only to be expected that they would be surprised at the discovery that incentives do shape education. But that surprise is itself the product of a belief that there is something inherently wrong with responding to incentives. A little careful thought will show that no one could really sustain that view consistently.

Imagine for a moment that your income was set on a fixed track for life, regardless of anything else. You still have the same job, but your income is no longer related to your performance. No matter what you do or what else happens, you can't be fired, and you will make an amount of money indicated by a set formula. You can't make any more or any less.

Would you keep showing up for work?

Maybe so, but one thing's for sure: you wouldn't do your job *in the same way*.

You might still work hard. You might still come in to work every day you're supposed to, not taking any additional days off beyond what company policy allows. You might still accept orders from your superiors. You might still sometimes work late or go the extra mile on a task. It would take an extraordinary dedication to do this and not slip, but it is possible.

But even if you possessed this abnormally rigorous self-discipline, ask yourself: Would you still work every bit as hard as you did before, knowing that you could sometimes slack off a little more than you used to and still be in no danger of losing anything? Would you take on all the same tasks and make all the same choices in every situation? Would you work late and go the extra mile just as often, knowing that your additional efforts will earn you no additional reward? Would you still defer to your superiors when you disagree with them about the way the job should be done, knowing that you could do the job the way you think is right and suffer nothing for it?

Any honest person would have to admit that at least sometimes—at some point, in some situations—the absence of financial incentives would make a difference. In fact, most people will probably concede that their behavior would be vastly different if they didn't stand to gain or lose anything tangible by it. The more you reflect, the more you'll realize how deeply financial incentives (and other, similar kinds of incentives) are imbedded into just about every aspect of human life.

To admit this doesn't mean admitting that you're a bad person. It just means admitting that you're a person. Responding to incentives is as much a part of being human as responding to physical stimuli, or responding to love, or responding to injustice. It's simply how we're built. A person who didn't respond to incentives would have to be cared for by others, since he wouldn't provide for himself.

In fact, people accept the legitimacy of financial incentives so intuitively that they are often offended if these incentives aren't properly aligned with good behavior. Suppose one person in an office is working much harder than the rest, staying long hours, and putting in extra effort when everyone else is doing only the bare minimum. Money comes into the office budget at the end of each year to pay for employee bonuses, to be distributed at the boss's discretion. Suppose that every year the boss divides the bonus money evenly among all the employees, never choosing to reward the one good employee any more than the clock-watchers. An outside observer would be likely to think that justice was not being served, that fairness requires a financial reward for the exceptional employee's contribution. And the employee whose outstanding diligence is not being financially rewarded will probably come to feel over time that he was being cheated—that he's being a sucker, that the company owes him. If there were really something inherently unacceptable about responding to financial incentives, people would not have this kind of reaction—or if they did, it would be very wrong of them.

All this is as true in education as it is anywhere else. Teachers respond to the incentives created by the teacher pay system, which is structured to reward certain characteristics and not others. School administrators respond to the incentives created by accountability programs that hold them responsible for producing results, and by school choice programs that allow students to leave if they fail to produce results. Students respond to the incentives created by promotion exams that don't let them advance unless they obtain at least a basic level of proficiency. This doesn't mean that incentives are the only thing teachers, administrators, and students respond to. It doesn't even mean that incentives are necessarily the most important thing they respond to. But incentives are one important thing that they respond to, consistently and substantially. Education policies that fail to take account of incentives will be less effective than those that do, and education policies that create adverse incentives can even end up doing more harm than good.

No one claims that incentives are the whole story. All too often, people reject the idea that incentives matter by pointing to something else that matters. When told that the teacher pay system rewards the wrong attributes, many respond by saying, "people don't go into teaching for the money." When told that schools are more likely to diagnose children as disabled when such diagnoses will earn them larger budgets, many respond by saying, "but the people who run special education want what's best for kids." The unconscious assumption is that if something other than incentives makes a big difference in education, incentives therefore can't make a big difference.

Once this assumption is brought to the fore, it's easy to see that it's false. It could be true that incentives created by the teacher pay system have important effects on teachers' behavior, and on the composition of the teaching labor pool, even if it is also true that people are attracted to teaching for reasons other than money. Consider a bright young college graduate who loves kids and is attracted to teaching because of the nonmonetary rewards it offers. She'll have to make less total salary because teachers only work nine months of the year, but she might be willing to make that tradeoff. During her three months off she could make money doing other work, or enjoy some other activity. Unfortunately, because the teacher pay system doesn't reward academic ability while the pay system in just about every other professional field does, if she chooses teaching our bright graduate also has to take a huge additional pay cut relative to what she would make elsewhere, on top of the lower income that is inherent in the nine-month school year. That can't help but make academically gifted people less likely to become teachers. If, on the other hand, teacher pay rewarded academic ability, our bright young graduate would not have to take as big of a pay cut to become a teacher, and we would expect people like her to be more likely to go into education.

Similarly, it could be the case that incentives created by the special-education funding system have an effect on diagnosis rates even if it is also the case that the people making the diagnoses are sincerely trying to help the children under their care. The greater diagnosis rate might be produced by the decisions of school administrators rather than by special-education professionals—for example, low-performing students might be sent to be tested for learning disabilities over and over again until a positive diagnosis results. In such a case the person making the diagnosis isn't following budgetary incentives, but the administrators are. Or it might be the case that those making the diagnoses actually are following financial incentives, and are doing so precisely because they want to help the children. They know that putting a "learning disabled" label on low-performing kids will generate state subsidies that will get them extra help.

The meta-myth that incentives don't matter to education is so widespread and has corrupted so much of education policy that tracing the various things that could be done to correct it would be a whole other book in itself. But the first step is obvious—we cannot overcome the meta-myth, and the various particular myths about specific educational questions that support it and are in turn supported by it, until we first show it to be false. Rigorously testing our educational beliefs against a full reading of the systematic evidence is the only hope for dethroning the meta-myth. The work is difficult, and will be opposed by powerful groups that have interests in protecting the prevailing mythology. But science has triumphed over mythology against all hope in many other fields, and there is no reason it can't do so here as well.

Notes

Chapter 1

1. NEA website, www.nea.org/lac/fy04edfunding/ (accessed September 9, 2003).
2. Sam Dillon, "Cuts Put Schools and Law to the Test," *New York Times*, August 31, 2003.
3. "A Matter of Church and State," *New York Times*, February 20, 2002.
4. Richard Rothstein, "Raising School Standards and Cutting Budget: Huh?" *New York Times*, July 10, 2002.
5. Ulrich Boser, "Middle-class Blues," *U.S. News & World Report*, April 28, 2003.
6. Derrick Z. Jackson, "The Realities of School Vouchers," *Boston Globe*, July 10, 2002.
7. *Digest of Education Statistics 2002*, National Center for Education Statistics, U.S. Department of Education, 2003, Table 166.
8. Jay R. Campbell, Catherine M. Hombo, and John Mazzeo, "NAEP 1999, Trends in Academic Progress: Three Decades of Student Performance," National Center for Education Statistics, U.S. Department of Education, August 2000.
9. *Digest of Education Statistics 2002*, Table 103.
10. Eric A. Hanushek, "School Resources and Student Performance," in *Does Money Matter? The Effect of School Resources on Student Achievement and Adult Success*, Gary Burtless, ed., Brookings Institution, 1996, pp. 54, 69.
11. Larry V. Hedges and Rob Greenwald, "Have Times Changed? The Relation between School Resources and Student Performance," in *Does Money Matter? The Effect of School Resources on Student Achievement and Adult Success*, Gary Burtless, ed., Brookings Institution, 1996.

12. Richard Rothstein with Karen Hawley Miles, "Where's the Money Gone? Changes in the Level and Composition of Education Spending," Education Policy Institute, 1995.
13. Eric A. Hanushek, et al., *Making Schools Work*, Brookings Institution, 1994, p. 37.
14. David C. Berliner and Bruce J. Biddle, *The Manufactured Crisis: Myths, Fraud, and the Attack on America's Public Schools*, Perseus Books, 1995, pp. 81–86, 216–23.
15. Jay P. Greene and Greg Forster, "The Teachability Index: Can Disadvantaged Students Learn?" Manhattan Institute, September 2004, p. 25.
16. Greene and Forster, "Teachability Index," p. 23; for a detailed reply to Berliner and Biddle's claims about poverty, see p. 5.
17. Greene and Forster, "Teachability Index."
18. Hanushek, et al., *Making Schools Work*, pp. 32–34.
19. *Digest of Education Statistics 2002*, Table 77. Compensation does not include benefits, and data on changes in teachers' benefits are not easily available.
20. *Digest of Education Statistics 2002*, Table 65.
21. Hanushek, "School Resources and Student Performance," p. 68.
22. Hanushek, et al., *Making Schools Work*, p. 31.
23. See Jay P. Greene, "Books and Bombers," National Review Online, May 22, 2003.
24. Jonathan Kozol, *Savage Inequalities: Children in America's Schools*, HarperCollins, 1991, p. 86.
25. Leonor Valencia with Molly Selvin, "Struggling and Succeeding," *Los Angeles Times*, September 7, 2003.
26. Jeff Orlinsky, "Vouchers Just Harm Public Schools," *Los Angeles Times*, September 30, 2000.
27. Abigail Thernstrom and Stephan Thernstrom, *No Excuses: Closing the Racial Gap in Learning*, Simon & Schuster, 2003, p. 153; see also pp. 152–56.
28. Richard Rothstein, "Does Money Not Matter? The Data Suggest It Does," *New York Times*, January 17, 2003.

Chapter 2

1. *Digest of Education Statistics 2002*, National Center for Education Statistics, U.S. Department of Education, 2003, Table 52.

2. See Jay P. Greene and Greg Forster, "Effects of Funding Incentives on Special Education Enrollment," Manhattan Institute, December 2002, p. 7.
3. For the estimate of less than 20 percent see Eric A. Hanushek, "Spending on Schools," in Terry Moe, ed., *A Primer on America's Schools*, Hoover Institution, 2001, pp. 79–81. For the estimate of almost 40 percent, see Richard Rothstein with Karen Hawley Miles, "Where's the Money Gone? Changes in the Level and Composition of Education Spending," Education Policy Institute, 1995, p. 49.
4. Richard Rothstein, "The Myth of Public School Failure," *The American Prospect*, March 21, 1993.
5. David C. Berliner and Bruce J. Biddle, *The Manufactured Crisis: Myths, Fraud, and the Attack on America's Public Schools*, Perseus Books, 1995, pp. 81–82.
6. Sheldon Berman, Perry Davis, Ann Koufman-Frederick, and David Urion, "The Rising Costs of Special Education in Massachusetts: Causes and Effects," in Chester E. Finn, Jr., Andrew J. Rotherham, and Charles R. Hokanson, Jr., eds., *Rethinking Special Education for a New Century*, Thomas B. Fordham Foundation and Progressive Policy Institute, May 2001.
7. *Digest of Education Statistics 2002*, Table 52. Some have argued that the dramatic reduction in students classified as mentally retarded is actually a result of improved diagnosis of autism—that many autistic students who used to be misdiagnosed as mentally retarded are now correctly diagnosed as autistic. However, the decrease in mental retardation is much larger than the increase in autism. Furthermore, a study of medical records and parent surveys in California provides strong evidence that no such shift in diagnosis from mental retardation to autism has taken place (see Robert S. Byrd, "Report to the Legislature on the Principal Findings from The Epidemiology of Autism in California: A Comprehensive Pilot Study," M.I.N.D. Institute, University of California at Davis, October 17, 2002).
8. See G. Reid Lyon, et al., "Rethinking Learning Disabilities," in *Rethinking Special Education for a New Century*, Chester E. Finn, Andrew J. Rotherham, Charles R. Hokanson, Jr., eds., The Thomas B. Fordham Foundation and the Progressive Policy Institute, May 2001.
9. Table 20 from the Annual Social and Economic Supplements of the U.S. Census' Current Population Survey, available on the Census website at www.census.gov/hhes/poverty/histpov/hstpov20.html.

10. See Jay P. Greene and Greg Forster, "Effects of Funding Incentives on Special Education Enrollment," Manhattan Institute, December 2002, p. 7.
11. Table F-3 from the Annual Demographic Supplements of the U.S. Census' Current Population Survey, available on the Census website at www.census.gov/hhes/income/histinc/f03.html.
12. See Table 1 from the Annual Social and Economic Supplements of the U.S. Census' Current Population Survey, available on the Census website at www.census.gov/hhes/poverty/histpov/hstpov1.html.
13. Hillary Rodham Clinton, "Now Can We Talk about Health Care?" *New York Times*, April 18, 2004.
14. See, for example, Steven F. Hayward, *2004 Index of Leading Environmental Indicators*, Pacific Research Institute and American Enterprise Institute, 2004, pp. 36–37 and 41–42.
15. See Joetta L. Sack, "Sharp Rise Seen in Identification of Autistic Pupils," *Education Week*, October 20, 1999. One highly-publicized study claimed to show that "some, if not all, of the observed increase [in autism diagnoses] represents a true increase in cases of autism" (Byrd, "Epidemiology of Autism in California"). However, the study's methodology does not justify this conclusion (see Greg Forster, "From Greg's Desk," *The Education Gadfly*, October 30, 2002).
16. *Digest of Education Statistics 2002*, Table 52.
17. See Donald Deere and Wayne Strayer, "Putting Schools to the Test: School Accountability, Incentives, and Behavior," Texas A&M University, March 2001; Donald Deere and Wayne Strayer, "Closing the Gap: School Incentives and Minority Test Scores in Texas," Texas A&M University, September 2001; and Donald Deere and Wayne Strayer, "Competitive Incentives: School Accountability and Student Outcomes in Texas," Texas A&M University, April 2002.
18. See David N. Figlio and Lawrence S. Getzler, "Accountability, Ability, and Diability: Gaming the System?" University of Florida, April 2002.
19. See Brian A. Jacob, "Making the Grade: The Impact of Test-Based Accountability in Schools," John F. Kennedy School of Government, April 2002; and Brian A. Jacob, "Accountability, Incentives, and Behavior: The Impact of High-Stakes Testing in the Chicago Public Schools," National Bureau of Economic Research, Working Paper 8968, June 2002.
20. See Eric A. Hanushek and Margaret E. Raymond, "Improving Educational Quality: How Best to Evaluate Our Schools?" in *Education in*

the 21st Century: Meeting the Challenges of a Changing World, Yolanda Kodrzycki, ed., Federal Reserve Bank of Boston, 2003.

21. See Jay P. Greene and Greg Forster, "Effects of Funding Incentives on Special Education Enrollment," Manhattan Institute, December 2002.
22. See Greene and Forster, "Effects of Funding Incentives."
23. Richard Rothstein with Karen Hawley Miles, "Where's the Money Gone? Changes in the Level and Composition of Education Spending," Economic Policy Institute, 1995, p. 51.
24. Julia Silverman, "Special Ed Students Skew Test Results, Make Schools Look Worse," Associated Press, December 2, 2003.
25. "Leaving Some Children Behind," *New York Times*, January 27, 2004.
26. *Digest of Education Statistics 2002*, Table 103.
27. Data available on the NAEP website (nces.ed.gov/nationsreportcard). NAEP exclusions for special education students were not tracked with precision before the 1990s.

Chapter 3

1. Richard Rothstein, "Does Social Class Matter in School?" *New York Times*, November 10, 1999.
2. Michael Winerip, "A Pervasive Dismay on a Bush School Law," *New York Times*, March 19, 2003.
3. Michael Winerip, "Good Teachers + Small Classes = Quality Education," *New York Times*, May 26, 2004.
4. Geoff Rips, "Public Schools: An Ideal at Risk," *The American Prospect*, February 14, 2000.
5. Richard Cohen, "Houston's Disappearing Dropouts," *Washington Post*, September 4, 2003.
6. James J. Heckman and Amy L. Wax, "Home Alone," *Wall Street Journal*, January 23, 2004.
7. On the absence of a relationship between racial isolation and academic performance, see Abigail Thernstrom and Stephan Thernstrom, *No Excuses: Closing the Racial Gap in Learning*, Simon & Schuster, 2003, p. 169–88.
8. Richard Rothstein, "An Economic Recovery Will Tell in the Classroom," *New York Times*, December 12, 2001.
9. Jay P. Greene and Greg Forster, "The Teachability Index: Can Disadvantaged Students Learn?" Manhattan Institute, September 2004.

10. Margaret E. Raymond and Eric A. Hanushek, "High-Stakes Research," *Education Next*, Summer 2003.
11. See chapter 10 for a detailed critique of the Amrein and Berliner study.
12. Martin Carnoy and Susanna Loeb, "Does External Accountability Affect Student Outcomes? A Cross-State Analysis," *Educational Evaluation and Policy Analysis*, Winter 2002, p. 305–31.
13. Jay P. Greene and Marcus A. Winters, "Competition Passes the Test," *Education Next*, Summer 2004.
14. See William G. Howell and Paul E. Peterson, *The Education Gap*, Brookings Institution, 2002, p. 161; Jay P. Greene, "Vouchers in Charlotte," *Education Next*, Summer 2001; Jay P. Greene, Paul E. Peterson, and Jiangtao Du, "Effectiveness of School Choice: The Milwaukee Experiment," *Education and Urban Society*, February 1999; and Cecilia Elena Rouse, "Private School Vouchers and Student Achievement," *Quarterly Journal of Economics*, May 1998.
15. G. Reid Lyon, et al., "Rethinking Learning Disabilities," in *Rethinking Special Education for a New Century*, Chester E. Finn, Andrew J. Rotherham, Charles R. Hokanson, Jr., eds., The Thomas B. Fordham Foundation and the Progressive Policy Institute, May 2001.
16. Lawrence J. Schweinhart, et al., "Lifetime Effects: The High/Scope Perry Preschool Study through Age 40," High/Scope Press, forthcoming; see also Lawrence J. Schweinhart, "Benefits, Costs, and Explanation of the High/Scope Perry Preschool Program," paper presented at the Meeting of the Society for Research in Child Development, Tampa, Florida, April 26, 2003.
17. Rebecca Herman, et al., *An Educator's Guide to Schoolwide Reform*, American Institutes for Research, 1999.

Chapter 4

1. "Our Apologies," *Arkansas Democrat-Gazette*, September 8, 2003.
2. Tracy Dell'Angela, "Schools Think Small, Win Big," *Chicago Tribune*, September 14, 2003.
3. "Houston's School Dropout Debacle," *New York Times*, July 21, 2003.
4. Jonathan Kozol, *Savage Inequalities: Children in America's Schools*, HarperCollins, 1991, pp. 88–89; see also pp. 133–37, 143.

5. "An Urgent Crisis, An Effective, Affordable Remedy," People for the American Way, September 2002.
6. NEA website, www.nea.org/classsize (accessed October 8, 2003).
7. AFT website, www.aft.org/issues/class_size.html (accessed October 8, 2003).
8. Eric A. Hanushek, "Some Findings from an Independent Investigation of the Tennessee STAR Experiment and from Other Investigations of Class Size Effects," *Educational Evaluation and Policy Analysis*, Summer 1999.
9. Eric A. Hanushek, "The Failure of Input-based Schooling Policies," *Economic Journal*, February 2003.
10. Alan B. Krueger and Diane M. Whitmore, "The Effect of Attending a Small Class in the Early Grades on College Attendance Plans," distributed at a Project STAR press conference, April 10, 1999.
11. For a more complete discussion of these see Hanushek, "Some Findings."
12. *Digest of Education Statistics 2002*, National Center for Education Statistics, U.S. Department of Education, 2003, Table 65.
13. For test scores, see Jay R. Campbell, Catherine M. Hombo, and John Mazzeo, "NAEP 1999, Trends in Academic Progress: Three Decades of Student Performance," National Center for Education Statistics, U.S. Department of Education, August 2000; for graduation rates, see *Digest of Education Statistics 2002*, Table 103. See also chapters 1, 8, and 9 for more discussion.
14. *Digest of Education Statistics 2002*, Table 70.
15. Michael Winerip, "Miracles of Small Class Size Unfold Each Day in California," *New York Times*, October 29, 2003.
16. George W. Bohrnstedt and Brian M. Stecher, eds., *What We Have Learned about Class Size Reduction in California*, RAND Corporation, August 2002, pp. 13–14.
17. Bohrnstedt and Stecher, *What We Have Learned*, p. 17.
18. For an overview of this research, see Abigail Thernstrom and Stephan Thernstrom, *No Excuses: Closing the Racial Gap in Learning*, Simon & Schuster, 2003, pp. 189–210; see also Steven G. Rivkin, Eric A. Hanushek, and John F. Kain, "Teachers, Schools and Academic Achievement," unpublished paper, April 2000.
19. Caroline M. Hoxby, "The Cost of Accountability," in *School Accountability*, William M. Evers and Herbert J. Walberg, eds., Hoover Institution, 2002.

Chapter 5

1. Bruce Fuller, Marytza Gawlik, Emlei Kuboyama Gonzales, and Sandra Park, with Gordon Gibbings, "Charter Schools and Inequality: National Disparities in Funding, Teacher Quality, and Student Support," Working Paper Series 03-2, Policy Analysis for California Education, University of California, Berkeley and Davis, and Stanford University, April 2003.
2. Nick Anderson, "Emergency Licenses Likely to Hit Record," *New York Times*, June 22, 1997.
3. Caroline Hoxby and Andrew Leigh, "Pulled Away or Pushed Out? Explaining the Decline of Teacher Aptitude in the United States," unpublished paper, December 2003.
4. Steven G. Rivkin, Eric A. Hanushek, and John F. Kain, "Teachers, Schools and Academic Achievement," unpublished paper, April, 2000.
5. For an overview of this research, see Abigail Thernstrom and Stephan Thernstrom, *No Excuses: Closing the Racial Gap in Learning*, Simon & Schuster, 2003, pp. 189–210.
6. For an overview of some of this research, see Abigail Thernstrom and Stephan Thernstrom, *No Excuses*, pp. 192–94 and 206–7; see also *Teacher Certification Reconsidered: Stumbling for Quality*, Abell Foundation, 2001; Harold Wenglinsky, "How Teaching Matters: Bringing the Classroom Back into Discussions of Teacher Quality," Educational Testing Service, 2000; and David W. Grissmer, Ann Flanagan, Jennifer Kawata, and Stephanie Williamson, *Improving Student Achievement: What State NAEP Test Scores Tell Us*, RAND Corporation, 2000.
7. An extensive review of about 150 studies found that this entire body of research was highly unreliable due to a variety of methodological failures; see *Teacher Certification Reconsidered*. For a response to this review of the research, see Linda Darling-Hammond, "The Research and Rhetoric on Teacher Certification: A Response to 'Teacher Certification Reconsidered'," National Commission on Teaching and America's Future, October 15, 2001. Unfortunately, most of Darling-Hammond's responses to the original review are tangential and fail to address the review's main arguments. For a defense of the original review, see Kate Walsh, "Teacher Certification Reconsidered: Stumbling for Quality: A Rejoinder," Abell Foundation, November 2001.

8. Eric A. Hanushek, "School Resources and Student Performance," and Larry V. Hedges and Rob Greenwald, "Have Times Changed? The Relation between School Resources and Student Performance," in *Does Money Matter? The Effect of School Resources on Student Achievement and Adult Success*, Gary Burtless, ed., Brookings Institution, 1996, pp. 54, 59, and 85.
9. Walsh, *Teacher Certification Reconsidered*, pp. 7–8.
10. Julian R. Betts, Kim S. Rueben, and Anne Danenberg, *Equal Resources, Equal Outcomes? The Distribution of School Resources and Student Achievement in California*, Public Policy Institute of California, 2000, esp. p. 195.
11. Rivkin, Hanushek, and Kain, "Teachers, Schools and Academic Achievement," p. 32.
12. Wenglinsky, "How Teaching Matters"; and Grissmer, Flanagan, Kawata, and Williamson, *Improving Student Achievement.*
13. Dan Goldhaber, "The Mystery of Good Teaching," *Education Next*, Spring 2002.
14. Paul T. Decker, Daniel P. Mayer, and Steven Glazerman, "The Effects of Teach For America on Students: Findings from a National Evaluation," Mathematica Policy Research, 2004.
15. Eric A. Hanushek, et al., *Making Schools Work*, Brookings Institution, 1994, p. 80.
16. *Digest of Education Statistics 2002*, National Center for Education Statistics, U.S. Department of Education, 2003, Table 69.
17. *Digest of Education Statistics 2002*, Table 70.
18. Grissmer, Flanagan, Kawata, and Williamson, *Improving Student Achievement*, p. 105.
19. Goldhaber, "The Mystery of Good Teaching."
20. See Walsh, *Teacher Certification Reconsidered*, pp. 5–6.
21. Hanushek, "School Resources and Student Performance," pp. 54 and 59.
22. Eric A. Hanushek, John F. Kain, and Steven G. Rivkin, "The Revolving Door," *Education Next*, Winter 2004, p. 77.
23. Betts, Rueben, and Danenberg, *Equal Resources, Equal Outcomes?*, p. 195.
24. Wenglinsky, "How Teaching Matters."
25. Walsh, *Teacher Certification Reconsidered*, pp. 5–6.
26. Rivkin, Hanushek, and Kain, "Teachers, Schools and Academic Achievement," p. 3.

27. Grissmer, Flanagan, Kawata, and Williamson, *Improving Student Achievement.*
28. Susan Snyder, "Minority Students' Rights Violated, Complaint Says," *Philadelphia Inquirer*, March 9, 2004.
29. Dana Tofig, "Teacher Certification Changes Debated," *Atlanta Journal-Constitution*, January 8, 2004.
30. Maureen Feighan, "Demand to Prove Skills Enrages Veteran Teachers," *Detroit News*, January 12, 2004.
31. Linda Saslow, "L.I. Charter Schools Still Lagging in Tests," *New York Times*, November 30, 2003.
32. Michael Dobbs, " 'No Child' Law Leaves Schools' Old Ways Behind," *Washington Post*, April 22, 2004.
33. David C. Berliner and Bruce Biddle, *The Manufactured Crisis: Myths, Fraud, and the Attack on America's Public Schools*, Perseus Books, 1995, pp. 336–37.
34. Eric A. Hanushek, et al., *Making Schools Work*, Brookings Institution, 1994, p. 79.

Chapter 6

1. Michelle Quinn and Jennifer Lafleur, "Money Money Everywhere So Why Don't You Feel Rich?" *San Jose Mercury News*, August 15, 1999.
2. Ramon G. Mcleod, Torri Minton, and Jonathon Curiel, "Making More, Having Less; Bay Area Families Struggle to Earn Middle-Class Status," *San Francisco Chronicle*, April 13, 1999.
3. Charles Piller, "Silicon Valley Paying the Price for Its Own Success," *Los Angeles Times*, September 20, 1999.
4. Elizabeth Rhodes, "Seattle Faces Crisis of Affordable Housing," *Seattle Times*, June 13, 1999.
5. Lori Aratani, "Santa Clara Might Build Apartments for Teachers: Below-Market Rent Could Make Hiring Easier," *San Jose Mercury News*, October 29, 1999.
6. Tracey Kaplan and Griff Palmer, "Teacher Housing Crisis a Myth," *San Jose Mercury News*, February 2, 2004.
7. Richard Cohen, "Leave No Teacher Behind," *Washington Post*, November 18, 2003.
8. Bob Herbert, "Only the Minimum," *New York Times*, June 27, 2002.

9. Lisa Snell, "Study Shows Teacher Hiring Practices Need Work," *School Reform News*, October 2003.
10. David M. Herszenhorn, "First Lady Campaigns for Teachers and Trainees," *New York Times*, September 3, 2003.
11. *Digest of Education Statistics 2002*, National Center for Education Statistics, U.S. Department of Education, 2003, Table 77.
12. Michael Podgursky, "Fringe Benefits," *Education Next*, Summer 2003, p. 73.
13. David C. Berliner and Bruce J. Biddle, *The Manufactured Crisis: Myths, Fraud, and the Attack on America's Public Schools*, Perseus Books, 1995, p. 251–52.
14. *National Compensation Survey: Occupational Wages in the United States, July 2002*, Summary 03-02, Bureau of Labor Statistics, U.S. Department of Labor, June 2003, pp. 6–7.
15. Robert C. Herguth and Chris Fusco, "Union Leaders' Salaries," *Chicago Sun-Times*, March 7, 2004.
16. *Digest of Education Statistics 2002*, Tables 69 and 79.
17. *Digest of Education Statistics 2002*, Table 70.
18. Frederick M. Hess, "Teacher Quality, Teacher Pay," *Policy Review*, April-May 2004.
19. Sylvia A. Allegretto, Sean P. Corcoran, and Lawrence Mishel, *How Does Teacher Pay Compare?*, Economic Policy Institute, 2004, pp. 35–37.
20. Allegretto, Corcoran, and Mishel, *Teacher Pay*, p. 35.
21. Richard DiPatri, "Three Cheers for Teachers," *Florida Today*, May 4, 2004.
22. Terry M. Moe, "Reform Blockers," *Education Next*, Spring 2003, p. 60.
23. Podgursky, "Fringe Benefits," p. 71.
24. Berliner and Biddle, *Manufactured Crisis*, p. 103.
25. Richard Vedder, "Comparable Worth," *Education Next*, Summer 2003, p. 16.
26. *National Compensation Survey*, Summary 03-02, pp. 5–13.
27. Allegretto, Corcoran, and Mishel, *Teacher Pay*, p. 34.
28. Podgursky, "Fringe Benefits," p. 72.
29. Richard Rothstein, "The Myth of Public School Failure," *The American Prospect*, March 21, 1993.
30. Berliner and Biddle, *Manufactured Crisis*, p. 103.
31. Vedder, "Comparable Worth," p. 16.

32. Vedder, "Comparable Worth," p. 16.
33. Podgursky, "Fringe Benefits," p. 74.
34. Data for teachers taken from "Employee Benefits in State and Local Governments, 1998," Bulletin 2531, Bureau of Labor Statistics, U.S. Department of Labor, December 2000; data for private professional and technical employees taken from "National Compensation Survey: Employee Benefits in Private Industry in the United States, 2000," Bulletin 2555, Bureau of Labor Statistics, U.S. Department of Labor, January 2003.
35. Richard Rothstein, "The Myth of Public School Failure," *The American Prospect*, March 21, 1993.
36. Berliner and Biddle, *Manufactured Crisis*, p. 103.
37. Caroline Hoxby and Andrew Leigh, "Pulled Away or Pushed Out? Explaining the Decline of Teacher Aptitude in the United States," unpublished paper, December 2003.

Chapter 7

1. The National Commission on Excellence in Education, *A Nation At Risk: The Imperative for Education Reform*, United States Department of Education, 1983.
2. Anna Mulrine, "Can You Read This Story? Half of All U.S. Adults Can't," *Christian Science Monitor*, September 10, 1993.
3. Jay R. Campbell, Catherine M. Hombo, and John Mazzeo, "NAEP 1999, Trends in Academic Progress: Three Decades of Student Performance," National Center for Education Statistics, U.S. Department of Education, August 2000.
4. *Digest of Education Statistics 2002*, National Center for Education Statistics, 2003, Table 134.
5. *Digest of Education Statistics 2002*, National Center for Education Statistics, 2003, Table 137.
6. *Digest of Education Statistics 2002*, Table 103.
7. Diane Ravitch, *Left Back: A Century of Failed School Reforms*, Simon & Schuster, 2000, p. 13.
8. David C. Berliner and Bruce J. Biddle, *The Manufactured Crisis: Myths, Fraud, and the Attack on America's Public Schools*, Perseus Books, 1995.
9. Richard Rothstein, *The Way We Were? The Myths and Realities of America's Student Achievement*, Century Foundation, 1998, p. 114.

Chapter 8

1. United States Census, "CPS Annual Demographic Survey: March Supplement," Table PINC-03, available at ferret.bls.census.gov/macro/032000/perinc/new03_001.htm.
2. Marilyn M. McMillen and Phillip Kaufman, "Dropout Rates in the United States: 1994," National Center for Education Statistics, U.S. Department of Education, July 1996.
3. "Correctional Populations in the United States, 1997," Bureau of Justice Statistics, U.S. Department of Justice, November 2000.
4. Phillip Kaufman, Martha Naiom Alt, and Christopher D. Chapman, "Dropout Rates in the United States: 2000," U.S. Department of Education, National Center for Education Statistics, 2001.
5. Stephen Cameron and James Heckman, "The Nonequivalence of High School Equivalents," *Journal of Labor Economics*, 1993, pp. 1–47.
6. Richard J. Murnane, John B. Willett, and Kathryn Parker Boudett, "Do High School Dropouts Benefit from Obtaining a GED?" *Educational Evaluation and Policy Analysis*, Summer 1995, pp. 133–47.
7. For example, see Pam Easton, "Definition of Texas Dropouts Leads to Discrepancies," *Associated Press*, September 5, 2003.
8. Pete Baylsma and Lisa Ireland, "Graduation and Dropout Statistics for Washington's Counties, Districts, and Schools: School Year 2000–2001," Office of Superintendent of Public Instruction, May 2002.
9. Jay P. Greene and Greg Forster, "High School Graduation and College Readiness Rates in the United States," Manhattan Institute, September 2003.
10. Jay P. Greene and Marcus A. Winters "Public School Graduation Rates in the United States" Manhattan Institute, November 2002.
11. Greene and Forster, "Graduation and College Readiness Rates."
12. Diana Jean Schemo, "Questions on Data Cloud Luster of Houston Schools" *New York Times*, July 11, 2003.
13. Texas Education Agency website, www.tea.state.tx.us/perfreport/aeis/hist/state.html (accessed October 16, 2003).
14. Greene and Forster, "Graduation and College Readiness Rates."
15. Greene and Forster, "Graduation and College Readiness Rates."
16. "Quality Counts 2004," *Education Week*, January 8, 2004.
17. The Education Trust, "Telling the Whole Truth (or Not) about High School Graduation," December 2003.

18. *Digest of Education Statistics 2002*, National Center for Education Statistics, U.S. Department of Education, 2003, Table 103.
19. Jay P. Greene and Marcus A. Winters, "The Effect of Residential School Choice on Public High School Graduation Rates," Manhattan Institute, April 2005.
20. Jay P. Greene, "Graduation Rates for Choice and Public School Students in Milwaukee," School Choice Wisconsin, September 28, 2004.

Chapter 9

1. United States Census, "CPS Annual Demographic Survey: March Supplement," Table PINC-03; available at ferret.bls.census.gov/macro/032000/perinc/new03_001.htm.
2. Calculated using numbers provided in, Jay P. Greene and Greg Forster, "Public High School Graduation and College Readiness Rates in the United States" Manhattan Institute, September 2003.
3. NAACP, "Call for Action in Education," NAACP Education Department, May 2003.
4. "The New Luxury Item: College," *Chicago Tribune*, June 22, 2002.
5. "Universities in Decline," *New York Times*, August 26, 2003.
6. Advisory Committee on Student Financial Assistance, "Empty Promises: The Myth of College Access in America," June 2002.
7. Charmaine Llagas, "Status and Trends in the Education of Hispanics," National Center for Education Statistics, U.S. Department of Education, April 2003, Supplemental Table 1.4c.
8. Lutz Berkner and Lisa Chavez, "Access to Postsecondary Education for the 1992 High School Graduates," National Center for Education Statistics, October, 1997.
9. Jay P. Greene and Greg Forster, "Public High School Graduation and College Readiness Rates in the United States," Manhattan Institute, September 2003.
10. Data taken from the NAEP High School Transcript Study, 1998, available from the National Center for Education Statistics.
11. Laura J. Horn, Xianglei Chen, and Chris Chapman, "Getting Ready to Pay for College: What Students and Their Parents Know about the Cost of College Tuition and What They Are Doing to Find Out,"

National Center for Education Statistics, U.S. Department of Education, September 2003.

12. See "College Costs Increase but Record Amount of Financial Aid Is Available to Students," College Board, October 23, 2001.

Chapter 10

1. "School Miracles vs. Reality," *Los Angeles Times*, August 16, 2003.
2. Gregory J. Cizek, "Cheating to the Test," *Education Matters*, Spring 2001.
3. Barbara Kantrowitz and Daniel McGinn, "When Teachers Are Cheaters," *Newsweek*, June 19, 2000.
4. Paul Wellstone, "Bush Plan May Set Students Up for Failure," *Los Angeles Times*, February 6, 2001.
5. Kantrowitz and McGinn, "When Teachers Are Cheaters."
6. Connie Langland, "Writer: Tests No Help to Learning," *Philadelphia Inquirer*, May 29, 2003.
7. Audrey L. Amrein and David C. Berliner, "High-Stakes Testing, Uncertainty, and Student Learning," *Education Policy Analysis Archives*, March 28, 2002.
8. Greg Winter, "Make or Break Exams Grow, but Big Study Doubts Value," *New York Times*, December 28, 2002.
9. Margaret E. Raymond and Eric A. Hanushek, "High-Stakes Research," *Education Next*, Summer 2003.
10. Raymond and Hanushek, "High-Stakes Research," p. 51.
11. Raymond and Hanushek, "High-Stakes Research," p. 53.
12. Jay P. Greene, Marcus A. Winters, and Greg Forster, "Testing High Stakes Tests: Can We Believe the Results of Accountability Tests?" *Teachers College Record*, Volume 106, number 6, June 2004, pp. 1124–1144.
13. Deborah Meier, *Will Standards Save Public Education?* Beacon Press, 2000, p. 85.
14. Alfie Kohn, *The Schools Our Children Deserve*, Houghton Mifflin Company, New York, p. 75.
15. See Holly Schmidt-Davis, Harold Kay, and Becky J. Hayward, "Basic Skills and Labor Market Success: Findings from the VR Longitudinal Study," U.S. Department of Education, 2001.

Chapter 11

1. Craig R. Barrett, "Education SOS," *Wall Street Journal*, March 4, 2004.
2. Marcus A. Winters and Greg Forster, "Meaningless Diplomas Hurt Hispanic Students," *Education Week*, January 21, 2004.
3. Robert L. Steinback, "The New College Try," *Miami Herald*, March 3, 2003.
4. Sonji Jacobs, "FCAT Protest Gains Steam in Broward," *Miami Herald*, May 16, 2003.
5. Tamar Lewin and Jennifer Medina, "To Cut Failure Rate, Schools Shed Students," *New York Times*, July 31, 2003.
6. Audrey L. Amrein and David C. Berliner, "High Stakes Testing, Uncertainty, and Student Learning," *Education Policy Analysis Archives*, March 28, 2002.
7. John Robert Warren and Krista N. Jenkins, "High School Exit Examinations and High School Dropout in Texas and Florida, 1971–2000," unpublished paper, 2003.
8. See Chandra Muller, "The Minimum Competency Exam Requirement, Teachers' and Students' Expectations and Academic Performance," *Social Psychology of Education*, 1998; John Robert Warren and Melanie R. Edwards, "High School Exit Examinations and High School Completion: Evidence from the Early 1990s," unpublished paper, December 2003; Brian A. Jacob, "Getting Tough? The Impact of High School Graduation Exams," *Educational Evaluation and Policy Analysis*, Summer 2001; and Chandra Muller and Kathryn S. Schiller, "Leveling the Playing Field? Students' Educational Attainment and States' Performance Testing," *Sociology of Education*, April 2000.
9. Sean F. Reardon and Claudia Galindo, "Do High-Stakes Tests Affect Students' Decisions to Drop Out of School? Evidence from NELS," presented at the Annual Meeting of the American Educational Research Association, April 2002.
10. Warren and Jenkins, "Exit Examinations and High School Dropout," p. 6.
11. Jay P. Greene and Marcus A. Winters, "Pushed Out or Pulled Up? Exit Exams and Dropout Rates in Public High Schools," Manhattan Institute Education Working Paper No. 5, May 2004.
12. Richard W. Cross, Theodor Rebarber, and Justin Torres, "Grading the Systems: The Guide to State Standards, Tests, and Accountability

Policies," Thomas B. Fordham Foundation and Accountability Works, January 2004.
13. Michael Cohen, Chester E. Finn, Jr., and Kati Haycock, "Creating a High School Diploma that Counts," *Education Week*, March 10, 2004.
14. Center on Education Policy, "State High School Exit Exams Put to the Test," August 2003.

Chapter 12

1. See Robert Dodge, "Federal No Child Rules Relaxed," *Dallas Morning News*, February 20, 2004; and Sam Dillon, "Utah House Rebukes Bush with Its Vote on School Law," *New York Times*, February 11, 2004.
2. Laura Scott, "Educated Rebellion; States Are Beginning to Resist Unfunded Mandate of No Child Left Behind," *Kansas City Star*, February 19, 2004.
3. William J. Mathis, "No Child Left Behind: Costs and Benefits," *Phi Delta Kappan*, May 2003.
4. James Peyser and Robert Costrell, "Exploring the Costs of Accountability," *Education Next*, Spring 2004.
5. Keith Gayler, Naomi Chudowsky, Nancy Kober, and Madlene Hamilton, "State High School Exit Exams Put to the Test," Center on Education Policy, August 2003.
6. Caroline M. Hoxby, "The Cost of Accountability," in *School Accountability*, William M. Evers and Herbert J. Walberg, eds., Hoover Institution, 2002.
7. Eric A. Hanushek and Margaret E. Raymond, "Lessons about the Design of State Accountability Systems," in *No Child Left Behind? The Politics and Practice of School Accountability*, Paul E. Peterson and Martin R. West, eds., Brookings Institution, 2003, p. 127–52.
8. Martin Carnoy and Susanna Loeb, "Does External Accountability Affect Student Outcomes? A Cross-State Analysis," *Education Evaluation and Policy Analysis*, Winter 2002.

Chapter 13

1. Tamar Lewin, "Chock Full of Choice," *New York Times*, June 29, 2002.

2. Justin Blum, "Voucher Plan Lacks Accountability," *Washington Post*, September 14, 2003.
3. Rebecca Winters, "Vouchers: More Heat Than Light," *Time*, October 9, 2000.
4. See Sarah Carr, "Voucher Debate Flares as Program Nears Its Limit," *Milwaukee Journal-Sentinel*, October 24, 2004.
5. Peter Beinart, "TRB from Washington," *New Republic*, July 29, 2002.
6. Ralph Neas, "Correspondence," *American Prospect*, August 12, 2002.
7. Brian P. Gill, P. Michael Timpane, Karen E. Ross, and Dominic J. Brewer, "Rhetoric versus Reality: What We Know and What We Need to Know about Vouchers and Charter Schools," Rand Corporation, 2001, pp. xiii, xiv.
8. Jay P. Greene, Paul E. Peterson, and Jiangtao Du, "School Choice in Milwaukee: A Randomized Experiment," in *Learning from School Choice*, eds. Paul E. Peterson and Bryan C. Hassel, Brookings Institution, 1998; see also Jay P. Greene, Paul E. Peterson, and Jiangtao Du, "Effectiveness of School Choice: The Milwaukee Experiment," *Education and Urban Society*, February 1999. The points described here as "percentile points" are actually normal curve equivalent points.
9. Cecilia Elena Rouse, "Private School Vouchers and Student Achievement," *Quarterly Journal of Economics*, May 1998. The points described here as "percentile points" are actually normal curve equivalent points.
10. Jay P. Greene, "Vouchers in Charlotte," *Education Next*, Summer 2001.
11. William G. Howell and Paul E. Peterson, *The Education Gap*, Brookings Institution, 2002.
12. Howell and Peterson, *Education Gap*.
13. Alan B. Krueger and Pei Zhu, "Another Look at the New York City School Voucher Experiment," Working Paper, March 2003.
14. Paul E. Peterson and William G. Howell, "The Latest Results from the New York City Voucher Experiment," *Education Next*, Spring 2004; for the table listing all Peterson and Howell's statistical models, see the unabridged version of the article, available at: www.educationnext.org/unabridged/20042/peterson.pdf.
15. John Barnard, Constantine E. Frangakis, Jennifer L. Hill, and Donald B. Rubin, "Principal Stratification Approach to Broken Randomized Experiments: A Case Study of School Choice Vouchers in New York City," *Journal of the American Statistical Association*, June 2003.

16. Howell and Peterson, *Education Gap*.
17. Common Core of Data, National Center for Education Statistics, U.S. Department of Education.
18. Howell and Peterson, *Education Gap*, pp. 91–92.

Chapter 14

1. Albert Shanker, "Private vs. Public Schools: What Education Gap?" *Washington Post*, February 2, 1992.
2. David Bernstein, "Tuition Tax Credits: Threat to Public Schools," *Washington Post*, January 2, 2000.
3. Kevin Smith and Kenneth Meier, *The Case against School Choice: Politics, Markets, and Fools*, M. E. Sharpe, 1995, pp. 65 and 124.
4. Marc Fisher, "Vouchers Don't Add Up to Real Choice," *Washington Post*, September 11, 2003.
5. "Public School Power," *Michigan Daily*, June 18, 2001.
6. Data collected from the NAEP website, nces.ed.gov/nationsreportcard/reading/results2003/natachieve-schooltype-gr8.asp.
7. Data collected from the NAEP website, nces.ed.gov/nationsreportcard/mathematics/results2003/natachieve-schooltype-gr8.asp.
8. Steven J. Ingels, et al., "Coming of Age in the 1990s: The Eighth-Grade Class of 1988 12 Years Later," Office of Educational Research and Improvement, U.S. Department of Education, March 2002.
9. *Digest of Education Statistics 2002*, National Center for Education Statistics, U.S. Department of Education, 2003, Table 61.
10. *Digest of Education Statistics 2002*, Table 166.
11. Stephen P. Broughman and Lenore A. Colaciello, "Private School Universe Survey: 1999–2000," National Center for Education Statistics, U.S. Department of Education, August 2001, Figure 2; and *Digest of Education Statistics 2002*, Table 61.
12. William G. Howell and Paul E. Peterson, *The Education Gap*, Brookings Institution, 2002, pp. 92–93.
13. Anthony S. Bryk, Valerie E. Lee, and Peter B. Holland, *Catholic School and the Common Good*, Harvard University Press, 1993, p. 128.
14. Howell and Peterson, *Education Gap*, pp. 67–76.
15. See Howell and Peterson, *Education Gap*, chapter 3, as well as Jay P. Greene, "Vouchers in Charlotte," *Education Matters*, Summer 2001.
16. Bryk, Lee, and Holland, *Catholic School*, p. 129.

17. Howell and Peterson, *Education Gap*, p. 83.
18. Quoted in Howell and Peterson, *Education Gap*, p. 83.
19. Jill DeVoe, Katharin Peter, Sally Ruddy, Amanda Miller, Mike Planty, Thomas Snyder, and Mike Rand, "Indicators of School Crime and Safety: 2003," National Center for Education Statistics, U.S. Department of Education, October 2003.
20. *Digest of Education Statistics 2002*, Table 39.
21. Bryk, Lee, and Holland, *Catholic School*, p. 129.
22. *Digest of Education Statistics 2002*, Table 53.
23. Broughman and Colaciello, "Private School Universe Survey," Table 16; and *Digest of Education Statistics 2002*, Table 42.

Chapter 15

1. "Florida's School Voucher Scheme," *New York Times*, May 1, 1999.
2. "The Price of Vouchers," *Boston Globe*, June 28, 2002.
3. "The Trouble with Vouchers," *Boston Globe*, December 26, 2000.
4. Two of the voucher programs, in Colorado and Washington, D.C., have not even begun yet as of this writing. The McKay Scholarship Program in Florida targets special-needs students, making an analysis of its effects on public-school student achievement difficult. Cleveland's voucher program is relatively small. Programs in Pennsylvania, Florida, and Arizona that give tax credits or deductions for contributions to organizations that in turn provide private-school scholarships are too diffuse for their effects to be easily studied. The voucher program in Milwaukee, the A-Plus voucher program in Florida, and the "tuitioning" vouchers in Maine and Vermont are large enough and sufficiently long-running to warrant serious study of their effects on public school student achievement.
5. See for example Patrick J. McEwan, "Private and Public Schooling in the Southern Cone: A Comparative Analysis of Argentina and Chile," Occasional Paper No. 11, National Center for the Study of Privatization in Education, December 2000; Fedrick Bergstrom and F. Mikael Sandstrom, "School Choice Works! The Case of Sweden," The Milton and Rose D. Friedman Foundation, January 2003; and Edward B. Fiske and Helen F. Ladd, *When School Compete: A Cautionary Tale*, Brookings Institution, 2000.
6. See Charles Glenn, *The Myth of the Common School*, University of Massachusetts Press, 1988.

7. Jay P. Greene and Marcus A. Winters, "Competition Passes the Test," *Education Next*, Summer 2004.
8. Martin Carnoy, "School Vouchers: Examining the Evidence," Economic Policy Institute, 2001, p. 25.
9. Carnoy, "Examining the Evidence," p. 52.
10. Rajashri Chakrabarti, "Impact of Voucher Design on Public School Performance: Evidence from Florida and Milwaukee Voucher Programs," unpublished manuscript, October 2003. See also Rajashri Chakrabarti , "Closing the Gap," *Education Next*, Summer 2004.
11. Caroline Hoxby, "Rising Tide," *Education Next*, Winter 2001.
12. Jay P. Greene and Greg Forster, "Rising to the Challenge: The Effect of School Choice on Public Schools in Milwaukee and San Antonio," Manhattan Institute, October 2002.
13. Christopher Hammons, "The Effects of Town Tuitioning in Maine and Vermont," *School Choice Issues in Depth*, January 2002, p. 2.
14. Jay P. Greene, Greg Forster, and Marcus A. Winters, "Apples to Apples: An Evaluation of Charter Schools Serving General Student Populations," Manhattan Institute, July 2003.
15. Hoxby, "Rising Tide."
16. Jay P. Greene and Greg Forster, "Rising to the Challenge: The Effect of School Choice on Public Schools in Milwaukee and San Antonio," Manhattan Institute, October 2002.
17. Clive R. Belfield and Henry M. Levin, "The Effects of Competition on Educational Outcomes: A Review of U.S. Evidence," National Center for the Study of Privatization in Education, March 2002, p. 2.
18. Belfield and Levin, "Review of U.S. Evidence," p. 11.
19. Belfield and Levin, "Review of U.S. Evidence," p. 39.

Chapter 16

1. Sandra Feldman, "No Bargain," May 1998. AFT website.
2. Barbara Miner, "No One Really Knows How Children in Milwaukee's Voucher Schools Are Doing: Who's Vouching for Vouchers?" *Nation*, June 5, 2000.
3. People for the American Way/Disability Rights Education and Defense Fund, "Jeopardizing a Legacy," March 6, 2003, p. 1.
4. Linda Perlstein, "Parents See No Humor in Skit on Special-Ed," *Washington Post*, March 31, 2004.

5. See Kenneth Lovett and Carl Campanile, "Staggering Fail Rate in Special Ed," *New York Post*, May 19, 2004.
6. For special-education spending see Exhibit II-6 of Thomas Parrish, et al., "State Special Education Finance Systems, 1999–2000, Part II: Special Education Revenues and Expenditures," Center for Special Education Finance, March 2004; regular-spending figure is authors' calculation based on data from Table 161 of the *Digest of Education Statistics 2002*, National Center for Education Statistics, U.S. Department of Education, 2003; and from "Statistics in Brief: Revenues and Expenditures for Public Elementary and Secondary Education: School Year 2000–2001," National Center for Education Statistics, U.S. Department of Education, 2003.
7. Jay P. Greene and Greg Forster, "Vouchers for Special Education Students: An Evaluation of Florida's McKay Scholarship Program," Manhattan Institute, June 2003.
8. As quoted in Howard Fuller and Kaleem Caire, "Lies and Distortions: The Campaign against School Vouchers," Institution for the Transformation of Learning, Marquette University, April 2001, p. 10.
9. Wisconsin Legislative Audit Bureau, "Milwaukee Parental Choice Program," Report 00-2, February 2000.
10. See Howard Fuller and George Mitchell, "Selective Admission Practices? Comparing the Milwaukee Public Schools and the Milwaukee Parental Choice Program," Current Education Issues, 2000–2001, January 2000, pp. 9–10.
11. PFAW/DREDF, "Jeopardizing a Legacy," p. 6.
12. Greene and Forster, "Vouchers for Special Education," p. 10 and Table 36; calculations for removing gifted students from the "exceptional" category are based on Florida Department of Education data available at www.firn.edu/doe/eias/flmove/florida.htm.
13. Calculations based on Florida Department of Education data available at www.miedresearchoffice.org/mckayscholarship.htm; figures for voucher students are for 2002–2003; figures for Florida student population are for Fall 2001.
14. Richard Rothstein, "Voucher Program Gets Failing Grade in Special Ed," *New York Times*, June 19, 2002.
15. See Greene and Forster, "Vouchers for Special Education," Table 38; and U.S. Census income data available at factfinder.census.gov/servlet/BasicFactsTable?_lang=en&_vt_name=DEC_2000_SF3_U_DP3&_geo_id=04000US12.

Chapter 17

1. Richard W. Riley, "What Really Matters in American Education," white paper prepared for Riley's speech at the National Press Club, September 23, 1997; available at www.ed.gov/Speeches/09-1997/matters.pdf.
2. "The Wrong Ruling on Vouchers," *New York Times*, June 28, 2002.
3. See *EIA Communiqué*, Educational Intelligence Agency, May 10, 1999.
4. Dorothy Shipps, "The Business Model Won't Fix Schools," *Los Angeles Times*, September 3, 2000.
5. Benjamin R. Barber, *Strong Democracy: Participatory Politics for a New Age*, University of California Press, 1984, p. 296.
6. Benjamin R. Barber, "Education for Democracy," *The Good Society*, Spring 1997, p. 1.
7. John L. Sullivan, James Pierson, and George E. Marcus, *Political Tolerance and American Democracy,* University of Chicago Press, 1982.
8. Terry M. Moe, "The Two Democratic Purposes of Education," in *Rediscovering the Democratic Purposes of Education*, ed. L. M. McDonnell, P. M. Timpane, and R. Benjamin, University Press of Kansas, 2000, p. 141.
9. Charles Leslie Glenn, Jr., *The Myth of the Common School*, University of Massachusetts Press, 1988, p. 285.
10. Patrick J. Wolf, "School Choice and Civic Values in the U.S.: An Evidentiary Review," presented at the 2002 American Political Science Association meeting in Boston.
11. David E. Campbell, "The Civic Side of School Reform: How Do School Vouchers Affect Civic Education?" Program in American Democracy Working Paper 4, Notre Dame University, May 24, 2002.
12. Jay P. Greene, Joseph Giammo, and Nicole Mellow, "The Effect of Private Education on Political Participation, Social Capital and Tolerance: An Examination of the Latino National Political Survey," *Georgetown Public Policy Review*, Fall 1999.
13. Jay P. Greene, Nicole Mellow, and Joseph Giammo, "Private Schools and the Public Good: The Effect of Private Education on Political Participation and Tolerance in the Texas Poll," *Catholic Education: A Journal of Inquiry and Peace*, June 1999.
14. Christian Smith and David Sikkink, "Is Private School Privatizing?" *First Things*, April 1999.

15. See www.unc.edu/~cssmith/firstthings/.
16. Jay P. Greene, "Civic Values in Public and Private Schools," in Paul E. Peterson and Bryan C. Hassel, eds., *Learning from School Choice Washington*, Brookings Institution, 1998.
17. Kenneth R. Godwin and Frank R. Kemerer, *School Choice Tradeoffs: Liberty, Equity, and Diversity*, University of Texas Press, 2002.

Chapter 18

1. AFT website, www.aft.org/research/vouchers/research/myths/myths .htm#d (accessed April 12, 2004).
2. Michael Hout, "Houses Divided," *Washington Post*, February 15, 2004.
3. David A. Bositis, "School Vouchers along the Color Line," *New York Times*, August 15, 2001.
4. Cited in Evan Thomas and Lynette Clemetson, "A New War over Vouchers," *Newsweek*, November 22, 1999.
5. Quoted in Zina Vishnevsky, "Education Needed to Thrive, Urban League President Says," *Cleveland Plain Dealer*, March 16, 2002.
6. Jesse Jackson, Jr., "Vouchers: Illegitimate Cure for Legitimate Concerns," *Madison Times*, July 5, 2002.
7. David Berliner, Walter Farrell, Luis Huerta, and Roslyn Mickelson, "Will Vouchers Work for Low-Income Students?" Education Policy Project, CERAI-00-37, University of Wisconsin-Milwaukee, December 19, 2000.
8. NEA website, www.nea.org/vouchers/ (accessed April 12, 2004).
9. AFT website, www.aft.org/research/vouchers/research/myths/myths .htm#d (accessed April 12, 2004).
10. There is also a "standardized" Index of Exposure that produces a single answer to the question of whether a school is segregated, but it does so by taking the racial composition of the district as a given, thereby introducing the same problems as are faced by the Index of Dissimilarity.
11. James Coleman with Thomas Hoffer and Sally Kilgore, *High School Achievement*, Basic Books, 1982.
12. Robert Crain, *Private Schools and Black-White Segregation: Evidence from Two Big Cities*, Institute for Research on Educational Finance and Government, Stanford University, Eric document #259 430, 1984.

13. See Karl Taeuber and David James, "Racial Segregation among Public and Private Schools," *Sociology of Education,* April/July, p. 133–43, 1982; and E. Page and T. Keith, "Effects of U.S. Private Schools: A Technical Analysis of Two Recent Claims." *Educational Researcher,* August 10, pp. 7–17, 1981.
14. Casey Cobb and Gene Glass, "Ethnic Segregation in Arizona Charter Schools," *Education Policy Analysis Archives,* January 14, 1999.
15. If the standard of comparison for Phoenix charter schools and nearby public schools is the racial composition of metropolitan Phoenix, we see that the charter schools are slightly better integrated than are their public-school neighbors. According to the 1990 U.S. Census, the school-aged population of metropolitan Phoenix is 67.4 percent non-Hispanic white. The average Phoenix charter school examined by Cobb and Glass deviates from this proportion of whites by 21.7 percentage points. The average nearby public school examined by Cobb and Glass deviates by 26.5 percentage points.
16. Amy Stuart Wells, "Beyond the Rhetoric of Charter School Reform: A Study of Ten California School Districts," UCLA Charter School Study, 1999, p. 48.
17. Wells, "Beyond the Rhetoric," p. 48.
18. J. Douglas Willms and Frank Echols, "The Scottish Experience of Parental School Choice," in *School Choice: Examining the Evidence,* Edith Rasell and Richard Rothstein, eds., Economic Policy Institute, 1993, pp. 63–65; Willms and Echols look at segregation by class, not race. But many people, probably correctly, believe that the results on class could apply to race as well because the two are strongly correlated.
19. Jeffrey Henig, "The Local Dynamics of Choice," in *Who Chooses? Who Loses?,* Bruce Fuller and Richard Elmore, eds., Teachers College Press, 1996, p. 103.
20. See Jay P. Greene, "Choosing Integration," paper presented at the 2000 meeting of the American Political Science Association, pp. 12–13.
21. See for example John E. Chubb and Terry M. Moe, "Politics, Markets, and Equality in Schools," in *Reducing Poverty in America,* Michael R. Darby, ed., Sage Publication, 1996.
22. See Jay P. Greene, Greg Forster, and Marcus A. Winters, "Apples to Apples: An Evaluation of Charter Schools Serving General Student Populations," Manhattan Institute, July 2003.

23. Jay P. Greene, "Civic Values in Public and Private Schools," in *Learning from School Choice*, Paul Peterson and Bryan Hassel, eds., Brookings Institution, 1998.
24. A racially mixed group was defined as one in which any of the five seats immediately adjacent to each student was occupied by at least one student who was of a different racial group from the student being observed.
25. Jay P. Greene and Nicole Mellow, "Integration Where It Counts," *Texas Education Review*, Spring 2000.
26. Sean Reardon and John Yun, "Private School Racial Enrollments and Segregation," Harvard Civil Rights Project manuscript, June 26, 2002, p. 3.
27. Reardon and Yun, "Private School Racial Enrollments," Tables C1 and C2.
28. See Chubb and Moe, "Politics, Markets, and Equality."
29. Gary Ritter, Alison Rush, and Joel Rush, "How Might School Choice Affect Racial Integration in Schools? New Evidence from the ECLS-K," *Georgetown Public Policy Review*, Spring 2002.
30. Howard L. Fuller and Deborah Greiveldinger, "The Impact of School Choice on Racial Integration in Milwaukee Private Schools," American Education Reform Council manuscript, August 2002.
31. Jay P. Greene, "The Racial, Economic, and Religious Context of Parental Choice in Cleveland," paper presented at the Association for Public Policy Analysis and Management meeting, November 1999.
32. See for example "Civic Values in Public and Private Schools" and "Lessons from the Cleveland Scholarship Program," both in Peterson and Hassel, *Learning from School Choice*.

Index

A+ Accountability Program. *See* Florida
Abell Foundation, 63, 65
academic coursework. *See* college readiness, teachers
accountability programs, 45–46, 48, 126, 143, 170, 180–81, 184, 189, 217, 220, 223; choice model, 181, 189; legal process-compliance model, 180–81, 184, 189; parental involvement, 181. *See also* NCLB, performance, spending, testing
accountability testing. *See* testing, high-stakes
ACSFA, 106. *See also* Department of Education, U.S.
ACT, 90–91, 107, 120
advanced degrees, 60–61, 63, 220; masters in subject taught, 63; student performance, 63; teacher classroom performance, 61. *See also* college entrance exams, SAT
Advanced Placement. *See* AP coursework
Advisory Committee on Student Financial Assistance. *See* ACSFA
Aesop, 1
affirmative action, 106, 111. *See also* college admissions
Allegretto, Sylvia, 75–76, 79–80
American College Test. *See* ACT
American Education Reform Council, 213
American Enterprise Institute, 75
American Federation of Teachers, 51, 77, 158, 179, 201, 204
American Indian students, 110. *See also* minority students
American Jewish Committee, 158
American Medical Association, 3
Amrein, Audrey, 45, 120–22, 128–29
anecdotal reasoning, 17–18
AP coursework, 120–21
Asian students, 110. *See also* minority students
at-risk students, 13, 210; charter schools, 210; programs for, 13
attendance control, 13
attention-deficit disorder. *See* disabilities
autism. *See* disabilities

bake sales, school, 7, 17
Barber, Benjamin, 193
Barnard, John, 153
Barrett, Craig, 127
Beinart, Peter, 149
Belfield, Clive, 177

Bennett, William, 14–15
Berliner, David, 14–15, 23, 36, 45, 69, 74, 77–78, 83, 92, 120–22, 128–29, 192, 195, 202
Berman, Sheldon, 24
Bernstein, David, 158
Betts, Julian, 63
Biddle, Bruce, 14–15, 23, 36, 69, 74, 78, 83, 92
bilingual education, 13
birth-weight, 24
black students, 40–41, 43, 46–47, 96, 102, 105, 109–10, 112, 151–52, 154, 204; college enrollment, 105, 110; college readiness, 109–10; graduation rate, 96, 102, 109–10, 112; parenting, 41; performance, 43, 46; Perry Preschool Project, 47; poverty, 40; private schools, 204; voucher programs, 151–52, 154. *See also* minority students
Bositis, David, 202
Boston Children's Hospital, 24
breakfast subsidies. *See* meals
broken homes, 39, 41–43, 47. *See also* family structure
Brown v. Board of Education, 204
Bryk, Anthony, 162–64
Bush, Laura, 72

California, 60, 66, 71–72, 139–41, 206, 229n7; charter schools, 60, 206; disabilities diagnosis, 229n7; NCLB cost, 141; NCLB goals, 139–40; San Francisco teacher housing crisis, 72; Silicon Valley, 71–72; student performance, 55–56, 66; teacher experience, 66
Cameron, Stephen, 97
Campbell, David, 197–98
Carnoy, Martin, 45, 143, 171
car seats, 24
Catholic schools, xi, 158, 160–64, 199, 205, 211; compared to Andover, xi; compared to Exeter, xi, 158; Index of Exposure, 205; parental voting rates, 199; segregation, 211. *See also* private schools
Catholics, voting rates, 199
Census, U.S., 27, 96, 98, 105, 110, 129
Center on Education Policy, 132
certification. *See* teachers
Chakrabarti, Rajashri, 172
charter schools, 60, 68, 147, 149, 167, 174–76, 205–6, 210, 220, 250n10; at-risk youth, 175, 210; California, 60, 206; dropouts, 174; non-certified teachers, 68; prison, 175; racial composition, 205–6, 250n10; segregation, 206
Chicago, 30, 74; schools, 30; teachers' union, 74
citizenship, 194
civic life, 191, 193
civil rights leaders, 202
Cizek, Greogry, 118
class rank. *See* college readiness
classroom performance, 50–57, 141, 188–89, 220; benefits over time, 53; California, 55–56; cost, 56, 141, 220; Florida, 50; graduation rates, 54; New York, 50; one-time benefit, 53; parents' education, 54; poverty, 54; private schools, 189; STAR Project, 51–57; teachers unions, 51; test scores, 54; voucher schools, 188–89. *See also* teachers
class size, 49–57, 84, 189, 219

Clinton Administration, 192
Clinton, Hillary, 27
Cobb, Casey, 205
Cohen, Michael, 132
Cohen, Richard, 41, 72
college admissions, 106, 108, 110–13; affirmative action, 106, 111–12; discrimination, 106; financial aid, 106, 111–13 (*see also* ACSFA); minority students, 106, 110–13; relationship to family wealth, 106; transcripts, 108
College Board, The, 113
college entrance exams, 9, 28, 52, 89–91, 120; representativeness, 9; special-education students, 28; STAR Project, 52. *See also* ACT, SAT
college readiness, 106–13; academic coursework, 107–9; class rank, 107; GPA, 107; literacy, 109; low-income students, 107; minority students, 107, 110, 113; NCES method of calculation, 107–8; transcript requirements, 108
community college, 108
completion, high school, 95, 97–99, 101–3, 217; GED, 97–99; rate, 95, 101, 103; rate versus graduation rate, 97, 101–2; tracking individual students, 98–99. *See also* dropout
Chubb, John E., xi
Coleman, James S., ix, xi, 205
Coleman Report, x
computer labs, 17
computer teachers, 17. *See also* teachers
Corcoran, Sean, 75–76, 79–80
Costrell, Robert, 136–38, 140, 143
counseling, 13, 161
CPS, 96–98, 129; graduation reporting, 96; prisoners' exclusion, 97, 129. *See also* Census, U.S.
Crain, Robert, 205
Current Population Survey. *See* CPS, Census, U.S.
curriculum. *See* testing

Danenberg, Anne, 63
Davis, Perry, 24
Dead Poets Society, 158
Decker, Paul, 63
deCODE Genetics, 153
Deere, Donald, 29, 31
democratic values, 191–200, 220
Department of Education, Florida, 248n6
Department of Education, U.S., 9, 45, 54, 87, 95, 99, 105–6, 109, 139, 142, 160, 163–64, 211. *See also* ACSFA
Department of Labor, U.S., 73–75, 78–80, 82, 127
Department of Planning and Budget, Virginia, 29
diminishing marginal returns, law of, 10, 18
diplomas, 95, 97, 100–101, 105, 108–9, 123, 127–28, 131–32; awarded, 100–101; economic success, 105; high-stakes testing, 123; quality control, 131–32; regular, 95, 97, 108; relationship to life outcomes, 105; worth to employers, 127–28
direct instruction, 48; achievement, 48; test scores, 48
disabilities, 13, 21–25, 27–28, 35–36, 47, 164, 179–90, 219–20, 223–24,

227n7, 230n15; attention-deficit disorder, 28; autism, 27–28, 164, 184, 187, 229n7, 230n15; blindness, 36, 164, 184–85, 187; deafness, 36, 164, 184, 187; deinstitutionalization, 24–25; diagnosis, 23, 27–28, 47, 164, 219, 223–24, 227n7, 230n15; emotional disturbance, 164, 184–85, 187; graduation rates, 22; improvement in medical technology, 24; IEP, 180–85, 188–89; IEP compliance, 182; lawyers, public-school, 182; learning, 25–27, 36, 47, 187, 224; low birth-weight, 24; neurological disorders, 24; parents, 181–83, 187–89; private schools, 164, 179–90; public-school versus private-school services, 179–90; retardation, 24–25, 27, 227n7; severity, 22, 25, 35–36, 184; speech or language impediments, 36, 187; students, 13, 21, 23, 35–36, 220; test scores, 22; voucher programs, 179–90. *See also* special education

disability rates, 14–15, 21, 23–25; car seats, 24; health-care needs, 14; increase, 14–15, 21, 23–24; lead-paint exposure, 24; non-English speakers, 14; poverty, 14–15, 24–25; prenatal medicine, 24

Disability Rights and Education Defense Fund, 180, 186

disciplinary problems, 34

discrimination, 106

districts, 31–33, 103, 220; graduation rate, 103; size, 103, 220; special-education funding, 31–33; dropout, 13, 97–99, 128, 130–33; definition, 99; prevention, 13; rates, 128, 132; relationship to exit exams, 131–33; reporting, 97, 99; dropouts, 95, 97–99, 127–29, 174; broken homes, 95; charter schools, 174; prison, 95, 129; salary, 95; unemployment, 127–28; welfare, 95

Du, Jiangtao, 151

early intervention, 47–48; minority students, 47; poverty, 47; Echols, Frank, 207

Economic Policy Institute, 13, 34, 75, 207

educational nihilism, 125–26

Educational Testing Service, 66

Education Commission of the States, 7

Education Law Center, 67

education policy, 2–3, 8

education reforms, effectiveness, 125

employment benefits. *See* teachers

English, 14–15, 29, 42, 44; Non-native speakers, 15; proficiency, 14, 42, 44; proficiency-testing exemption, 29

enrollment, college, 105–14; barriers, 105–6; minorities, 108–12. *See also* college readiness

enrollment, high school, 99–101, 109; incentives to report, 100; population change, 100; relationship to funding, 100; Texas, 101. *See also* graduation rate

Equality of Educational Opportunity Report. *See* Coleman Report

evolution, 70

exit exams, 127–33; consequences, 129; Florida, 128; New York, 128; relationship to dropout, 130; relationship to graduation rates, 128
expulsion rates, 157, 162–64; private-school, 157, 162–64; public-school, 163–64

failure stigma, 170–72
family structure, 44. *See also* broken homes
Feldman, Sandra, 179, 184
Figlio, David, 29
financial aid. *See* college admissions, funding, voucher programs
Finn, Chester, 132
Fisher, Marc, 159
Flanagan, Ann, 66
Florida, 123, 128, 131, 170–74, 177–78, 183, 186–89, 244n4; A+ Accountability Program, 123, 170–72; dropouts due to testing, 131; exit exams, 128; family income, 187; FCAT, 123; high-stakes testing, 123; McKay Scholarship Program, 186–89, 246n4; voucher competition, 170–74, 177–78; voucher programs, 123, 170–74, 177–78, 183; Florida Comprehensive Assessment Test. *See* FCAT
Fordham Foundation, 131
Forster, Greg, 15, 31, 33, 44, 108–10, 122, 125–28, 173, 183, 186–89
Frangakis, Constantine E., 153
Fuller, Howard, 213
funding, 100, 117, 186, 224; high-stakes testing, 117; relationship to enrollment, 100; special-education, 186, 224

Galindo, Claudia, 130
GED, 97–99, 129; NCES method, graduation rates, 97–98; recipients' life outcomes, 97; versus diploma, 97. *See also* completion, high school; dropout
General Educational Development. *See* GED
Getzler, Lawrence, 29
Giammo, Joseph, 198
Gini Index. *See* integration
Glass, Gene, 205
Glazerman, Steven, 63
Glenn, Charles, 196
Glennie, Elizabeth, 171
Godwin, Kenneth, 200
Goldhaber, Dan, 63, 65
GPA. *See* college readiness
grades, 9. *See also performance*
graduation rates, 11, 22, 37, 47, 91–93, 95–104, 109–10, 112, 117, 127–33, 139–40, 169, 177, 220, 233n13; calculation, 96–103; disabilities, 22; effect of exit exams, 127; enrollment figures, 99, 101; high-stakes testing, 117; Houston scandal, 101; incentive to distort, 99; Milwaukee voucher students, 103; minorities, 96, 102, 109–10, 112; NAEP scores, 11, 37; NCES method of calculation, 96–98; NCLB, 139–40; preschool, 47; private schools, 103; relationship to exit exams, 128–33; school district size, 103. *See also* completion, high school

Greene, Jay, 15, 31, 33, 44, 46, 99, 108–10, 122, 125–26, 130–31, 151–52, 170–72, 183, 186–89, 198–200, 208, 210–13
Greiveldinger, Deborah, 213
Grissmer, David, 66

Hammons, Christopher, 174
Hanushek, Eric, 11, 16, 31, 45, 51, 61–62, 64–66, 121–22, 142
Harvard Civil Rights Project, 211
health, student, 14, 44
Heckman, James, 41–42, 97
Henig, Jeffrey, 208
Herbert, Bob, 72
Hess, Frederick, 75
High/Scope Educational Research Foundation, 47
high-stakes testing, 1–2, 28–31, 45–46, 117–26, 135–42, 217; cost, 135–42, 217; curricula changes, 118, 124–25; Florida, 29, 46, 118, 123–24; reliability, 122; teacher response, 2, 118, 123
Hill, Jennifer, 153
Hispanic students, 46, 96, 102, 105, 109–10, 112, 127–28, 151, 198, 204; college enrollment, 105, 110; college readiness, 109–10; graduation rate, 96, 102, 109, 112; private schools, 204; tolerance, 198; unemployment, 127–28; voucher programs, 151. *See also* minority students
Holland, Peter, 162–64
Homer, 1
home-schoolers, 199
Hoover Institute, 121
Hout, Michael, 201–2
Howell, William, 161–63
Hoxby, Caroline, 56, 60, 83, 141, 172–73, 175

identity, 194–95; cultural, 195; civic, 194
incentives, 12, 21, 31–34, 77, 83, 99–100, 124, 132, 170, 174, 177–78, 184, 193, 218–24; accountability, 221; bounty system, 33; dropout reporting, 99; economic, 218; enrollment reporting, 100; funding, 100, 184, 220, 224; graduation rates, 99; institutional, 12; high-stakes testing, 124; lump-sum system, 33; performance, 77, 83, 170, 174, 177–78, 218, 221; private, 193; special-education funding, 21, 31–34, 184; special-education labeling, 29, 184; income, family, 15, 126, 158–59, 164, 172, 187; Florida, 187; poverty, 15; private schools, 158–59, 164; relationship to basic skill, 126; voucher programs, 172; income taxes, 72, 169
Index of Dissimilarity. *See* integration
Index of Exposure. *See* integration
Individual Education Plan. *See* disabilities, IEP; public schools, IEP
individualism, 193
Individuals with Disabilities in Education Act, 180, 184. *See also* disabilities; special education programs
inefficiencies, structural, 12, 19
integration, 201–16, 220, 250n10; effect of choice in Scotland, 207; classrooms, 212, 216; Cleveland,

214; definition, 208; discipline, 215; Gini Index, 204; Index of Dissimilarity, 204, 211, 250n10; Index of Exposure, 204–5, 211, 248n10; measures, 203–10; Milwaukee, 215; parental choice, 207; private schools, 201–2, 205, 209, 213, 216; public schools, 201–2, 205, 215; safety, 215; school choice, 209, 214; secondary schools, 212; voucher programs, 209–10, 216. *See also* resegregation; segregation
interest groups, 2–3, 219

Jackson, Jesse Jr., 202
Jacob, Brian, 30
Jenkins, Krista, 129–31
Joint Center for Political and Economic Studies, 202

Kain, John, 61
Kawata, Jennifer, 66
Kemerer, Frank, 200
Kohn, Alfie, 119, 125
Koufman-Frederick, Ann, 24
Kozol, Jonathan, 7, 17–18, 50

labor force, 81, 127, 223
Ladd, Helen, 171
Latino National Political Survey,
lead contamination, 27
Lee, Valerie, 162–64
Leigh, Andrew, 60, 83
legal process-compliance model, 180–82, 184, 189; labeling of students, 184; parental advocates, 182; parental ignorance, 181; problems, 181–84; lessons, planned, 48
Levin, Henry, 177
licensure, professional, 68–69; doctors', 68; lawyers', 68; quality of practitioners', 68–69
literacy, 87, 109–10, 126
Loeb, Susanna, 45, 143
lunch subsidies. *See* meals
Lynch, Deborah, 74
Lyon, G. Reid, 47

magnet programs, 176, 208–9, 215
Manhattan Institute, 15, 31, 44, 46, 99, 108, 122, 127, 130, 152, 170, 173, 175, 183, 208
Massachusetts, 24, 136, 138; Association of School Superintendents, 24; Board of Education, 136; NCLB cost, 138
Mathematica Policy Research, 63
Mathis, William, 136
Mayer, Daniel, 63
McKay Scholarship Program. *See* Florida
McNeil, Linda, 118
meals, 13, 161; private school, 161; subsidies, 13
Meier, Deborah, 125
Meier, Kenneth, 158
Mellow, Nicole, 198
mercury contamination, 27
Mfume, Kweisi, 202
Milwaukee, 103, 148, 150–51, 172–73, 213, 215; graduation rate, 103; integration, 215; private schools, 103, 213; school choice program, 215; segregation, 213; voucher competition, 172–73; voucher program, 103, 148, 150–51, 172–73, 213; Miner, Barbara, 180, 184

minority students, 29, 40–42, 46–48, 67, 96, 102, 105, 107, 109–13, 126–28, 143, 151–52, 154, 203–6, 209–10, 213; affirmative action, 112; basic skills, 126; charter schools, 205–6; college enrollment, 105, 110, 112–13; college readiness, 107, 109–11, 113; dropout, 127–28; early intervention, 47; financial aid, 112; graduation rate, 96, 102, 109–10; integration, 203, 209; learning to read, 47; math skills, 40; parenting, 40–41; performance, 46, 143; Perry Preschool Project, 47; private schools, 204–5, 213; poverty, 40–42, 47–48, 151, 213; public schools, 205; racial composition, classrooms, 210; school choice, 46; teacher certification, 67; testing exemption, 29; unemployment, 127–28; voucher programs, 151–52, 154
Mishel, Lawrence, 75–76, 79–80
mortality rate, child, 14
Mosteller, Frederick, x
Moynihan, Daniel Patrick, x
Moe, Terry M., xi, 195
myth(s), 1–2, 17–18; anecdotal evidence, 17–18; definition, 1; interest groups, 2;

NAACP, 106, 202
NAEP, 10–11, 37–38, 45–46, 63–64, 65, 88–90, 109–10, 120–22, 142–43, 160; math scores, 11, 37, 45, 88, 121, 160; minority students, 46, 143; private-school students, 160; reading scores, 10, 38, 88, 90, 110, 121, 160; science scores, 11, 88; students with disabilities, 37–38
National Assessment of Educational Progress. *See* NAEP
National Center for Education Statistics. *See* NCES
National Education Association, 7, 51, 72, 202
National Education Household Survey, 199
National Education Longitudinal Study. *See* NELS
National Football League, 111
National Institutes of Health, 47
National Press Club, 249n1
Nation at Risk, A, 87–88, 90, 92
Nation's Report Card. *See* NAEP
Neas, Ralph, 149
NCES, 95–98, 101, 103, 107–9, 112; method, college readiness, 107–8; method, graduation, 96–98, 101, 103; NELS, 107
NCLB, 40, 117, 135–41
NCLB costs, 141
NELS, 107, 130, 160, 199, 210–12
Neurological disorders. *See* disabilities
New Mexico state legislature, 192
New York: City schools, 7, 17, 51, 148, 150, 152–53, 156, 183; student volunteerism, 200
No Child Left Behind Act. *See* NCLB
numeracy, 126

OC, The, 158
overcrowding, 42, 50
overtime. *See* salaries, teachers, workday

INDEX

Paine, Thomas, 203
parental choice, 103, 107, 207–8; district size, 103; integration, 208; segregation, 207
parenting, 39, 41
parenting, teenage, 41
pedagogical theory, 62, 70
pedagogy courses, 70
People for the American Way, 149, 180, 185–86
performance, 8, 11, 30, 36–39, 43–46, 48, 54–56, 59, 61, 63–66, 83, 87, 93, 118, 123–24, 137, 140–41, 143, 157–60, 167–68, 175–76, 177–78, 183, 217, 220–21, 234n4; black students', 43, 46; California, 55–56, 66; charter-school competition, 175–76, 178, 220; class size, 55, 217; direct instruction, 48; evaluation of, 36–38; improving, cost of, 140–41, 143; incentives, healthy, 124; math, 64; overcrowding, 42; parents' education, 54; poverty, 42, 54; private-school versus public-school students, 157–60, 220; public schools, 93, 157; reading, 64; relationship to parenting, 39; relationship to school choice, 217; relationship to school spending, 8, 11, 36–38, 87, 168, 177, 217; school, 118, 124, 137; school choice, 167–68, 221; special-education labeling, 30; student, 123, 183, 234n4; student advantage, 44; student-teacher ratio, 54; teacher, 83; teacher certification, 59, 63; teacher master's degrees in subject, 63; teacher credentials, 63; teacher education, 63, 65; teacher experience, 65; teacher quality, 61; Texas, 66; versus teachability, 44–45; voucher competition, 169–74, 177–78, 220, 246n4. *See also* accountability, testing
Perry Preschool Project, 47
Peterson, Paul, 151–54, 161–63
Peyser, James, 136–38, 140, 143
Podgursky, Michael, 73, 80
political participation, 191–95, 198–200
poverty, 15, 26, 37, 39, 41–44, 47–48, 107, 149, 151–52, 155, 172–73, 203; change in, 15, 26; college readiness, 107; definition of, 26; disabilities, 26; early intervention, 47; family income, 15, 37; learning to read, 47; minorities, 40–43, 47–48; Paine, Thomas, 203; performance, 41–42; relationship to the economy, 15; special-education enrollment, 26; standard of living, 39; voucher programs, 149, 151–52, 155, 172–73
prejudice, 74, 202, 216; racist, 202, 216; sexist, 74
prep schools. *See* private schools
preschool, 15, 47; attendance, 15; broken homes, 47; employment, 47; high-school graduation, 47; income, 47; marriage, 47; minority students, 47; reading intervention, 47; Price, Hugh, 202
principals, 40
prison population, 95, 97, 129; Census exclusion, 97, 129; dropout, 95, 129

privacy restrictions, 99
private schools, 103, 147–48, 150–65, 167–70, 174, 176, 179–201, 204–5, 206–18, 220; admissions, 157, 159, 162–64; barriers to attendance, 213; black students, 204; Choate, 158; Cleveland, 213–14; democratic values, 191–200, 220; disabled students, 164, 179–90, 220; discipline, 216; donations, 160–61; expulsions, 157, 162–64; Georgetown Day, 158; graduation rate, 103; Hispanic students, 204; Hispanic tolerance, 198; integration, 201–3, 205, 209, 213–16, 220; kindergarten, 212; low-income students, 151, 155; Milwaukee, 103, 148, 150–51, 185–86; minority students, 205; NELS, 160; parental confidence, 216; parental satisfaction, 154–56, 187–89; parental wealth, 158–59; prep schools, 158–59; primary education, 212; racial composition, classroom, 210; racial composition, lunchrooms, 211; racial homogeneity, 205; religious, 213; random-assignment research, 165; safety, 154, 188–89, 216; scholarships, 160–62; school choice, 213; segregation, 201, 211–15, 218; selectivity, 157–59, 162–64; shared sense of purpose, 195–96; special education programs, 161; teacher quality, 154, 156; tuition, 158–60; voucher programs, 103, 148, 151–55, 157–59, 162, 165, 167–70, 174, 176, 179–90, 214, 220; white students, 204. *See also* Catholic schools, religious schools
proficiency, student, 117–18, 123, 125–26, 133, 138, 140, 142, 223
Public Policy Institute of California, 63
public schools, 98, 148, 151, 153–56, 167–78, 180–85, 188–89, 191–201, 205, 210–14, 217–18, 220, 250n10, 250n18; admissions, 176; charter-school competition, 175–76, 178, 220; democratic values, 191–200; efficiency, 177; IEP, 180–85, 188–89; IEP compliance, 182; Index of Exposure, 205; integration, 201, 205; kindergarten, 212; main objective, 98, 192–93; minority students, 205; racial composition, classroom, 210, 250n18; racial composition, lunchrooms, 211; safety, 188–89; secondary students, 212; segregation, 201, 211–14; shared sense of purpose, 195–96; voucher competition, 169–74, 177–78, 220

Quality Counts report, 103

racial composition, 205–11, 215, 250n10; broader community, 208, 211, 250n10; charter schools, 205–6, 250n10; choice schools, 209; classrooms, 208–11; lunchrooms, 208–9, 211; school districts, 206–7, 215, 250n10; schools, 208; school systems, 209; urban schools, 208
Rand Corporation, 55, 149
RAND Foundation, 66

random assignment. *See* class size; school choice; voucher programs
Ravitch, Diane, 92
Raymond, Margaret, 31, 45, 121–22, 142
reading, 47; learning-disability diagnosis, 47; learning to, 47
Reardon, Sean, 130, 211–12
regression to the mean, 170–72
regression modeling, 122
religion, 192, 194–95
religious schools, 192, 199, 211; segregation, 211, 213. *See also* Catholic schools; private schools
Renzulli, Joseph, 119
resegretation, 208, 212–13. *See also* integration; segregation
retardation. *See* disabilities
Riley, Richard, 88, 192
Rips, Geoff, 41
Ritter, Gary, 212–13
Rivkin Steven, 61
rote drilling, 118–20, 124. *See also* testing
Rothstein, Richard, 13, 17, 23, 34–36, 40–43, 46, 80, 83, 92, 187
Rouse, Cecilia, 151
Rubin, Donald B., 153
Rueben, Kim, 63
Rush, Alison, 212
Rush, Joel, 212

salaries, 73–74, 77–81, 228n19; doctors', 77; lawyers', 77; professional specialty workers', 78–81; teachers', elementary, 74; teachers', Japanese, 81; teachers', secondary, 74; teachers', starting, 73, 80–81. *See also* teachers
San Francisco housing crisis, 72
SARS, 119
SAT, 90–91, 107, 120, 122. *See also* ACT; college entrance exams
scholarship programs. *See* private schools; voucher programs
Scholastic Assessment Test. *See* SAT
school board associations, 3
school choice, 1, 46–48, 158, 163, 167–78, 203, 207–10, 213–15, 217, 220–21, 223;integration, 207, 209, 214; Milwaukee, 215; minority participation, 208; minority students, 46; private schools, 213; segregation, 1, 203, 210; standard of living, 46–47; white participation, 208. *See also* voucher programs
science teachers, 17. *See also* teachers
Seattle Chamber of Commerce, 71
security in schools, 13–14
segregation, 192–93, 195, 201–18, 250n10, 250n18; charter schools, 206; Cleveland, 214; definition, 212; housing, 207, 214–15; kindergarteners, 212–13; private schools, 201–2, 211–15, 218; public-school system, 202–3, 211–14; racial homogeneity, 204; school choice, 210; school systems, 204; voucher programs, 210, 213; white racial privilege, 201. *See also* integration; resegregation
Shanker, Albert, 158
Shipps, Dorothy, 193
sick days, 80
Sikkink, David, 199
Silicon Valley, 71–72
skills, 112, 120, 126; analytical, 126; basic, 112, 126, 129, 220; critical thinking, 126; higher-order, 120;

minority students', 126; Smith, Christian, 199
South Carolina: cost of NCLB, 141
special education, 13, 21–25, 28–35, 161, 180–89, 223–24, 231n27, 246n4, 248n6; enrollment funding incentives, 33, 224; enrollment and parental pressure, 28; enrollment in programs, 22–23, 26, 35; enrollment nationwide, 30; enrollment testing, 29, 31; funding, 13, 21–23, 33, 183, 185–86, 223; harassment of students, 188–89; outcomes, 22; private schools, 161; programs, growth of, 21, 23; spending, 183, 248n6; student outcomes, 23, 35–36, 183; students, graduation rates, 37; students, labeling of, 21, 23–25, 28, 30, 32–35, 183–86, 224; teachers, 32; testing, 28–29, 31, 183; voucher programs, 183, 186–89, 246n4. *See also* disabilities
speech therapist, 33
spending, 8–9, 11, 14–17, 22–23, 34, 42, 87, 137, 141, 160–62, 168–69, 177, 183, 248n6; military, 17; per student, 17, 42, 141, 160–62, 168–69; relationship to school performance, 8, 11, 137; relationship to student performance, 87, 168–69, 177; school cost-effectiveness, 160–62; special education, 22–23, 34, 183, 248n6; students, total, 9, 17; student teachability, 15–16; test scores, 14. *See also* accountability programs
standardized tests, 9, 88, 92, 117, 119, 123, 125–27, 130, 135, 137–38, 143, 151, 153; condition of graduation, 127; math gains, 151, 153; reading gains, 151; spending on schools, 9. *See also* NAEP, Stanford-9, testing
standard of living, 39, 46–47
Stanford-9, 123, 170. *See also* testing
STAR Project, 51–57
Strayer, Wayne, 29, 31
Stuart Wells, Amy, 206
student behavior, 48
student-teacher ratio, 16, 54, 228n19
suburban schools, 2, 17; funding gap, 17; student achievement, 2
Supreme Court, 147, 192

teachability, 15, 36, 44–45; change in over time, 15; disabilities, 36; English proficiency, 44; evaluation, 15; family structure, 44; health, 44; poverty, 44; versus test scores, 44–45
Teachability Index, 15–16, 44; Louisiana, 44–45; Texas, 44
teachers, 3, 14, 16–17, 32–33, 49, 51–52, 55, 59–84, 118, 136, 185, 210, 218–20, 223–24, 228n19, 234n7; acquisition of skills, 69; advanced degrees, 60, 62, 220; aides, 51–52; certification, 59–70, 220, 234n7; certification effectiveness, 59; charter schools, 60; classroom performance, 61, 70; class size, 49, 84; cohorts, 65; computer, 17; contracts, 66; credentialing, 59–60, 62; dental coverage, 82; disability insurance, 81; effectiveness, 59–61;

employment benefits, 14, 73, 81; enthusiasm, 61; experience, 60, 62, 65–67, 220; grading, 76; health care, 81–82; home ownership, 71–72; hourly wage, 73–74, 78, 81; household incomes, 78; Japanese, 81; job security, 82; life insurance, 81; master's degrees in subject, 63; new, 55; noncredentialed, 64; offsite work and overtime, 75–77; pay systems, 61, 64, 71–84, 220, 223–24; performance incentives, 83; planning, 76; prescription drug insurance, 82; prospective, 64; qualifications, 81, 136; qualification standards, Michigan, 68; quality, 16, 49, 56, 59–61, 66, 68, 83, 136, 220; response to high-stakes testing, 118; retirement benefits, 81–82; salaries, 14, 16, 49, 60, 73–75, 77–81, 83, 228n19; science, 17; special education, 32–33, 185; Teach for America, 63–64; tenure, 66, 82; tuition costs, 64, 74; unions, 3, 49, 72, 74, 78, 219; veteran, 60, 65–66, 68; vision coverage, 82; women, 16

testing, 1–2, 14, 22, 28–31, 45–46, 48, 53, 87, 92–93, 117–26, 129, 135–42, 147, 154–55, 169–173, 175–76, 217, 220, 233n13; accountability, 29, 117–26, 129, 135, 141–42, 220; cheating, 118–19, 123–24, 126, 217, 220; economic differences, 46; low-stakes, 123, 125; point-of-entry, 53; requirements, 176; rigor, 131–32; special-education students, 28–29; state, 138; stress, 119, 123; student exemption, 29; teaching to the test, 118–19, 123, 220; Texas, 29, 118. *See also* accountability programs; high-stakes testing; test scores

test scores, 14, 22, 87, 92–93, 118, 121–22, 129, 138–41, 147, 154–55, 169–73, 175, 233n13; changes, state, 121–22; improvements, 138–41, 147, 154–55, 170–73, 175; disabilities, 22; spending, 14, 169. *See also* accountability programs; testing

test-taking strategies, 118

Texas, 29, 44, 61, 66, 99, 101, 118, 129, 131, 141, 198, 200; cheating, 118; cost of NCLB, 141; dropouts due to testing, 131; dropout reporting, 99; enrollment figures, 101; exit exams, 129; graduation-rate reporting, 101; high-stakes testing, 118; student performance, 66; student volunteerism, 200; Teachability Index, 44; teacher experience, 66; teacher quality, 61; testing, 29; voting rates, 198; textbooks, 14

textbook shortage, 17

Thernstrom, Abigail, 17

Thernstrom, Stephan, 17

tolerance, 191–98, 200

trade school, 108

transcripts, 108–9. *See also* college admissions

transferring schools, 135, 163–64, 176

tuition, 64, 74, 112–13; costs for teachers, 64, 74; parental overestimation, 112–13

tuitioning programs, 148, 173–74, 246n4
tutoring, 135

unemployment, 42, 127–28; dropouts, 127; minorities, 127–28; whites, 127–28. *See also* poverty, childhood
Urban Institute, 63
Urban League, 202
urban schools, 17, 17, 113, 163, 175, 208, 215; funding gap, 17; racial composition, 208
Urion, David, 24
Utah House of Representatives, 136

vacation days and holidays, 73–75, 80, 82
Vedder, Richard, 78, 82
Vermont, 136, 148, 173–74, 246n4; legislature, 136; Society for the Study of Education, 136; tuitioning programs, 148, 173–74, 246n4
Vietnam War, 40
violence in schools, 13–14, 188–89, 216
volunteerism, 191, 199–200
voting rates, 198–99
voucher programs, 46, 103, 123, 147, 150–59, 162–63, 165, 167–94, 197, 200–202, 207, 209–10, 213–14, 216, 220, 246n4; Charlotte, 148, 150, 152, 155, 163; Cleveland, 147, 163, 192, 213–14, 246n4; competition for public schools, 169–74, 177–78, 220; Dayton, 148, 150, 152, 155, 162–63; disabled students, 179–90; foreign, 169; Florida, 123, 173, 190, 246n4; high-stakes testing, 123; housing, 207; integration, 201, 209–10, 214, 216; low-income students, 151–52, 155; Maine, 173–74, 246n4; Milwaukee, 103, 147–48, 151–52, 155, 163, 173, 185–86, 190, 213, 246n4; minorities, 151–52, 154; New York City, 148, 150, 152–53, 156, 162–63; Paine, Thomas, 203; parental satisfaction, 154–56, 187–89; performance improvements, 150–53, 155–56; privately funded, 148, 152–55; private schools, 147, 157–59, 162, 165, 167–70, 174, 176, 179–90, 213–14, 220; publicly funded, 148; random assignment studies, 46, 150–56; San Antonio, 163; scholarship programs, 152, 169, 246n4; segregation, 201–2, 210, 213; tuitioning programs, 148, 173–74, 246n4; Vermont, 173–74, 246n4; Washington, D.C., 148, 150, 153–55, 162–63, 246n4. *See also* private schools, school choice

Warren, John, 129–31
Wax, Amy, 41–42
welfare, 95
Wellstone, Paul, 119
Wenglinsky, Harold, 66
white Americans, 201–2; preference for segregation, 202; racial privilege, 201; wealth, 202
white students, 41, 46, 102, 105, 109–11, 127–28, 201, 204–6; college enrollment, 105, 111; college readiness, 109–11; graduation rate, 102; performance,

46; private schools, 204–6; public schools, 205–6; racial privilege, 201; unemployment, 127–28. *See also* minority students
Williamson, Stephanie, 66
Willms, J. Douglas, 207
Winerip, Michael, 40–43, 45–56
Winters, Marcus, 46, 122, 125–28, 130–31, 170–72
Wisconsin Legisative Audit Bureau, 185
Witte, John, 151, 163
Wolf, Patrick, 197, 200
workday, 75–77, 81, 84; nonteaching professions, 76–77; teachers', 75–76, 81, 84
women, 16; career opportunities, 16; education, 16; teaching workforce, 16
World War II, 9

Yun, John, 211–12

About the Author

Jay P. Greene is a Senior Fellow at the Manhattan Institute's Education Research Office, where he conducts research and writes about education policy. He has conducted evaluations of school choice and accountability programs in Florida, Charlotte, Milwaukee, Cleveland, and San Antonio. He has also recently published research on high school graduation rates, charter schools, and special education.

His research was cited four times in the Supreme Court's opinions in the landmark *Zelman v. Simmons-Harris* case on school vouchers. His articles have appeared in policy journals, such as *The Public Interest*, *City Journal*, and *Education Next*, in academic journals, such as *Teachers College Record*, *Georgetown Public Policy Review*, and the *British Journal of Political Science*, as well as in major newspapers, such as the *Wall Street Journal*, *Los Angeles Times*, and *Washington Post*.

Greene has been a professor of government at the University of Texas at Austin and the University of Houston. He received his B.A. in history from Tufts University in 1988 and his Ph.D. from the Government Department at Harvard University in 1995. He lives with his wife and three children in Weston, Florida.